GARDEN ROUTE TRAVELS

TRAVELS

OVERBERG & LITTLE KAROO ROUTE 62

URSULA STEVENS

Wanderlust Books
A division of Wanderlust Tours CC
www.wanderlust.co.za
E-mail:wanderlust@iafrica.com
Reg.No.CK 1997/011464/23

P.O.Box 303 Paarden Eiland 7420
South Africa

ISBN
0-620-34227-7

First published: 2005

Cover Photos:
FRONT: Genadendal street   *BACK:*   Knysna Lagoon
Outeniqua mountains
Cape Honeysuckle

INDEMNITY: While every effort has been made to ensure the accuracy of the maps, routes described and all information given in this book, the author and publishers accept no responsibility for consequences arising from any error and/or omissions.

Publisher   Wanderlust

Illustrations   Renate Stitfall

Photographs   Ursula Stevens

Cover design and Reproduction   Eva Tucek

Printing   CTP Book Printers (Pty)Ltd
Cape Town

CONTENTS

ACKNOWLEDGEMENT

To discover the diverse attractions, history, natural and man-made wonders of the Garden Route, Overberg and Little Karoo regions, involves journeys of thousands of kilometres and the assistance of many individuals and organisations too numerous to mention here. My thanks therefore, goes to those who so willingly assisted me, especially to my colleagues in the travel industry, coach drivers, tourism information officers, church and museum guides. In particular, I would also like to thank the staff of the National Library for their assistance with my research; Jabedi Mapping, Cape Town, who kindly assisted with the maps; Eskom for providing and allowing me to use their technical information on the Palmiet River Scheme; Cape Nature Conservation and SA National Parks for permitting me to use information on the parks falling under their jurisdiction.

My thanks also to the many authors who captured the beauty and challenges of the region in their books, providing insight and laying a foundation on which to build and draw.

INTRODUCTION

The vast area described in the following pages is like a second home to me. With my family I have spent unforgettable holidays in the region. I have guided hikers and tourists into the mountains and forests, and along various routes between Cape Town and Port Elizabeth. I have also lived in Knysna, which I think of as the heart of the Garden Route.

Some of the most memorable and enjoyable hikes and walks are the Otter Trail, the Robberg Peninsula circuits, the Swellendam and Outeniqua Trails, the Harkerville coastal walks,the Kingfisher and Mole Rat trails, the Brenton-on-Sea walk to Buffel's Bay and from there on towards Gericke Point. In the deep Knysna forests look for louries and elephants, bushbuck and lynx and, if you have the time and inclination, follow the tracks trodden by gold miners on the Jubilee Creek and Millwood walks. In the Overberg wheatfields look for blue cranes and storks; in the ocean for whales, dolphins and seals. If you are lucky you may swim with otters, if not, you may be chased by baboons.

You will discover striking mountain passes traversing the majestic Tsitsikamma, Outeniqua and Swartberg peaks, crossing from the Great Karoo into the Little Karoo, the 'Thirstland' and into the green coastal belt. In the Little Karoo you can stand in awe in the Cango Caves and, if you're not too big, ride an ostrich.

If you enjoy steam trains, ride the Choo-Tjoe between George and Knysna; watch the surfers ride the giant waves at Victoria Bay, St Francis and Jeffreys Bay; look for the narrow gauge "Apple Express" in the Longkloof Valley. View the magnificently constructed bridges spanning deep gorges with their rivers far below, winding their way from the mountains to the sea.

The various routes can be seen as a day's journey or linked to others – it all depends how much time you have to explore. Travellers with only a couple of days to spare would best be advised to drive on the national road N2 and the major link roads. Those at leisure should endeavour to get off the N2 as much as possible and venture on to minor roads.

I hope I have inspired you to read a little deeper into this book and plan your visit of a lifetime.

ROUTE ONE

CAPE TOWN - SOMERSET WEST – GRABOUW – ELGIN – CALEDON – GENADENDAL/GREYTON - RIVIERSONDEREND - SWELLENDAM

Only forty-six kilometres away from Cape Town, the greener, open country-side of the Somerset West area welcomes the traveller.

The attractive town of

SOMERSET WEST

spreads out leisurely in the foothills of the Helderberg and Hottentots Holland Mountains which climb to some considerable height.

In the days under Dutch East India Company rule, its first Commander at the Cape, Jan van Riebeeck, comments in his diary *"they, the Chainoukwa-Khoikhoi called this place of exceptionally rich pasturage their Holland or Fatherland, to give our men an idea of the abundance of food and excellent pasturage to be had there"*.

Thus, the indigenous Khoikhoi, the 'Men of Men' considered this area their home, just as Holland meant home to the settlers who moved into the foothills of these mountains, dominated by the Helderberg, Guardian Peak, Pic Sans Nom, New Year Peak, The Triplets, Sneeuwkop, Sugar Loaf, Landroskop, Langkloofberg and Moordenaarskop peaks. By about 1672, the Chainoukwa Khoi surrendered their land – though the Company officially termed it *sold..*

Before official settlement in the region got off the ground, four Company deserters had made their way towards these mountains, hoping to march overland to Mozambique and there to find a homeward-bound ship. Cheese and a little fish sustained them, a dog kept them company and two pistols offered safety. All should have gone well, but the mighty mountains which barred their passage inland, frustrated their plan, forcing them to turn back.

> ### Jan van Riebeeck
> was born in 1619 in the Dutch town of Culembourg. He died in 1677 in Batavia, the Dutch East Indies. Van Riebeeck joined the services of the Dutch East India Company or VOC in 1639 as assistant-surgeon. Accompanied by his French born wife Maria de la Queillerie, his fleet reached the Cape on 6 April 1652, signalling the beginning of European settlement in South Africa.
> The VOC – Vereenigde Oostindiese Companjie – governed the Cape from that date to 1795.

Impenetrable bush and trees covered the mountain slopes and wild animals roamed free. Van Riebeeck, the first commander at the Cape, mentions lion and *wolf* attacks on the cattle outpost which he had set up, killing close to one hundred sheep one night. Against all odds, the post survived and in the late 1670s the Company settled a handful of hardy men in the area.

In the early 19th century H.Alexander, the Colonial Secretary, steered the small settlement towards genuine development. Intuitively he sensed that his own estate in the area was well positioned for further exploration and trade with the interior. Accordingly, he divided his land situated '*on the great thoroughfare over the kloof to the interior*' into plots of varying size and offered to construct small houses for tradesmen. The offer appealed to numerous tradesmen who made the Somerset West region their home.

A church site was selected around which the town developed, named on 13 February 1820 after Governor Lord Charles Somerset.

Lord Charles Henry Somerset (1767 – 1831)
He was born in Gloucestershire and died in Brighton.

Lord Charles Somerset was a relation of the British royal family. He started out in life with a career in the army. Attracted by politics, he changed direction and became a member of Parliament in 1796. Following the Second British Occupation of the Cape (1806), he was offered the governorship of the Cape in 1813. This was a time of strife at the Cape between the settlers on the expanding eastern border and the Xhosa nation. The Frontier Wars had broken out, dominating political development. To secure the eastern border and deal with the problem of its defence, Lord Charles Somerset recommended to settle British immigrants in the eastern Cape. In 1820 more than 4000 settlers stepped ashore at today's Port Elizabeth. Earlier he had tried to negotiate with the Xhosa, recognising Ngqika as paramount chief, but after the war of 1819, Lord Charles Somerset forced Ngqika to give up the land between the Keiskamma and the Fish rivers, which became so-called neutral territory.
Somerset was of an autocratic nature and intolerant of dissent.

Somerset West, home to the famous Vergelegen Wine Estate, once the property of the dishonourably dismissed Governor Willem Adriaan van der Stel in the early 18th century, developed at a leisurely pace. The pace quickened when an enterprising Mr Roos introduced an omnibus service between Cape Town and Somerset West and finally, when the railways reached the town in 1889.

Modern Somerset West is a lively and prosperous town on the banks of the Lourens River which is named after a man who drowned in it.

The national road sweeps past Somerset West and its new commercial and light industrial centre, past Lwandle township and crosses the Sir Lowrys Pass River. Then it begins to climb towards the mountains, sweeping uphill in broad bends, with wide views of False Bay and below, of Gordon's Bay. False Bay earned its name in the days of the early voyages around the Cape. Sailors approaching from the east coast frequently spotted the unmistakable outline of Table Mountain and steered into the bay – to discover to their dismay that they had sailed into the *false bay*.

The route across the mountains was forged long ago by migrating animals. The indigenous Khoikhoi -'The Brave Men' - knew it as *Gantouw* (Elandspad). It was steep, so incredibly steep that much later, European settlers were forced to unload the wagons at the foot of the pass. Some even dismantled the wagons completely and hauled the goods to the top. Scars of wagon wheels can still be seen on some of the rocks.

Happily, the modern traveller's journey is a leisurely crossing as the scenic **Sir Lowry's Pass** no longer follows this torturous track. Problematic only are the occasional troupes of baboons, strong winds and frantic traffic.

The Chacma baboon

The indigenous people called the gregarious animal choa kamma, also choachamma. This name was later adopted by the French zoologist, Baron Cuvier, and became widely accepted from 1819.

The male grows to a height of 1,5m, including the tail whilst the female reaches a height of 1,2m. The male weighs in at about 40kg, and the female tops the scales at only 20kg. Females may be distinguished from other similar sized males by their brightly coloured ischial callosites on the rump, when in season.

Males reach maturity at 8 years, and females at about 3 to 4 years. A young is born after a gestation of six months and weaned after six to eight months.

Mid-morning and afternoon are taken up by feeding activities: the diet is essentially vegetarian.

Feeding is strictly forbidden as baboons lose the ability to forage for themselves and are condemned to death through starvation. Heavy fines are payable.

The pass bears the name of Governor Sir Lowry Cole. Impatient with the authorities in England who dragged their heels over what he deemed a necessary expenditure, he authorised and partially paid for its construction out of his own pockets.

Nearer the summit, turn off to the right to a view point. From a height of 452 metres marvel at False Bay's vast expanse, the ragged mountains, green plains and sprawling towns, with Table Mountain visible in the distance.

Baboon

You may be lost in wonder, but probably not alone as baboons regularly enthrone themselves on the surrounding rocks. Keep car doors closed – the dangerous four-legged passengers may join the onward excursion.

On the descent, signs point to **Steenbras Dam.** Not only is the dam a major recreational area, set in terraced rock gardens along the steep riverbed, it is also a major supplier of drinking water to the greater Cape Town area. The dam was constructed in 1921 and covers some 380 hectare. Its wall rises to just over 22 metres. Three pipelines feed its water into Newlands Reservoir in Cape Town.

At the bottom, once across the Steenbras River and past the turn-off to North Pineview and Rockview Dam, you enter a different world. Behind lie the majesty of False Bay and Table Mountain, ahead the fruit gardens of the Western Cape. The road leisurely traverses the valley, we are joined by the R321 for Grabouw, Elgin and the Theewaterskloof Dam and shortly cross the Palmiet River. The river takes its name from a sedge *Prionium serratum,* known by the Khoikhoi as *houtema* which describes a winding river.

Near the town of Grabouw is situated the **Palmiet Pumped Storage Scheme,** a joint venture between Eskom Holdings Ltd and the Department of Water Affairs and Forestry.

Eskom provides 95% of the country's electricity, most of which (90%) is produced by coal fired thermal power stations.

South Africa is rich in coal, but water is a precious resource. To make optimal use of it, the Palmiet Hydroelectric Power Station plays an important double role: not only does it provide peaking power for the Eskom National Grid, it also provides water for Cape Town which is achieved through its reversible pump turbines that are components of an intercatchment water transfer.

The power station of a pumped storage scheme is situated on the waterway which links an upper and lower reservoir. The Palmiet scheme comprises two new dams, the lower Kogelberg Dam on the Palmiet River and the upper Rockview Dam on the watershed between the Palmiet and Steenbras rivers. In peak demand periods, a conduit between the two reservoirs conveys the water stored in the upper reservoir to the reversible pump turbines in the 400MW station on the bank of the Kogelberg reservoir to generate electricity. In periods of low demand water is pumped back from Kogelberg to Rockview Reservoir. From here, water allocated to the Department of Water Affairs flows by gravity into the Steenbras Reservoir via a separate conduit. This supplements Cape Town's annual water supply by an average of 30 million m³, which will ultimately be increased to 140 million m³.

The power generated at the Palmiet Pumped Storage system is fed into the national transmission network at the Bacchus substation near Worcester.

The Scheme was commissioned in 1988. To discover more about it, call at the Visitors Information Centre at Palmiet or join a tour organised by the Elgin Tourism Bureau. The tours last between 2 to 3 hours and booking is essential.

The national road by-passes the towns Grabouw and Elgin.

GRABOUW
is cornered by the Hottentots Holland and Groenland Mountains where Mount Lebanon Peak reaches a height of 1201 metres.

Grabouw is the commercial centre for the export fruit producing area, but wine production is steadily increasing. Though surrounded by natural beauty, the busy town itself is somewhat unattractive. Its roots go back to 1856 when Wilhelm Langschmidt acquired the farm *Grietjiesgat*. He re-named it after his home, *Grabow*, in Germany. Not surprisingly the region's population flourished, as Langschmidt himself was head of an extraordinarily large family of 23 children which included 3 sets of twins.

Commercial rivalry between Grabouw and Elgin has developed over the years.

Though Grabouw is the region's commercial hub, it is the Elgin name that has become internationally known, particularly for its apples. When the railway line across Sir Lowry's Pass finally linked Cape Town to the Overberg in

1902, Grabouw was by-passed by a paltry 1.5km. Instead, it led to a station named 'Elgin' on the farm *Glen Elgin*, owned by the Molteno brothers.

Sir John Charles Molteno

Born in London in 1814 Sir John began his career as a wealthy merchant, wool farmer and banker in the Beaufort distric where he was known as the 'Lion of Beaufort.

He fought in the Sixth Frontier War in the Eastern Cape (1846) and in 1854 became a member of the Cape Legislative Assembly. In support of liberal politics, Sir John headed the move for responsible government and became the Cape's first Prime Minister (1872-1878).

During his term of office, the Cape enjoyed an economic boom and Molteno encouraged the building of harbours, bridges and the railways. Advances were also made in educational matters under his government which strongly rejected imperial intervention in the affairs of the Colony. He opposed the annexation of Griqualand West and clashed with Governor Sir Bartle Frere over the use of British troops in the Ninth Frontier War of 1877. His opposition earned him his dismissal in 1878.

ELGIN was intended as a despatch point for the produce of the region. Wheat, oats and everlasting flowers were loaded, destined for the export market, particularly Germany. To develop into a prime apple producing district, the region needed the extraordinary Dr. Antonie Viljoen.

Dr. Viljoen, born in Caledon, obtained his medical degree at Edinburgh University. Initially he practised in the Transvaal but later returned to the Cape. In 1899 he acquired part of the *Palmietriver Farm* which he renamed *Oak Valley*. The outbreak of the Anglo-Boer War in the same year took him back to the Transvaal where he served on the Boers' side. The British captured and returned him to his Cape farm on amazing terms: he had to pay the salary of his two guards in return for his freedom! In no time at all, his farm became the centre for numerous crop experiments, but none delivered positive results. At the end of the hostilities, Dr Viljoen

---

John X. Merriman 1841–1926

On completion of his education in England, Merriman returned in 1862 to the Cape and became a minister in Sir John Molteno's government in the mid 1870s. He became also a cabinet minister in Rhodes's government in 1890 and gained himself the reputation of being a 'Cape Liberal'. He opposed both the Jameson Raid of 1895 and the ensuing Anglo-Boer War which erupted in 1899. He travelled to London to plead for peace and after the war supported full self-government for the Transvaal and Orange River colonies.

was elected to the Cape Legislative Assembly where he made the acquaintance of the Minister of Agriculture, John X. Merriman.

apples

On the minister's recommendation, he launched into apple farming. Dr. Viljoen followed the advice, purchased assorted apple trees and planted them out near his homestead on *Oak Valley*.

The first crop filled the baskets in 1912 and there was no turning back now: the excellence of the product convinced Dr. Viljoen to embark on large scale apple farming. His ambitious project was interrupted by the First World War. Sadly, Dr. Viljoen died in 1918 and never witnessed the roaring success of his enterprise.

In time the local farmers formed the Elgin Co-operative Fruitgrowers Ltd (1923) and implemented systematic education in apple cultivation.

A handful of farmers formed the Elgin Fruit Company as a joint venture in marketing and packing. Yet again, progress in the industry was slowed, this time by the outbreak of the Second World War.

After the war, the fruit industry advanced in leaps and bounds due largely to technical progress.

Advancement was sparked by the introduction of a sprinkler irrigation system, made possible by the waters of the Palmiet River. Improved fertilisers and realisation that natural grass left between the trees enriches the soil with humus, retains water and prevents erosion, increased production enormously. Another leap forward came in 1959 when Edmond Lombardi introduced the Italian palmette system of cultivation on his farm *Applethwaite*. According to this ancient practice fruit trees are planted in close proximity to each other, the main branches being tied down into a horizontal position. This technique quickens apple production: the trees bear after 4 years instead of the usual eight. In spring this continuous wall of apple trees is easily seen from the roadside.

A by-product of the apple industry is the delicious *Appletiser* juice, developed on Lombardi's farm in 1966, in association with Professor H. Luthi, from Switzerland. It solved the problem of what to do with lower grade fruit!

Today, the district not only grows apples in abundance but also pears, plum and nectarines.

The **Elgin Apple Museum** on the banks of the Palmiet River allows a glimpse into the history of apple farming from its beginning in 3000 BC in Mesopotamia to modern day production. Photographs and old machinery, tools and carts mirror the past when the cultivation of apples was certainly a physically cumbersome endeavour. The restored shoemaker's cottage houses part of the collection.

The N2 proceeds easterly through fruit orchards and past farm stalls where fruit, juices, cheeses, meat, farm delicacies, cookies and cakes tempt the traveller.

The drive is particularly enchanting in spring when the fruit trees, in full blossom, don their most beautiful colours.

Soon the huge packing sheds of the Kromrivier Apple Co-Operative **Kromcro** line the road.

Just beyond these packing sheds **Valley Road** turns left into the attractive farming area of the Krom Rivier. 'Krom' means 'Bent, Crooked'. The N2 meanwhile continues east and a couple of kilometres further on passes the Lebanon Forestry Station. The huge letter 'K' staring from the slope indicates the farm *Korteshoven*.

Just as the eyes grow accustomed to the sight of fruit orchards, a sign alerts to another delicious product of the valley, **Paul Cluver Wines.** Dr Paul Cluver identified the Elgin region in the mid-1980s as a wine growing area and established the De Rust Estate which has been in the family since 1896. The estate on the banks of the Reebok River, is also home to popular summer-concerts. The original homestead *Opstal,* more than 250 years old, has been turned into a guesthouse. Since the first plantings of vineyards in 1986, Paul Cluver wines have earned many international accolades.

Mountains keep you company, forcing the road to wind gently uphill on the **Houhoek Pass** which climbs to a height of 341 metres.

Below stretches the lovely Houhoek valley, home also to the curiously named **Houhoek Inn**.

The Swedish adventurer Oloff Bergh first crossed these treacherous mountains in 1682 by way of a route that became known as *Hout Hoek,* or 'Timber Corner' or *Houw Hoek*, which means 'Hold Back' as the oxen had to be held back on the steep descent. A few years later, Ensign Schrijver was dispatched from Cape Town on a cattle bartering trip. He too followed the twisting, rising and falling track which eventually was improved by Major Charles Mitchell and ultimately re-directed by Andrew Geddes-Bain in 1846. He led it diagonally up the slopes, thus eliminating the torturous ascent or descent.

The Jakkals River and the railway line snake through the deep valley over which the 896m-high Houwhoekberg stands guard. The Jakkals eventually flows into the Bot River.

Once a route had opened up, early Cape government officials followed the trail for journeys into the interior where they hoped to purchase cattle from the Khoi. Transport wagons regularly outspanned near the river bank and an inn was built. It became a favourite staging post. This prompted the VOC, never averse to making money, to erect a toll gate.

One of the more illustrious visitors to the Inn was Lady Ann Barnard (see page 55)who sojourned here whilst exploring the region with her husband. Much later, in the 1900s the Houw Hoek Inn looked after the welfare of Cape Town judges whilst they conducted Circuit Courts in the nearby town of Caledon (see page 22).

The building's ground floor dates back to the late 1770s. The upper floor was added in 1860. Extensions have been progressively added over the years. The Inn's adjoining old farm buildings have been converted into dining rooms and conference rooms, retaining their old character.

Gracious old oaks, towering poplars and a gigantic eucalyptus tree planted in 1859 by the innkeeper Beyers to celebrate his daughter's birth, afford the visitor welcome shade.

The Houhoek Inn is the oldest licensed hotel in South Africa.

On the descent the eye feasts on sweeping views of rolling wheat fields. Nearer the bottom and in the distance, the Jakkals River joins the *Bot River*. The small town of **Botrivier** takes its name from *botter* or *bot* from the days when the Khoi living there supplied the traders with butter. Just beyond Botrivier, the R43 (exit 90) branches off to **Hermanus and Kleinmond (**see page 45)

The national road continues easterly, whilst the R43 also heads in a northerly direction towards **Villiersdorp** (31km away), a thriving farming community at the foot of the Blokkop Mountains. It was established in 1834 by Veldkornet P.H. de Villiers on portion of his farm *Bo-Radyn*. It was later re-named to De Villiersdorp to reflect the French influence amongst the inhabitants of whom many were of Huguenot descent.

Further along the N2 the **Boointjieskraal Farm** is easily recognised by its low whitewashed ring wall. The farm was at one stage one of Governor Willem van der Stel's stock posts, popular with travellers because of its good water and grazing.

A few kilometres further on, the R406 takes you on a 46km-long picturesque country route to **Genadendal** and **Greyton.**

A visit to Genadendal is well worth the detour, to marvel at the strength of faith which guided the missionaries.

GENADENDAL, the 'Valley of Mercy', naps in the shadow of the Riviersonderend Mountains, the 'River without an End Mountains'. Once known as Baviaan's Kloof, the village is the oldest missionary station in the

country, established by the Moravian Missionary Society, the Herrenhuter Brudergemeinschaft. Its first active missionary, Georg Schmidt, began working among the Khoikhoi population in 1737. Laboriously he dug an irrigation canal, laid out a garden and planted a pear tree of which shoots still grow. Seven years later his missionary zeal bore fruit when he baptised his first converts in 1742.

Field cornet Jan Marthinus Theunissen befriended the missionaries. He was in charge of the Company's outpost *Oude Post* east of Swellendam and was genuinely interested in the welfare of the Khoikhoi. His caring earned him the nickname

Genadendal canal

Hottentotsgod amongst his friends. Theunissen provided the Herrenhuters with transport from Cape Town to Baviaanskloof and rendered assistance wherever he could. His most precious gift was a large church bell which he bought in Cape Town. The bell was hung in a tree, but its joyful sound was soon smothered by the Dutch Reformed Church. The Rev. Meent Borcherds of Stellenbosch whose parish included Genadendal, was so angered by the sound of the 'Moravian' bell that he requested the government to stop this 'sect'. The Reverend alleged that the Genadendal bell could be heard in far away Stellenbosch!

Genadendal Pear Tree

Genadendal street

Dutch Reformed Church, the only Christian church permitted by the Company, forced Schmidt to abandon his work. In 1743 he returned, dejected, to his native Germany. In 1792, twelve years after the Lutherans were granted religious freedom at the Cape, the Moravian Brotherhood returned. Missionaries Schwinn, Kühnel and Marsveld picked up the threads left behind by Schmidt. Imagine their joy when they met Magdalena, one of Schmidt's converts, now an old woman. Proudly she presented to the missionaries the New Testament (printed 1694 in Amsterdam), still in her possession. Her granddaughter Hannah read from the sheepskin-wrapped bible the first service in the shade of the pear tree planted by Georg Schmidt. She read from the 2nd chapter of St. Matthew, the story of the three wise men. Hannah was one of the forbears of Bishop Habelgaarn who led the Moravian Brotherhood until his death in 1980.

Incidentally, the story of the banished bell found a happy ending during the First British Occupation when Lord Macartney allowed the bell to be used to call 'together the members of your congregation in the Baviaanskloof'.

No longer was it necessary for the bell to peal out from a tree. With their own hands the congregation built a bell-tower, completed in 1798.

Genadendal began to flourish. Wisely, missionary Beinbrecht built a bridge over the Riviersonderend River. Soon a church and school graced the valley and a printing work was started which produced interesting pamphlets.

One of the earliest children's periodical *De Kinder Vriend*, or 'The Children's Friend' and *De Bode*, 'The Messenger', were written and, interestingly, a brochure warning against alcohol abuse *De Drank,* 'The Drink'.

The missionaries were hands-on people, practical and accomplished craftsmen. Under their guidance the villagers became skilled smiths, coopers and shoemakers. One product became particularly well-known, the *Herneuter*

Knife. (Herneuter is a contraction of Herrenhuter)

A path around the central village, past the school, bell-tower, church, water channel, pear tree and cemetery has been laid out.

The First British Occupation 1795 – 1802

The First British Occupation was a direct result of the French Revolution. In 1793 Britain and Holland joined forces to fight France. A year later, the French had over-run the Austrian Netherlands and invaded Holland where the liberal French politics appealed to the people. The 'Patriotic Party' which sympathised with France was formed. When Amsterdam was captured in 1795, Holland formed an alliance with France and became known as Batavia. The Prince of Orange, still allied to England through the Coalition Treaty of 1793, fled across the Channel to seek English protection for the settlement at the Cape.

His request was granted as Britain in turn, was anxious about the safety of its Indian possessions.

Thus, in 1795, Admiral Sir Keith Elphinstone and Maj.-Gen. J.H. Craig sailed for the Cape with a force of about 1600 soldiers. In June, the fleet reached False Bay and anchored at Simon's Town. The Prince of Orange's demand to the commander of the Company's forces to submit to British protection was handed over, but declined. In fact, Commander Sluijsken who had anticipated a Dutch-French alliance broke off negotiations with the English, and war was imminent.

The British totally outnumbered Sluijsken's men, particularly after the landing of additional soldiers under the command of Gen. Clarke which swelled the English forces to over 5000 men. The Company surrendered on 16 September 1795 at Rustenburg, Cape Town.

The First British occupation ended in 1802 when England and France signed the Treaty of Amiens which returned the Cape to Batavian (Dutch) rule.

The Genadendal Hiking Trail

The trail falls within the Riviersonderend Conservation Area which extends to over 69 500 hectare between the towns of McGregor, Greyton, Riviersonderend and Villiersdorp. It is part state, part privately owned land. The walk is fairly strenuous but affords spectacular views of the Overberg and the Worcester-Robertson Karoo. The 25-km long circular route requires overnighting at 'Die Hoek', which is just over 14km away from the starting point, the Moravian Mission Church. Overnight facilitities are available at the Church.

The first day leads past two pools at Groot and Klein Koffiegat before it reaches Die Hoek. On day two you walk about 7 km back to Genadendal.

Only 4 kilometres separate Genadendal from popular and fashionable

GREYTON

which dates back to 1846 and was named after Sir George Grey, Governor of the Cape for a few years till 1861. From tranquil roots Greyton has developed into a fashionable retreat for city folk. The first plots of today's Main Street were sold in 1854. Oak trees and quaint cottages still line the Main Street, curious little shops rub shoulders with fashionable boutiques and restaurants – the past and present meet harmoniously.

The Posthouse

Greyton street

Vegetables drying in the sun...

The town is also an extremely popular starting or ending point for the splendid Boesmanskloof Hiking Trail which links Greyton to McGregor, beyond the Riviersonderend Mountain. There is no road from Greyton to McGregor – you have to put on your hiking shoes!

Do not rush the walk if you want to enjoy the varied, typical mountain fynbos vegetation and the riverine vegetation along the water courses. Maybe you are lucky enough to spot the common duiker, klipspringer, caracal or small spottet genet.

The Boesmanskloof Hiking Trail

A permit is necessary to walk the trail. It covers a distance of about 15km and can be managed in five to six hours. You must be fit to enjoy it.

The walk starts north-east of Greyton, just outside the village. Should you opt to walk it from McGregor the starting point there is at Die Galg, 'The Gallows', about 14km away from McGregor town centre. Transport arrangements must be made in advance. At either end of the trail private accommodation await the weary.

At one stage the Boesmanskloof Trail route which winds through the Riviersonderend Mountains was the only link between the villages of Greyton in the south and Mcgregor in the north. It passes through the Riviersonderend Conservation Area which is a declared mountain catchment area of state-and privately owned land.

Cape sugarbirds and malachite sunbirds feast on the sugarbush and common pincushion, whilst jackal buzzards and black eagle circle above. Crystal clear pools for swimming will happily detain you. In winter the spectacular Oakes Falls plunge into the river from considerable height – the daring have even plunged themselves into the pools below. Flowers accompany the hiker all the way. A little warning for those walking towards McGregor – near the end is rather unexpected steep climb. Manageable, of course, but testing.

A sparkling pool on the trail

From Greyton, heading towards Caledon in a south-easterly direction, the R406 turns into a gravel road – after rains extremely slippery and muddy. It connects after 36km with the national road N2.

The speedier re-connection to the N2 is the way you came, back along the R 406 which reaches the national road 4km outside the town of Caledon.

You are now in the **Overberg,** literally meaning *Over the Mountain.*

In 1662 members of the Hessequa Khoi arrived with cattle at the Castle in Cape Town for barter. When quizzed where they came from, they replied 'from over the mountain', a name the area was never to loose. The Dutch boldly described it in the past as a place *waar die macht der hoog edel Compagnie endig –* an *area where the might of the illustrious Company ends.*

To the north-east the lush Overberg is bounded by the Langeberg mountain range at the foot of which one finds Swellendam and to the south by the sea. It is a winter rainfall area and watered by many perennial streams.

The constant need for slaughter stock led to the exploration of the Overberg. A report of 1666 mentions the arrival of 12 French ships in Table Bay and states, almost in despair that 'they ate everything, leaving little for the return fleet from Batavia'.

In 1667 Corporal Cruse led a barter trip from Cape Town to trade with the Hessequa. It is uncertain with how much success he met. But from a second trip which took him as far as the Gouritz River (see page 81) where he traded with the Gouriquas, he returned with 150 cattle and 310 sheep.

Incidentally, Cruse's daughter was to become the mother of the first Cape born governor, Hendrik Swellengrebel. (see page 28).

After 1707 the number of farmers permitted to graze cattle beyond the mountains increased steadily -'gepermitteerd met zijn vee te gaan leggen en weijden'. Their families were large, their children married young. Because of the vast distances, it was not unusual for parents to present themselves and their children simultaneously for their own marriage ceremony and their sometimes adult children to be baptised in the Groote Kerk (Mother Church), in Cape Town!

Growth and development of the Overberg was unhurried though it was soon denuded of its forests. Wagonloads of timber rumbled to the Castle where the authorities had issued *placaaten*, or orders, forbidding anybody to chop wood for personal use. Forests were considered Company property, and commanders in charge of woodcutters' posts were required to deliver wood regularly.

First steps towards development occurred when Colonel Jacob Gordon introduced in 1789 Spanish merino sheep which were to make the Overberg a major wool producing region. The Cape sheep of the Khoi had fat in their tails but bore hair and not wool.

The N2 continues its stride through wheat fields and valleys which are clad in juicy green after the winter rains, glow gold in spring, but look cheerless and quite drab in summer. At the entrance to Caledon, to the left of the national road, lie the **Caledon Botanical Gardens,** a major attraction of the town.

The Gardens are linked to the National Botanical Gardens and cover about 50 hectare of land. They are host to a remarkable collection of indigenous flowers which are best admired in September, the month of Caledon's Wild Flower Show.

Before venturing into the Gardens the term *fynbos* needs to be explained.

What is fynbos?
Fynbos stems from the Afrikaans language and means simply *fine bush*. It describes the fine-leaved heathland vegetation which grows on the infertile soils of the Cape mountains and near the coast. Within the Cape Floristic Kingdom it is species-rich vegetation though its major component is made up of three plant families. These are the erica or heath family, which is joined by the protea and restio families. Not to be left out of the floral splendour of this grouping, other species join, such as the gladioli, irises, orchids and many others. Fynbos is essentially a knee-to-shoulder-high vegetation which has adapted well to the climatic conditions of the Cape: cold and wet winters, and dry, mostly windy summers.

The protea genus, of which about 350 species are counted in South Africa, is probably the best known plant within fynbos. It was named by the Swedish botanist Linnaeus after the Greek god Proteus who, to avoid unwanted visitors or perhaps detection by evil-doers, assumed different forms and shapes. An

The King Protea

apt description of this lovely plant which appears in equally many different colours, sizes and shapes.

The King Protea *(Protea cynaroides)* is the country's national flower.

The entire nature reserve on the slopes of the Swartberg extends to just over 200 hectare. It was established in 1927, largely the fruit of a group of ardent nature lovers' enthusiastic, hard work.

To fully enjoy nature's treasure chest, a 10km-long walk through the reserve with its panoramic views is highly recommended.

After this visit, the national road approaches, but by-passes Caledon, readily recognised by its massive silos. A downhill drive past the Museum, Standard Bank building and the 'Theewaterskloof Municipality' leads to the centre of

CALEDON (110km from Cape Town)
The town is enfolded by appealing surroundings, dominated by the 1089m-high Swartberg near the town's entrance, and the 1167m-high Tower of Babel in the south (along Shaw's Pass, the R320). It lies at the heart of an agricultural area that produces wheat, barley and wool.

The discovery of **hot springs** led to Caledon's development. The 7 iron-rich springs (one cold and six hot) were known to the San and Khoikhoi long before the European settled in the Cape. They called these springs bubbling to the surface d*isporekamma,* or 'Hot Water', and the river into which they flowed was the Hacqua (Zebra) River.

> ### Shaw's Pass
> *is named after ex-Indian army officer, Lt.Col. William Shaw.*
> *He settled in the area in 1839 and was very involved in furthering agriculture. He lived on the farm 'Muirton', after his family home in Scotland. The original farm name was 'Tryuntjierivier'.*

In the 1650s settlers chanced upon the springs, and fifty years later Ferdinandus Appel was granted land nearby on condition he build a guest house and vegetable garden for travellers. One wonders why he was so privileged. Appel had been chosen to guide a high ranking official, Cnoll, to these iron-rich springs in 1710. Cnoll suffered from severe rheumatism and sought relief from these medicinal waters.

The first baths were simply hollowed out on the slopes with pick and shovel and allowed to fill. After 1710, the water was led into permanent baths in a special bath house. The baths proved immensely popular and few dignitaries visiting the country missed the chance to seek relief at the baths.

In 1785 a Dr John Frederick Hassner arrived at the Cape. A visit to the baths in 1804 prompted him to submit a report which detailed his recommendations on how to improve and expand them. Hassner built a 14-roomed guesthouse in 1806 and developed a European styled spa.

Forty slaves saw to the comforts of the sick, maintained the buildings and laboured on the fields around the property.

In 1817, Hassner suffered the tragic loss of his wife who died in childbirth. By then a town had been established which bore the name *Swartbergbad*, but was subsequently renamed after an early English governor at the Cape, the Earl of Caledon. When Sir Lowry's Pass opened in 1830, transport improved and greatly boosted economic activities in the area. In 1899 the railway line reached Caledon, again facilitating transport of agricultural produce.

At about the same time the brothers J.G. and W.J. Walsh acquired the land on which the old VOC and Dr Hassner's guesthouse had once stood. An extensive renovation and redevelopment programme was launched. Soon the new sanatorium with its magnificent views lured the visitors to the town. Residents were now advised by physicians on the nature of their disease and hydrotherapy programmes prescribed. Caledon had become the focus of social life in the Overberg until flames destroyed the sanatorium in 1946.

Today, the baths have become the setting for an elegant hotel, sanatorium and casino

Caledon Mineral Spring Water samples were submitted in 1893 in the Chicago World Fair and won First Prize.

A walk down the historic Mill, Church and Constitution Streets reveals some historic architecture. Mill Street, a declared conservation area, is part of the Old Wagon Road which entered the town over the Bath River, near the hot springs. The bridge spanning the river has been restored. The first residential plots stretched to the Bath River and houses were built above the Wagon Road. The oldest building in Caledon stands probably in 35-37 Mill Street. It dates back to 1817 and is easily recognised by its high *stoep* or terrace, and front gable built in the tradition of Cape Dutch gables. By contrast, 24 Mill Street is a splendid example of a Victorian-styled home. It has a hipped roof and central covered gable, two projecting gables with bay windows.

Particularly attractive is the green striped verandah roof.

Church Street is the town's first official street. Near the corner with Mill Street stands the old Town Hall which dates from 1906. Today this fine building is home to the Tourism Information Office and Museum. The Museum has many historical displays, including a house museum at 11 Constitution Street which is a building of the late Victorian period. On Fridays, the hungry visitor can buy bread here, baked in the traditional wood-burning oven.

In March, Caledon celebrates the harvest of wheat and other cereals, like barley.

The production of barley contributes enormously to the wealth of the Overberg area. In 1978 the Southern Associated Maltsters was founded to develop a local malting industry. This company is now the largest malt producer for South African lager beer.

Barley is a winter cereal crop and is a member of the grass genus *Hordeum*. It is characterised by strong germination, a high protein content and plumpness of grain. Not all of it goes into the production of beer: some barley is also used for pearling, ground into small grains, familiar in soups and stews. Smaller quantities of barley are converted to yeast and malt extracts, and some barley is also grown as forage. Altogether about 140 000 tons of barley are produced annually.

Nature does not only please the eye, it also spoils the palate. In Caledon grows a fine onion species, favoured by climate and latitude: the **Caledon Globe onion**, developed through cross-breeding and selection. The quality onion is harvested in January.

Caledon House Museum

> ### Geological formation of the springs
> #### *(Extract from the leaflet 'Caledon's Historic Walk')*
>
> *The hot springs owe their existence to the geological structure of the region. The Caledon fault, an ancient zone of rock fracture and movement, cuts steeply through the earth's crust along the southern foot of the Swartberg. This fault separates the Table Mountain sandstone uplands from the gently undulating country to the south, which are underlain by more easily-weathered mud rocks of the Bokkeveld group. Rainwater falling on the southern Swartberg and perhaps also on the Steenboksberg south of Caledon, finds its way deep underground via many cracks and fissures in the sandstone. The groundwater is warmed by the earth's internal heat to over 53ºC at enormous depths of at least two kilometres. In these hot waters metallic impurities in the sandstone, such as iron and manganese and a little silica, are dissolved. The recycling of groundwater to the surface is blocked in the lowlands by the overlying barrier of impermeable Bokkeveld mud rock. But when hot, mineralised groundwater (now under great pressure) meets the zone of shattered rocks along the Caledon Fault, they can ascent rapidly to the surface emerging as chalybeate (iron-rich) hot springs along the fault line. Rapid oxydation and cooling of the water causes precipitation of previously dissolved minerals as various ores of iron, manganese and silica around the spring eyes, at least seven of which have been identified. These mineral deposits have accumulated over time to form a mound of rusty to coffee-brown earths and silvery-grey metallic ores about 6m thick which extends northwards across the N2 from beneath the modern Spa.*

CONTINUATION: CALEDON/N2 TOWARDS SWELLENDAM:

From Caledon town centre, return to the national road. In a continual see-saw motion it winds its way past endless fields where sheep and cattle graze contentedly, small white egrets hover near the cattle, blue cranes gather and the odd buzzard circles overhead, out to spot its prey.

Forty kilometres outside Caledon, the R326 heads off south-westerly towards the coast and the small town of Stanford (see page 52). Shortly afterwards it reaches

RIVIERSONDEREND (163km from Cape Town)
was once known as the *Zoete Melks Valley*, the 'Sweet Milk Valley'.

The young town – it dates back to 1923 – is named after the mountains and the eponymous river: 'River Without End'. The Sonderend River has its origin in the Theewaterskloof near Villiersdorp. Even the Khoikhoi must have been overawed by its sheer length as in their language *Kanna Kam Kanna* expressed the same. This name was adopted and translated by the traveller and horticulturist Jan Hartogh, employed by the Dutch East India Company, when he visited the region in 1707.

Today, Riviersonderend is a farming centre and renowned for the many sightings of the elegant Blue Crane. Although large colonies of Blue cranes gather on the surrounding fields, the bird is threatened by extinction. Its decline is mainly due to poisoning incidents.

The Blue Crane – Bloukraanvoel (Anthropoides paradisea)

The large Blue Crane has a distinctive blue-grey plumage, a bulbous head and long slate-grey tertials that curve elegantly to the ground. It lives on the midland and highland grassveld, the edge of the Karoo, cultivated land and edges of vleis in the eastern and southern regions of South Africa.

The Blue Crane is a strong flier and soars well, often calling with a fairly high-pitched rattling croak from great heights.

It roosts on the ground or in shallow wate. the birds seem to enjoy displaying their beauty as they can often be seen 'dancing' in groups or in pairs.
Frogs,insects, reptiles, fish, grain and green shoots make up the diet

It breeds from October to February, lining its simple nest sometimes with pebbles, bits of plant material or even sheep droppings.

Of the estimated 10 000 to 14 000 surviving birds, almost 7 000 are found in the Overberg region.

One normally sees it in pairs or family groups as it is a highly gregarious bird when not breeding. Flocks number usually from 30 to 40 birds, sometimes up to 300.

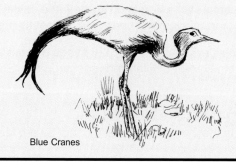

Blue Cranes

Kleinberge Hiking Trail

The 7km-long trail is situated on the historical farm Tygerhoek, 'Tiger's Corner'. The Sonderend River splashes by at the foot of the hiking trail, where weary hikers can cool down on a hot summer day.

Along the trail one passes a signal cannon used during the days of the Dutch East India Company. In 1734 the Company moved cannons to the high points of the Overberg area. This original cannon chain started at Sir Lowry's Pass, stretched across to Houw Hoek, to the Swartberg and the Hessequakloof beyond Storms River. Later additional cannons were placed at Tygerhoek, Luiperdsberg and Swellendam.

When the alarm was raised, the signalman posted near the cannon, fired a shot and made smoke until he received a reply from the nearest farm. The field-cornet then mustered his men and commandeered the necessary supplies. This was a laborious but efficient system: in 1806 it alerted the people of Swellendam of the 2nd British occupation. It took just 8 hours for the signal to reach the town. The well-maintained cannons in the Overberg area were only fired twice: 1795 and 1806.

The journey continues past vast wheatfields where considerate farmers have erected bright yellow boards to educate the traveller: Wheat, Rye, Barley…. After about 20km, the national road meets with a turnoff to the R317. In a northerly direction it leads past the small village of **Stormsvlei** to **Bonnievale**, and in a southerly direction to **Bredasdorp** (see page 61).

The terrain assumes a somewhat more rugged character. Aloes cover the hills, ahead rise the immense Langeberg Mountains, with the Breede River, (Broad River) cutting a south-easterly course along the foothills of the mountains. We cross this river just a few kilometres outside the town of Swellendam, 40km away from Stormsvlei.

SWELLENDAM (221km from Cape Town)
stretches out on the banks of the Koringland Rivier, the 'Cornland River'.

By 1743 numerous farms had been established in the Overberg region, extending as far away as Mossel Bay (see page.88). The arduous journeys undertaken by the farmers and their families to reach Cape Town for official business or to attend church could take more than two months. The decision therefore to establish another magisterial district in 1745 was welcomed, as was also the siting in Swellendam of its administrative centre, known as a *drostdy*.

Swellendam lies 'where there dwells a shower of rain, where there is a river with a fertile valley and the Great Wagon Road passes through it', used by stock bargaining expeditions into the interior.

Early trade focused on transport, the *wagenmaakers end smeeden*, the wagon-makers and smithys. By the time wagoneers entered the village from the west they had crossed torturous mountain ranges and hazardous rivers such as the Sonderend, Brëe, Leeu and the Klippige rivers. Their battered wagons certainly needed an overhaul and their weary animals a rest.

Swellendam,today a lively farming centre, bears the name of Governor Hendrik **Swellengrebel** and his wife, Helena ten **Damme**. It became the centre of political strife in 1795. The townsfolk, aggrieved by the slack and often corrupt conduct of the Dutch East India Company dismissed the land-drost in 1795 and proclaimed Swellendam an independent republic! Its somewhat reluctant first president was Herman Steyn. 'Independence' last-ed for just over four months: when the British landed in 1795, the Swellendam Republicans swore allegiance to King George III, and the land-drost was duly re-instated.

The Drostdy buildings throughout the Cape were sold by the British govern-ment in 1846. The Swellendam Drostdy remained in private hands until 1931 when it was re-purchased by the government.

Swellendam's fortunes received a major boost in 1820 when Joseph Barry and his two nephews established their business in the town. At the time, a disastrous drought threatened the survival of man and beast. The govern-ment called for tenders for the delivery of emergency supplies to the Overberg. The tender went to Joseph Barry whose transportation proposal proved the most efficient and fastest: his investigations had established the Brëe Rivier's navigability to about 33 km from its mouth. With the successful tender documents in his pocket, Barry purchased the cutter 'Duke of Gloucester' and shipped supplies to the river mouth, instead of following the tedious landlocked mountain route. From here his little ship 'Kadie' trans-ported goods up-river before being loaded on to ox-wagons to complete the journey to Swellendam. The Barry empire prospered, leading also to the establishment of two small villages, **Malgas** and **Port Beaufort** (see p.77)

For now, explore Voortrek Street, the Old Wagon Road, starting at the western end where some of the town's oldest buildings exude a happy mix of mostly Cape Dutch, Georgian and Victorian styles. An excellent booklet on the architecture of Swellendam is available at the Tourism Information offices in Voortrek Street. Let's look at some of them.

The Old Boys School cnr Nr 147 Voortrek and Moolman Streets

This appealing building in the Cape Georgian style, stands on land that had been granted in 1818 to the town's well know wagon maker, Jacobus Wessel van Dijk. He built a thatch-roofed house seven years later on the mountain slope with expansive views of the valley.

A double flight of steps leads to the front door, flanked on either side by two half and two full sash windows. The beautiful fanlight allowed light to penetrate to the interior of the house. The impressive end gables with their convex curves round off a picture of harmony and symmetry.

The sloping ground of the property lent itself to the building of a cellar which became van Dijk's workshop.

The Old Boys School

The building accommodated the Swellendam Grammar School after 1870.

Christ Church

The church was built of dressed stone in 1911. Neo-romanesque and neo-gothic elements, popular styles at the time, are in strong evidence. Christ Church stands on the site of an earlier thatched church, designed in 1860 by Sophie Gray, the wife of the first Anglican bishop, Robert Gray, in the Cape.

Bishop Robert Gray arrived in 1848, accompanied by his wife and four children. Until then, the Anglican community had held its services in Dutch Reformed churches whose hospitality had been gratefully accepted. Under the Bishop, a tireless worker, the Anglicans embarked on an intense church building programme, enthusiastically supported by Mrs Gray, a skilled draughtswoman. The next few years witnessed a mushrooming of 'Sophie Gray' designed churches in the country.

72 Voortrek Street, Old St. Luke's Church

(The first church services were held in the Drostdy until the Dutch Reformed Church was built in 1802). This church dates back to the middle of the 19th century. St. Luke's was deconsecrated when the Anglican parish moved to the new St. Luke's in Railton in the 1970s. It is today an Apostolic church. In style it blends Cape Dutch and Revival Gothic features.

No 36 Voortrek Street, Oefeninghuis – Meeting House

in the Cape Dutch style is certainly eye catching with its flowing end gables. This modest building, standing almost on an island in the middle of the street, dates back to 1838. Under the supervision of the Rev. Dr. William Robertson it was built for educational and religious purposes. The school was controlled by a Board of Directors made up of leading inhabitants of the town. When independent mission churches and schools were established, the 'Oefeninghuis' lost its purpose and became redundant. It was sold in 1922 by the Directors who stipulated that it may never be used as 'a canteen or dance hall'.

The glazed frame beneath the false clock in the west gable once housed a real clock.

Today it is home to the Swellendam Information Bureau.

Oefeninghuis

Not far away, the

Dutch Reformed Church

towers over the street. An unorthodox mixture of Gothic, Renaissance, Baroque and Cape architectural elements lend the building distinction and magnificence. It was built in 1911 on the site of an earlier thatched church of 1802. The arched gateway in the front right hand corner of the property is all that remains of the original church.

It is open to visitors and its breathtaking interior is well worth a visit.

Dutch Reformed Church Swellendam

Opposite the church stands a simple plinth of dressed stone, bearing a lamp and an inscription. This is a memorial to the coronation of King George V. in 1911.

Nearby and on the same side of the street one finds the 'Barry' buildings:

No 4, 6 Voortrek Street - 'Barry House'
This building, originally single storeyed, was the 'Barry & Nephews Company' store. At some later stage, the double storeyed 'Barry Bank' was added to the back portion which ultimately led to the overall increase in height in the late 19th century Cape Victorian style.

The Barrys lived next to their store in

Auld House, 2 Voortrek Street
This Cape Dutch-Cape Georgian home was built in 1802 with an unusual double-T ground-plan and interesting end gables. The façade may have been restored after the fire of 1835. The extension on the left of the front wing is late 19th century.

Barry House

The Batavian Period at the Cape (1802-1806) and the Second British Occupation

At the end of the First British occupation, the Cape was returned to Dutch rule. Two highly principled and capable men were appointed to govern the Cape. Advocate J. de Mist became the Commissioner-General, and General Janssens the Governor. Both had imbibed the liberalism that was sweeping Europe, but believed also in a strong, central government. Extensive journeys acquainted them with the conditions at the Cape, but sadly, their endeavours remained unsuccessful as renewed hostilities broke out in Europe. This time it was Napoleon I, whose military and political ambitions plunged Europe into war. France, with its allies Spain and the Batavian Republic, challenged British maritime supremacy, only to be defeated by Nelson in 1805 at the Battle of Trafalgar.

Despite her mastery upon the oceans, Britain feared for the safety of her Indian possessions. To secure the Cape as a supply point on the passage to India, England dispatched a large fleet under the command of Sir Home Popham. Close to troops who totally outnumbered the defenders led by Governor Lieutenant-General Jan Willem Janssen. A few kilometers outside town, the warring parties clashed. Janssen, in the face of the overwhelming odds, withdrew his men to Hottentots Holland whilst Colonel von Proplahow surrendered Cape Town. The capitulation was signed at Papendorf (Woodstock) on 10 January 1806.

The Batavian era had ended and the **Second British Occupation** *began. It lasted until 1814 when the Treaty of Paris formally ceded the Cape to Britain.*

Near the two 'Barry' houses, **Gelderblom Street** joins Voortrek Street, opposite. Here one finds a very interesting cluster of buildings, a row of *tuishuise* or farmers' town houses and 'The Cottage', in the shade of ancient oaks.

The little square developed probably when the Dutch Reformed Congregation was established in 1798. It was difficult for farmers to find accommodation in the small town when they came to attend church services, particularly *nagmaal*, Holy Communion. They either built their own small townhouses or hired them, the famous *tuishuise* – homes from home. These became a feature of many country towns in the interior.

Walking on, where 'Van Oudtshoorn Road' joins Voortrek Street a name change occurs: Voortrek Street now becomes **Swellengrebel Street.** .

As you cross the **Koringland River,** picture a narrow footbridge in the old days over which the *burghers* walked to consult the magistrate on the other side of the river. The drift for the wagons was a little higher up the river.

No 18 Swellengrebel is a double-storeyed, formal house which was converted in the middle of the 19th century from a single-storey structure. It accommodates the offices of the Drostdy Museum. Striking is the cornice with the stepped parapet, heavy rusticated quoins and window surrounds and the unusual fanlight. It is built in the Cape Georgian style.

Turn into **Hermanus Steyn Street** which abuts Swellengrebel opposite this elegant building to visit

Mayville, No 4 Hermanus Steyn Street (part of the Drostdy Museum complex)

The Mayville ground formed originally part of the Drostdy property which was acquired in 1846 by Daniel de Bruyn.

The new owner sub-divided the lower sections of the Drostdy land into six portions. Of these he sold five in 1853 but kept one for himself on which he built the house now known as Mayville. De Bruyn sold the Drostdy in 1855 and moved into his new home. Mayville reflects Cape Dutch and Cape Georgian details. This can be seen in the T-plan design and the semi-circular fanlight which is elegantly echoed by the small dormer window above the front door. The thatched roof has half-hipped ends instead of traditional gables. French windows with louvered shutters and tall sliding sashes are features of the Victorian era.

When his wife died ten years later, de Bruyn married Maria Constantina Wahl. On his death in 1873, his widow retained the property until 1885 when she sold it to the Civil Commissioner and Resident Magistrate Frederick Hodges. Hodges sadly died shortly after taking up his appointment. In 1887 his widow sold the house to Gertruida Jacomina Steyn.

Gertruida's husband, Pieter Gysbert, was a wainwright and blacksmith. The couple had two children, Cornelia, nick-named Nina, and Nita. The Steyn family had the longest association with the house and probably also gave it its name.

The two daughters inherited Mayville. In 1927 Nina sold her half share to her sister. The property originally extended right down to the river. During Nita's ownership, various parts were either sold or given away by her. In 1974 the Drostdy received Mayville in a bequest from Miss Nita Steyn. It included the furniture and household objects. It was also Nita's wish that a rose garden for the pleasure of visitors to the museum' be established.

After extensive renovations in the 1970s, Mayville is now furnished to represent a Swellendam home of the late Victorian period. It was opened to the public in 1978.

Return to Swellengrebel Street to enter the

The old gaol: 24-28 Swellengrebel Street
built 1746, shortly after the Drostdy. The long front section housed the Landdrost's Secretary to the left of the door, whilst to the right one would have entered the Deputy Sheriff's home.

The prison cells are at the back of the gaol. In the middle of the yard once stood a pillory where offenders were exposed to public ridicule. Many of the heemraaden and landdrosts in the countryside, responsible for meting out justice, could barely read or write. They mostly handled smaller incidents and

Swellendam gaol

referred criminal cases to Cape Town.

The werft buildings
a more recent addition of 1969, display the tools formerly used by craftsmen and artisans.

Step into the old Drostdy building across the street.

The Drostdy, with its grand views from the eastern bank of the Koringland

Swellendam Drostdy

River across the valley towards the Langeberg Mountains was built in 1747. It served the double purpose of offices and residence for the magistrate.

The Drostdy was extended to its present size and appearance by Landdrost Buissine in 1813. Clay and unburnt bricks were used for the walls, whilst the surrounding forests delivered the masses of yellowwood required for the framework, rafters, ceiling and most floorboards, except those in the work-shops, the kitchen and the painted sitting room floor. From the smithy of Hermanus Steyn came the locks and hinges.

Several internal doors are crafted out of yellowwood and stinkwood. The same woods were utilised for much of the exquisite furniture displayed which mirrors the styles then in vogue at the Cape, varying from baroque to neo-classical and regency.

In the entrance hall, paintings by Thomas William Bowler (1812-1869) allow us a glimpse of the surroundings of Swellendam and the the Breede River. They were commissioned by the Barry & Nephews Company.
The modern housewife would probably not want to work on the open stove in the kitchen, nor wish to polish the copper kitchenware which was mostly

made by local craftsmen, whilst the ironware was imported.

The resident and his family were assured of a good night's rest in the elegantly appointed bedrooms. The house servant, or perhaps the teacher, would have to be satisfied with the far more unpretentious bedroom next to the kitchen.

The Administration Building

The building was sold by the English colonial government in 1846 and became the property of the Steyn family who owned it until the 1930s when the Drostdy was acquired by the government and refurbished as a museum.

After the Drostdy visit, relax at

Zanddrift, 32 Swellengrebel Street

situated opposite the Drostdy. This building was originally the homestead on the farm *Zanddrift*, near Bonnievale. In 1976 it was completely dismantled and rebuilt, stone by stone, in its present setting. An amazing achievement, if one considers that the earliest section of the front wing dates from about 1757.

To reach the **BONTEBOK NATIONAL PARK** continue beyond Zanddrift along Swellengrebel Street which joins the national road in a broad uphill swing. Beware of fast moving traffic either direction! Watch for the turn-off immediately to the right. The access gravel road crosses the railway line and Swellendam airfield, before it comes to the entrance gates to the park.

The bontebok occurs naturally only in the Overberg, from Bot River to Mossel Bay, between the ocean and the Riviersonderend Mountain ranges.

In 1689, Izaq Schrijver, on one of his exploratory trips up the coast, reported seeing '1000 bonte harte bokken loopen'. In coming years passing travellers recorded sightings of increasingly smaller herds. By 1803 a mere ten bontebok were spotted near Swellendam. Clearly the antelope was loosing its battle against human encroachment. Not only was its meat highly favoured, but increasing land cultivation robbed the bontebok of its habitat.

By 1837 legislation was introduced to protect the bontebok. Alexander van der Byl, owner of the farm *Nachtwacht* south of Bredasdorp, placed 27 bontebok on his farm in an enclosure to safeguard them from extinction. His example was followed by neighbouring farmers, such as the van Breda,

Albertyn and Uys families. Their numbers slowly recovered, but their survival was still threatened: by 1927 just over 115 bontebok could be counted on Bredasdorp and Swellendam farms. Drastic action was needed and just in the nick of time, the government stepped in. It acquired the farm *Quarrie Bos* near Bredasdorp in 1931 for the protectection of the buck.

Though the bontebok population grew, the unfortunate discovery-was made that the soil lacked essential trace elements and that para-sitic infections in the vleis impacked nega-tively on the animal. It was decided to re-locate the park to the south of Swellendam where the National Parks Board re-established the bontebok in 1960. It has flourished ever since. Today the park is also home to springbok, rhebok, duiker and grysbok.

The Breede River forms the southern boundary for the park. Beyond the park it meanders across the coastal plain towards the sea.

Langeberg Mountains

Marloth Nature Reserve

The magnificent Marloth Nature Reserve huddles in the Swellendam mountain range, between the towns of Swellendam, Ashton, Barrydale and Suurbraak. It extends over 14 123 hectare to which must be added an additional 16 532 hectare of privately owned proclaimed mountain catchment land.

The name honours the pioneer botanist, Marloth, who petitioned the Minister of Lands & Forestry in 1928 to set aside part of the mountain as a nature reserve. The initial request was for a mere 190 hectare.

Mountain fynbos and patches of afro-montane forest welcome the hiker. Yellowwood, stinkwood, Cape beech, wild olve, assegaaibos, cherrywood and hard pear are amongst the most typical tree species encountered.

Overexploitation of timber for the local furniture industry, wagon making and the need for fuel were the main culprits in reducing the once large forested areas to their present size.

Grey rheebuck, klipspringer, baboon, common duiker, dassie, porcupine, mongoose and hare may dart across the paths whilst hopefully the leopard keeps out of sight!

Birdlife is equally diverse, fish eagle, woodpeckers and Cape vulture may circle overhead, whilst on the ground puffadders, Cape cobra and mountain adders may slither by.

Duiker

Eight day walks and the six-day Swellendam Hiking Trail have been laid out. On the longer trail, overnight accommodation consists of rustic huts equipped with mattresses accommodated the hiker. All trails start and end at the Reserve office, which is about 1,5km outside of Swellendam. Take a turn-off to Andrew Whyte Street to reach it.

Leopard

ROUTE TWO

CAPE TOWN(N2), COASTAL ROUTE(R44/R43) HERMANUS, THE OVERBERG – ELIM - BREDASDORP – CAPE AGULHAS – ARNISTON - SWELLENDAM

On this route follow first the national road N2 from Cape Town towards Somerset West. Just before the entrance to the town **exit 43, 'Broadway Boulevard/R44' and turn right.**

The road swings past the Strand Golf Club, bears right and crosses the *Lourens River*. As it enters the town of **Strand**, it becomes known as Beach Road. Magic views of False Bay and Table Mountain in the distance open up.

The 3km-long sandy beach is overlooked by modern high rise apartments which detract somewhat from the natural beauty and disguise the town's humble beginnings.

During the middle of the 19th century landdrost van Ryneveld of Somerset West, fond of the sea, moved here and allowed farmers to erect holiday shacks on his farm. Soon the place became known as *van Rhyneveldsdorp*. Once the road over the Cape Flats was complete and the railway line extended, the area's popularity grew. By 1896 the municipality of Somerset West-Strand came into being, changing in 1913 to Somerset Strand, to be finally known as 'Die Strand' in 1913, and today simply as Strand.

Soon Beach Road reconnects with the R44, but the sea and mountain magic continues as the road hugs the coast for another 5km and then reaches the little town of

GORDON'S BAY

Huge letters 'GB', laid out in white stones, gaze down from the mountain slopes. These are not the town's initials, but stand for the 'General Botha' training ship. Though the ship is now out of commission, naval and merchant marine officers are still trained in Gordon's Bay.

Gordon's Bay Yachting Harbour

Near 'Bikini Beach', the older part of Gordon's Bay and yachting harbour sparkle in the sun.

From the eastern shores of False Bay, the town enjoys superb views over the immense bay.

The road rises steeply above Gordon's Bay and follows the popular coast-line, particularly with fishermen. But this stretch of coast is also dangerous. A deadly backwash and monstrous waves have claimed the lives of many fishermen. Memorial crosses along the road mark the disaster spots.

The Steenbras River, named after a fish species, and crossed via a narrow bridge, enters False Bay waters just 3km outside Gordon's Bay. The coastal road, ever more spectacular, climbs around the cliffs before descending again to sea level at Koeël Bay (Bullet Bay), at the foot of the 1269m-high mountain of the same name. Again, the endless sandy beach is tempting, but swimming is not safe. At the end of the bay, the road rises once more to round Blousteenberg, the 'Blue Stone Mountain', site of earlier attempts to mine manganese.

The Rooi Els River mouth is reached, named after a red alder tree which once thrived here. The river enters the sea at Rooi Els Bay, a popular and fairly safe swimming spot.

Travelling towards Cape Hangklip

Just beyond Rooi Els take the turn-off to the right for

PRINGLE BAY
named after Rear-Admiral Thomas Pringle, commander of the Royal Navy at the Cape from 1796 to 1798. Pringle Bay is situated between the mouth of the Buffels River and a small peninsula known as The Point. Originally it was to be developed as a port to ship farm produce across False Bay to Simon's Town, but instead developed into a popular, if overbuilt holiday resort.

In the late 18th century, Cape Hangklip caves sheltered dangerous d*rosters,* or deserters. From their hide-out they attacked unsuspecting farmers, stealing their cattle. They murdered herdsmen and kidnapped children, atrocious deeds that were to lead to their capture as the search for the children led the pursuers eventually to the *drosters'* hideout. The children were found alive.

The **Cape Hangklip Lighthouse** is operated by remote control from Cape Point at the opposite, western coast of False Bay. It was installed in 1960 and has a range of 25 sea miles from 34 metres above high water. There is a revolving optic of 800 000CD, flashing once every 10 seconds.

At least six to seven shipwrecks are known to have occurred in the lighthouse area. Reputedly the *De Grundel*, a Dutch ship of 90 tons of the Delft Chambers of the VOC was the first. She went down on 20 February 1673. No lives were lost.

Cape Hangklip Lighthouse

Return to the R44 which cuts through the foothills of Cape Hangklip (453m) 'The Hanging Rock'. Cape Hangklip is the most easterly point of False Bay which stretches about 35km from east to west, and the same distance from north to south. Soon you reach

BETTY'S BAY
named after *Betty* Youlden, daughter of a property developer in the Hangklip area. Sadly, property development has caused irreparable scars on the mountain slopes and coastline. De
spite this attack on the visual senses, holiday makers are attracted in their droves to the sandy beaches. Others enjoy the tranquil lakes and foot paths meandering through the hills of the *Kogelberg*, the 'Bullet Mountain', or visit the Harold Porter Gardens. Enthusiasts of marine life can explore the rock pools along the shoreline which has long been a coastal reserve. Near **Stony Point**, once a whaling station established by a Captain Cook in 1907 and which operated until the 1930s, a colony of African Penguins, endemic to the south-western coast of southern Africa, has found a home. Watch them in the early morning or late afternoon when they return from fishing.

The African Penguin - *Speniscus demersus*

The bird's survival is threatened. Over the past 60 odd years the penguin numbers declined by nearly 90%, leaving a total adult population of approximately 170 000. Before the discovery of the suitability of guano in the manufacture of fertilisers, the African Penguin dug its nest several metres deep into guano. When commercial exploitation of guano began in the 19th century, the penguin was forced to nest in sand or under protective ledges, making them vulnerable to predators. They breed throughout the year, normally laying two eggs. Adult birds feed during the day, whilst the chicks have to wait for their meal of re-gurgitated fish until the late afternoon. Parent birds normally take turns in their duties: one guards the nest, the other swims out in search for food.

The attractive black-white feathered penguin moves rather awkwardly ashore, but once in its watery element, it shows off its prowess as an agile swimmer and first class diver. Nature has equipped the penguin with wonderful camouflage: the black back protects it from predators swimming above them, whilst the white front shields it from being easily spotted by sharks looking up!

The birds are not totally defenceless: they can inflict nasty bites. Do not agitate them by clapping hands or running.

Harold Porter Botanical Gardens

welcome nature lovers, professional and amateur botanists. The nature reserve covers 188 hectare and displays a wealth of remarkable wild flowers, including the exquisite Red Disa orchid, indigenous to the Cape. The rich and diverse flora thrives on the dunes, on the mountain slopes and in dark, deep gorges with their relict forests.
Strolls across the lawns or along paved walkways under shady trees towards Disa Kloof appeal to all ages. The more energetic may seek out the somewhat rugged path up Luiperds Kloof, the Leopard's Ravine.
The birdlover too will be richly rewarded by the twitter of the 88 species recorded in the reserve, among them the rare Protea canary and the orange-breasted sunbird.
The land was a bequest in the late 1950s by Harold Nixon Porter, a co-owner of the Cape Hangklip Beach Estate Company.

Helichrysum vestitum

Leucospermum cordifolium

Kogelberg Nature Reserve

UNESCO recognised Kogelberg as the country's first biosphere reserve, which is an acknowledgement that people can live in harmony with nature, especially those living near protected areas. The reserve covers the entire coastal area from Gordon's Bay to the Bot River, and inland as far as Grabouw and the Groenland Mountains.

Kogelberg is home to over 1600 plant species of which 77 are endemic, and small patches of indigenous forest.

Nearly 18 000 hectare are kept pristine and natural where the conservation of the immense biological diversity is the priority. Only activities which do not impact negatively on the area nor on the wildlife are permitted, such as hiking, mountain biking and bird watching.

Beyond the border of this area, the surrounding plantations, farmlands, towns and villages are a transition zone where conservation is actively promoted.

Permits are needed for all activities in the reserve which is open from 07h30 to 19h00 in summer, and in winter from 08h00 to 18h00.

The Palmiet River mouth is crossed just outside Bettys Bay, and 3km beyond the bridge

KLEINMOND

is reached. Kleinmond means 'Little Mouth' and describes the lesser water run of the **Bot River**, the 'Butter River'. 'Bot' is a literal translation of the ancient Khoi word for the river, *Gouga*. The Bot River, first mentioned in the Company's Register of 22 July 1672, rises south of the Theewaterskloof Dam, forms a marsh near its mouth and then an expansive stretch of water known as the Bot River Lagoon.

Though humans have walked the shores near Kleinmond some 20 000 years ago – stone hand axes have been found – development was tardy. One formidable barrier to human intrusion on a large scale was the Kogelberg mountain which isolated the coastal plains.

In 1739 the first grazing land, *Welgemoet,* was granted to one Andries Grove. A hardy traveller to the area records some thirty years later sightings of wild animals, but no encounters with human beings. A Cape lion charged a travelling party led by William Paterson at the Palmiet River mouth, hippos threatened them near the Kleinmond Lagoon, herds of kudu delighted them at Bot River.

By the middle of the 19th century a small fishing community had entrenched itself at Jongensklip, near todays fishing harbour. Then too, the Albertyn family from Caledon was attracted to the sea at Kleinmond and built a holiday home in 1861. In 1899 and 1912 respectively, the authorities allowed the Albertyns to erect a further two buildings near the river mouth. Inevitably this development lured other families to the area. About 1919, the Kaplan brothers from Bot River acquired portion of the Lamloch Farm on which the town was laid out. Until the Second World War, Kleinmond slumbered peacefully. But when Cape Hangklip became the look-out post for the ever present menace of U-boats, life changed abruptly.

Italian prisoners-of-war built the coastal road from Gordon's Bay which would have been a wonderful link to the world had it not been damaged by a massive veld fire and then washed away by ensuing torrential rains, isolating Kleinmond. Travellers crossed the Palmiet River by ferry once more. This quaint mode of transport ended in 1952 when the Palmiet River was bridged.

Cape River Frog

As a holiday destination, Kleinmond spoils the nature lover: a network of hiking trails leads into the Kogelberg Nature Reserve; wild horses bound through the Rooisand Reserve – these horses may have been abandoned by the British during the Anglo-Boer War, or formed part of a Boer commando, or their ancestry may even be linked to the Great War; the rare Strawberry Rain Frog, (*Cape Platanna*) may be spotted in the estuaries and marshes near the town; and of course, swimming, angling, mountain biking and golfing can be enjoyed.

Beyond Kleinmond, the coastal road (R44) turns easterly and finds its way along the foot of the *Palmietberge* (593m) with magnetizing views of Sandown Bay's vast sandy beach. Then it points sharply north as it swings past the Botriver Lagoon. Alien vegetation, such as eucalyptus and acacia species, has infested the natural fynbos, and the tranquility of the vlei seems disturbed by the enormous 'Arabella' development on its shore. About 12km outside Kleinmond, the R44 meets with the R43 which, in a northerly direction, links with the national road N2 near Botriver (see page 14).

You follow the easterly arm of the R43 which swings around the Botriver Lagoon and then along the coast via Hawston, Vermont, Onrus to Hermanus

Very soon the Bot River is crossed and the view of the Botriver Lagoon broadens considerably as the route travels southward. Fields and meadows roll by, then the road becomes busy again as it approaches the fishing village of

HAWSTON

named after a civil commissioner of the Caledon district, C.R. Haw. A seemingly endless beach is tempting, but swimming can be hazardous. Take care. An annual sea festival is celebrated at the beginning of December at the Hawston camping site.

A number of turn-offs point to **VERMONT** and **ONRUS**, the latter meaning 'Restless'. People disagree whether the incessant, restless droning of the sea is responsible for the curious name, or the energetic little river which bubbles forth from the Babilonstoring Mountain,'Tower of Babel' (1167m) above the resort and *restlessly* enters the sea.

Heavy surf pounds the rocky coastline and the small beach popular with surfers and body-boarders alike, despite strong currents. For safe swimming one should head for the tranquil lagoon at the mouth of the Onrus River.

Fast traffic rushes towards Hermanus. In fact, in summer, particularly during the Christmas Holidays, the motorist must expect long delays and traffic queues when the whole world appears to descend on

HERMANUS

stretching out at the foot of the Kleinriver Mountains, with Maanskynkop rising to 964 metres. An itinerant teacher and shepherd, Hermanus Pieters from the Caledon farm of Boontjieskraal (Little Bean), lent the lively town its name.

One day he passed through the peaceful Hemel en Aarde, *(*Heaven and Earth) valley hiding behind the Kleinriver Mountains. Here a leper station had been established in 1814. (The patients from this station were transferred to Robben Island near Cape Town in 1845). From the lepers, Pieters learned about the *Elephant's Path* which led towards the coast. Doubtful but eager, he set off and, to his joy, the path eventually took him to the edge of the sea, but also to a fresh spring. The magnificent bay became his camp site, *Hermanuspietersfontein,* to which he returned time and again to tend his flocks.

The news of good grazing land behind the mountains and fresh water near the sea spread rapidly and not before long, the German settler Michael Henn and his large family, wife Henrietta, 5 sons and 5 daughters, ventured to the bay. The family fished and burned shells to make lime. One of their shell collecting forays led them close to Skilphoek, the Shell Corner, where the Henns decided to move. Hermanus Pieters had gained new neighbours. Ox wagons and the boat 'Nellie', the gig used by the ship's doctor of the ill-fated Birkenhead, (see page 58)transported their worldly goods to the new abode.

Increasing numbers of fishermen and settler families put their roots down at *Hermanuspietersfontein* which soon was shortened to Hermanus. By 1863 the first church was built, St. Peter's, shortly afterwards a school. The rustic settlement reached village status by 1891, governed by a management board. Thirteen years later, Hermanus became a municipality whose fame as a fashionable retreat even reached England. One of the town's first regular visitors was the general manager of the South African Railways, Sir William Hoy. He was so enamoured by the surrounding splendour that he successfully blocked the extension of the Bot River railway line – an amazing bequest: Hermanus Station has no trains or railway lines.

The hotel trade blossomed early (the Marine Hotel was established in the 1900s), as did the fishing industry. Henn's old 'Nellie' and others worked from the unique **Old Harbour** - a rocky cove with a dangerous entrance. Frequent damage to boats, even shipwrecks led to the construction of the new harbour, at the western end of town.

Hermanus Old Harbour

What to do in Hermanus

Beaches
Magnificent beaches, from soft white sands – perfect for that lazy walk -to rock protected coves, cater for the sun worshippers.

Grotto Beach is the town's longest and largest beach. It stretches east to the mouth of the Kleinrivier Lagoon and beyond to 'Die Plaat'.

Voelklip Beach is a little closer to town. The nearby Kammabaai, also known as Nanny's Beach and Lover's Cove, is popular with the surfers.

Sandbaai Beach lies to the west of Hermanus. Its coves and rock pools are popular during low tide; a favourite snorkel beach.

Walks

The Hermanus Cliff Path

is undoubtedly one of the most popular walks. It stretches for 12km from the new harbour in Westcliff along the stunning coastline to Grotto Beach and is accessible from many different points. The walkway will be heavily congested during the ten day **Whale Festival** in spring which celebrates annually the arrival of the magnificent Southern Right Whale to Walker Bay and turns Hermanus into a lively hub of culinary and cultural attractions.

The town's famous **whale crier** alerts visitors of their arrival.

The Southern Right Whale – *Eubalaena australis*

The Southern Right whale has no teeth. It eats by filling its huge mouth with water and then sieving it through the hairy baleen plates that hang from the roof of its mouth. Enormous quantities of tiny crustaceans called krill are caught in these baleen plates and swallowed – often accompanied by small fish and squid. Its stocky body is black, with occasional white markings along the back and underside. It has neither dorsal fin nor any ridge along the back. The adult whale grows up to 18 m and weighs on average 41 000kg. Whales normally produce one young after a gestation of about twelve months; it measures 5 to 6 metres at birth. They are born tail first.

It was judged 'right' to catch because it is rich in oil and floats when killed.Its slow average speed of 2 to 3 knots made it soon the world's most ruthlessly hunted whale species. Threatened by extinction, this species falls under international protection since 1935.

The whale inhabits sub-antarctic waters. During the cold winter months it migrates north to mate, calve and rear its young; during summer it moves south again when food supplies are more bountiful.

The whale can easily be recognised by its V-shaped 'blow' and the callosities on or around its huge head which are outgrowths of tough skin and form different patterns on each individual whale.

Whales are large brained and sensitive creatures with strong bonds between the females and their calves. They are normally non-aggressive and gentle.

Walks in the Fernkloof Nature Reserve

The Fernkloof Reserve, guarded by its highest mountain 'Aasvoelkop' (824m), was established in 1957 and has since then grown from a mere 100 hectare to some 1400 hectare. The untiring efforts to eradicate its invasive alien vegetation, has turned Fernkloof into a fynbos paradise. The reserve is managed by the Hermanus Botanical Society which welcomes its members and visitors to regular slide shows and talks in the Fernkloof Hall.

Fernkloof lies at the extreme west end of the Kleinrivier Mountains, the magnificent mountain backdrop to the town. These ancient mountains of Table Mountain sandstone were formed over 400 million years ago and knew their first flowering plants at the time of the Gondwanaland split-up which occurred about 70 –100 million years ago. Ever since then plants have been able to develop and evolve more or less undisturbed.

Disa cornuta

Aspalatus capensis

Some 1100 plant species are known to grow in the reserve. Their splendour is displayed in the September wild-flower festival.

A network of well graded walking paths traverses the reserve as well as a mountain bike trail. If you are looking for views of Hermanus and wish to test your endurance, then probably you would want to tackle Aasvoelkop. To reach its commanding height of 824 metres allow between 4 – 5 hours for a round trip, excluding rests.

Most other walks are of the gentler kind. Bear in mind that you may not necessarily walk alone, as troops of baboons enjoy the rocky outcrops as much as you. Klipspringers, steenbock and grysbock can be spotted and, be careful, also snakes. Please do not feed the animals.

Bird lovers too will enjoy the strolls as over 100 bird species have been recorded, amongst them Black eagle, steppe buzzard, sunbirds, Cape sugarbirds, jackal buzzards and ground woodpeckers and many 'little brown jobs'.

Steppe Buzzard

Naturally, you can simply relax with a picnic basket on the lawns opposite the Fernkloof offices.

The motorist reluctant to step out of his car can enjoy the views from Rotary Way. To find its start, head westerly towards Cape Town: about 4-km out of central Hermanus you find the turn-off 'Rotary Way'. Allow about an hour for a round trip.

Walks in the Walker Bay Nature Reserve

which lies east of Hermanus. The reserve consists of five coastal areas between Hermanus and Die Dam on the way to Struisbaai. The main section known as Walker Bay, extends from the Klein River estuary to De Kelders at Gansbaai and covers about 1000 hectare with a coastline of 17km. This fantastic beach with its white sands and rocky limestone outcrops is known as 'Die Plaat'. The northern boundary of the reserve is made up of stabilised dunefields.

Traces of human habitation going back some 85000 to 65000 years have been uncovered in the eastern section, in the Klipgat Cave, the 'Stone Hole' Cave. Here the Middle Stone Age people sheltered as did afterwards the Khoikhoi people some 2000 years ago. Fish, shellfish, plants and game in the area made up these ancient people's diet.

The main type of vegetation in the reserve is known as strandveld, a lowland coastal fynbos. It is characterised by plants such as blombos, bietou, sour fig and waxberry. In the 1900s until the 1980s rooikrans and Port Jackson (plants native to Australia) were planted out to stabilise the dunes. Invasive alien vegetation and increasing coastal development are a serious threat to the indigenous strandveld.

Blombos -Metalasia muricata

Along the banks of the Klein River one still finds dense thickets of old milkwoods, a protected species.

Tracks of the Cape clawless otter, bushbuck, duiker, grysbok and steenbok may be found.

Marine fish include the galjoen, kabeljou and steenbras which the lucky angler may catch at Galjoensbank, Sopiesklip, Skeurbank and other sites along the coast.

Day hikes are encouraged, angling, swimming and picnics are permitted – but no fires or overnight camping is allowed in the Walker Bay Reserve.

A permit for entry is obtainable from the Walker Bay Nature Reserve office at Voëlklip during office hours.

Normal restrictions apply for marine angling – permits are available at post offices.

Entry to the Reserve is from sunrise to sunset.

Whale watching in Hermanus

Fierce competition erupts annually between the towns and villages along the

South African coast: where is the best whale watching spot? Certainly, Hermanus counts amongst the leaders: the rocky cliffs offer breathtaking viewing of the Southern Right whales which start arriving in Walker Bay from June. By December they usually have disappeared. The best month for viewing is probably October.

From the rocks on Cliff Path, with a little luck, one may watch their antics almost from touching distance.

What do they do?

They breach: when they lift their massive bodies completely out of the water and leap joyously into the air. Whether this is an expression of sheer joy or a means of communication is still uncertain

spyhop: when they lift their head and part of their body vertically out of the water. Curiosity? Certainly a perfect 360° view to survey the scene

lobtail: when they slap their tails on the water's surface producing loud clapping noises. This could be a warning signal

sail: when they lift their tails clear out of the water. This could be a way of catching the wind to 'sail', or merely to cool down

blow: when they expel air from the lungs through the blowhole, producing a hollow, echoing sound

grunt: mainly at night - a loud, bellowing sound.

The pleasures of the sea
Legislation regarding the harvesting of marine organisms may change from time to time. Please inform yourself of these regulations before setting out on diving or angling trips. Telephone the Sea Fisheries on (028) 312 2609.

Abalone and Rock Lobster
Divers must be in possession of a valid permit available from the Hermanus Post Office.

Observe the closed seasons, the dates vary from year to year.

Sailing
The Hermanus Yacht Club, on the Klein River Lagoon, welcomes day visitors and for

Boating
visitors can hire boats on the Klein River Lagoon at Prawn Flats. Paddles-skis, kayaks and motorboats provide great entertainment.

The Old Harbour
Once this harbour witnessed the coming and going of fishing boats, the gutting of fish on the cement tables which were built in 1936, the banter of fishermen – today it is the stage for cultural events.

From the cliff-top entrance to the old harbour a marvellous view of Walker Bay welcomes the visitor. During whale time whales cavort about in the waters below, keeping you glued to the spot!

Before strolling down the slipway to the absorbing museum and the fishing boats which were in use from 1855 to 1961, note the cannons and the war memorial. The roll of honour names Roger Bushell, a Hermanus resident. His heroics in the Second World War were immortalised by the film 'The Great Escape' in which Steve McQueen played the lead rôle.

The history of the harbour and fishing and whales is depicted in the fascinating **Olde Harbour Museum**. Whether it is information

War Memorial

on marine life, old buildings in the town or old Hermanus families – the Museum has the answers at its fingertips.

Wine Tasting in Hermanus: The Hermanus Wine Route

Tucked away in the lovely Hemel-en–Aarde Valley, enjoy a unique wine tasting experience. Africa's southernmost vineyards delight in the cool maritime climate and correct soil combinations to produce outstanding Pinot Noir, Chardonnay and Sauvignon Blanc wines.

Near the intersection of the R43 and R320 one finds the

Wine Village and **Whalehaven Wines** on the Caledon road. Tastings are possible during the week and on public holidays

Continue along the R320, follow the signs to reach **Hamilton Russel Vineyards.** Its tasting rooms are open to the public daily.

The **Bouchard Finlayson** estate is about 6km away from the intersection, offering superb wines created by the renowned winemaker Peter Finlayson. Visitors are welcome to taste the Pinot Noir, Chardonnay, Sauvignon Blanc and Blanc de Mer.

Cape Bay and Southern Right wineries are also found along the same route, as is **Sumaridge,** the youngest kid on the wine 'block'.

FROM HERMANUS TO STANFORD (24km)

The R43 leaves Hermanus in an easterly direction and follows the Klein River Lagoon shoreline for some kilometres. A short roller coaster drive, wedged in between the Kleinriviers Mountains and the water's edge, and then it is flat countryside as the valley gradually widens near the small town of

STANFORD

In 1792 a Caledon farmer, Juriaan Appel, gazed in awe upon this fertile plain at the foot of the Akkedis Mountains. He applied for, and was granted a grazing permit on this wonderful stretch of land.

Over the years this grazing permit changed hands frequently. In 1801 it passed into the possession of a Christoffel Brand who built the first farmhouse (in today's Church Street). The most distinguished owner of this farmhouse was Captain Robert Stanford who bought the land in 1838 when he retired from the British army on half pay.

From Stanford's 'Klein River' farmland, the village developed in the 1850s and took on the owner's name. He became embroiled in the anti-Convict protests which had erupted in Cape Town against the British government's decision to settle convicts in the Cape. Though supportive of the agitation, as an army officer he could not openly demonstrate his feelings. The villagers learned that Stanford provisioned the convict ship 'Neptune', albeit not willingly – and chased him and his labourers off the farm. The community completely ostracized the family. His children were expelled from school and his one seriously ill child refused medical help. Robert Stanford went to England, seeking help from the government – but all he received was a knighthood and £5000. On his return to the Cape, he discovered to his dismay that documents relating to his property had been falsified and the farm sold by auctioned in 1857 to Phillipus de Bruyn. It was the latter who sub-divided the land into erven for a new town to be laid out.

It was rumoured that Sir Robert Stanford paid de Bruyn some money to have the town, which gained municipal status in 1919, named after himself.

What to do in Stanford
A stroll through the village reveals some interesting architecture dating from the 17th century onwards.

The **Anglican Church** (cnr Longmarket/Morton Streets) on the village commonage is one of the village landmarks and setting for many country weddings since 1892.

First School and post office (13 Morton Street) circa 1870. The first teacher and postmaster, a Mr James Goetz, ran the school and the post office from his own home. He charged a mere penny, or an 'oulap' a day per child, needless to say his school became the 'Oulap' school.

In 19 Morton Street, you find **Bachelor's Hope**. This was originally a 'tuishuis' built by Pieter Erwee circa 1902. Years later it accommodated lady teachers and many a local bachelor met his wife there.

In Queen Victoria Street stands **Stanford House**, once known as 'Die Langhuis'. It is believed that this building was one of the farm sheds on the original farm and subsequently converted into a house, later into a hotel.

Victorian influence is evident in some of the buildings in Stanford. On the outskirts, stands the **Spookhuis** (Haunted House), built about 1890. This former grand lady of a homestead is set behind a grove of old milkwood trees along the neck of the lagoon. Transport riders passing the farm reported seeing a little old lady sitting under the milkwood trees. But when they approached, nobody was there.

To enjoy nature's splendour, particularly fynbos, farmers in the area will, on request, lead groups across their land. Most of the fynbos is exported in either fresh or dried flower form. Stanford is the home of one of the largest dried flower exporters in South Africa.

Bird and watersport lovers can paddle down the Klein River to the bird sanctuary some 5km downstream. Blue cranes and fish eagle may glide overhead.

Just outside Stanford, on the R326 the country's only beer and wine estate welcomes visitors. At the **Birkenhead Brewery** savour splendid views of the Klein River Mountains as you sample the slow-brewed beer made from crystal clear spring water.

On the same stretch of road, the **Erica Vineyards** set amidst the fynbos hills and on the banks of the Klein Rivier, offer their wines. Ring the bell, should you arrive too late or too early for the tasting.

Ask the **Visitors Bureau in Queen Victoria Street** for more information of what to do and what to see.

Salmonsdam Nature Reserve

The reserve was established in 1962 and is probably named after the captain of the ill-fated iron-sided steamer 'Birkenhead', Captain Robert Salmond. The ship sank off Danger Point in 1852 with the loss of 454 souls (see page..).

Situated in the steep valley of the Perdeberg River, the reserve, extending over 840 hectare, is home to some magnificent mountain and floral splendour, is best explored on foot. The hiker can choose between three neither dangerous nor too arduous daywalks: the Mountain, Waterfall or Ravine Trail.

Keen mountain bikers can follow the many existing and quite exciting jeep tracks.
The enthusiastic motorist may embark on a mountain drive – but a word of caution, the drive is hazardous in places.

Three modest overnight huts at the foot of the Perdeberg cater for visitors.

Camping is possible but the sites have no electricity.

Possible Deviation:
From Stanford a short detour along the R326 leads to the **Salmonsdam Nature Reserve** *(18km). The road, also known as the Caledon Road, meets up with a signpost after about 4km 'Salmonsdam/Elim'. Approx. 7km down this road take the left fork towards Salmonsdam.*
One can return to the N2 from Stanford: the R326 leads in a northerly direction via Springerskuil and reaches the national road about 11km outside Riviersonderend. The total distance is approx. 55km

Your route, though, continues with the coastal experience from Stanford along the R43 which heads in a southerly direction across an unspoilt countryside. It swings and rolls gradually back towards the sea, traversing for about 20 kilometres the open fynbos veld. Then it makes contact with the sea at

DE KELDERS
which means 'The Cellar', quite a misnomer as the eye feasts on the stunning views of Walker Bay, across the endless white sands of the Strandveld shore, shielded by the coastal mountains. The curious name relates to an underground cavern traversed by a stream. The doughty Lady Ann Barnard (see page 14)whose husband Andrew was Secretary to Governor Lord McCartney, explored the cavern in 1798, then called *Drupkelder,* the 'Stalactite Cave'.

In her letter of 8 May 1798, she writes: (abbreviated)
Having heard of a curious cave for petrifications called the Drup Kelder........we determined to go, the road being heavy beyond all description, some time along the edge of the river, opposite to that where we had our disaster. A quantity of game bolted out on us, of various sorts.

On these banks there grows the Cokima-cranki (Kukumakranka – Gethyllis afra), or what I call Hottentot pineapple; it has the same flavour, same colour and is filled with an aromatic juice and seeds which I do not recommend to be bruised with the teeth as they leave a taste of garlick in the mouth. The Dutch are so fond of this fruit that they give twopence apiece for them to the black children who pick them in the country and bring them to the town.

We passed through a low brushveld afterwards, the trees so close that they met over the backs of the oxen. When we had pierced through this and travelled a few miles further we met with our fresh oxen and soon plunged into a pathless world, but covered high with evergreens of various descriptions. How many various plants might not a botanist have discovered here! Sometimes we went over bushy mountains, sometimes dipped into sandy holes. At last there appeared the stupendous hills of white sand which I had before observed no mortal surely could have courage to pass, but cross them we must, or no Drup Kelder.. The first remarkable thing I saw was a range of rocks, in one of which there was a natural porch, the sea having beat through it an opening in one of them for its foaming surge.

Many tremendous mounds of sand did we ascend and descend before we reached the top of the cliff where was the cavern…we sought for the path to the cave immediately. Mr Barnard called to me that he had discovered the way but was afraid I could not follow him – he bid me try and not be afraid. I did, cautiously grasping the bushes and in this way I descended the precipice which hangs over the sea, under which is the cavern till Mr B. called to me "Follow me up this road and don't look back at anything below'. I vigilantly followed his advice – I felt all my danger; it was even greater than he knew of as the soft, woolly cloth of my great-coat adhered to bushes and sadly retarded my progress. 'You turn your face to the rock, as I do and hold fast by the shrubs; the road is narrow'. When safely at the top I thanked God with a trembling heart. No part of the ascent of the Table Mountain was equal to the dangers or horrors of this.

We afterwards found the right path, and got down to the cave. In a cavity of the rock, we saw an immense hive of bees…and a noble porch is to be seen in a contiguous rock, through which the sea appears. At the cave's mouth there lay scattered bones, but we could not judge what animal they had belonged to. Tigers often infest it and it is therefore necessary to fire a gun before entering it. We had fortunately brought a tinder box and the gloom of the recess was soon illuminated with a set of wax candles.

The pointed drip stones descended from the roof in great numbers and sometimes met with others which had risen from the ground to meet them. The largest piece of petrification that has ever come out of the cavern is in the possession of Mr Cloete at Constantia.

The journey continues towards

Egyptian Goose

GANSBAAI
at the foot of the Franskraal se Berge (356m). A colony of Egyptian geese who nested in the rushes near a fresh water fountain in the harbour area, gave the town its name, 'Goose Bay'.

The busy fishing town with its colourful harbour

enjoys sweeping views of Walker Bay. Throughout the year, shore and boat based anglers are lured to Gansbaai, their catch hardly ever disappointing.

Gansbaai Harbour

Four kilometres from the town centre, the white, sandy Franskraal beach blinds the eye. Swimming, as almost everywhere along this coast, is dangerous, but the Uilenkraal River lagoon is safe.

The wanderer can enjoy the Duiwelsgat Hiking Trail (Devil's Hole). It follows the amazing coastline from Gansbaai to De Kelders through to the *Plaat* which is Walker Bay's stunning coastal nature reserve. It has the only fresh water caves on the African coast. Middle Stone Age people inhabited the area some 80 000 years ago as archeological excavations at Klipgat Caves, the 'Stone Hole Caves' have revealed.

On the outskirts of Gansbaai lies Kleinbaai, (Little Bay), prolific with milkwood trees. Here the younger beachgoer can frolick safely in a large tidal pool. It is also the site of Gansbaai's second harbour and the starting point for whale watching excursion boats, as well as boats heading for **Dyer Island,** a bird sanctuary to many species of coastal birds, particularly to penguins, and **Geyer Island**, home to a colony of Cape Fur seals. The channel between these two islands is known as **Shark Alley**, a popular feeding area for the Great White shark, which has earned Gansbaai the enviable reputation of Great White Shark capital of the world. The Great White is protected in South Africa since 1990.

Cape Fur Seals

The reefs and sunken rocks along **Danger Point** make it a dangerous place for ships coming too close inshore.In 1852, Danger Point, 6km from Gansbaai, was the scene of a major shipping disaster when the **HMS Birkenhead** went down with the loss of over 400 lives.

HMS Birkenhead

The steam troop ship HMS Birkenhead was conveying re-enforcements from Simon's Town (near Cape Town) to serve in the 8th Frontier War in the Eastern Cape. When it struck a submerged rock, its bottom was literally torn open and many soldiers drowned as they were asleep in their hammoks at the time of the disaster at 02h00.

The British officers and crew, aware of their fate, obeyed the order to 'Stand Fast' allowing women and children to board the life-boats first. Two boats were launched which lifted 7 women and 13 children, along with as many men as the boats could hold. Within 20 minutes of striking the rock, the Birkenhead went down. The gig was also launched which eventually reached the coast near Hawston . A coastal schooner encountered the other two lifeboats, rescued the occupants and then steamed on to the scene of the disaster. About 50 men, clinging to the remnants of the Birkenhead, were taken aboard. Altogether 116 survivors finally reached Simon's Town. The command 'Women and children' first was born here at Danger Point.

Low tide reveals the notorious Birkenhead Rock, just a few kilometres off Danger Point.

Tours to the Lighthouse, the Birkenhead Memorial and into the surrounding area can be arranged through the local tourism office in Main Street.

Gansbaai is only a short, but dusty distance away from **Elim**, a colourful mission station. Plans are afoot to tar the inland roads, but until that happens, be prepared for a fairly bumpy ride along the gravel roads.

Immediately outside Gansbaai, ignore the turn-off 'Elim/Baardskerdersbos', ('Beard Shaver's Bush). Instead drive on towards **Pearly Beach,** about 17km away, and then turn-off at the sign-post marked 'Elim/Napier'. The clearly marked route across fairly dry farmland and wide valleys is about 27km.

ELIM
was established by the Moravian Missionary Society, the Herrenhutter (see page 15) on the banks of the Nuwejaars River (New Year's River). In 1824, the missionaries acquired the farm Vogelstruyskraal (Ostrich Corral) from Johannes Schonken. They celebrated the first service on 31 July of the same year in the old farmhouse which had been built by the Huguenot descendent,

Louis du Toit, in 1796. Within a short time three families from Genadendal (see page 15) and others from the neighbourhood were permitted to settle on the farm, renamed to Elim by Bishop Hallbeck on Ascension Day 1825.

Elim is the name given to the second station or camp of the Israelites, after crossing the Red Sea (Exodus 15:27 '*and they came to Elim, where were twelve wells of water, and threescore and ten palm trees: and they encamped there by the waters'*.) The spirit of the past lingers on.

Elim Main Street houses

Neat and modest homes line the main street which leads to the plain, but large church. The church has a particularly strong link with the Herrenhutter Brotherhood in their home town of Herrenhut (today's Czech Republic). There, the Herrenhut church clock had faithfully served its congregation for over 140 years, when it was given its deserved rest. Unwanted it lay, until the Rev. Will from the Cape visited the Brotherhood just before the First World War. He heard about the clock, procured and shipped it back to Elim where it has told the time ever since 1914.

Interior of Elim Church   *Elim Church*   *Church Clock*

The massive water mill (1828) was originally constructed of wood alone. In 1881 parts were replaced by iron machinery so that today only the wheel remains of wood. The mill was restored and, since 1990 is grinding corn again.

Elim children

Elim home

Elim homes

Slave Emancipation Memorial

Home near the creek

Elim remains the property of the Moravian Church. Village life is administered and lived almost unchanged from the early days. It is here that the only memorial in the country is found that celebrates the emancipation of the slaves. This occurred in 1834 but an apprenticeship of four years was introduced so that final freedom was gained in 1838.

The local tourism bureau offers interesting guided tours which focus on life and conservation in Elim.

From the idyllic setting at Elim, the journey continues, still along a gravel road, towards **Bredasdorp**.

Overberg countryside

Drive south-easterly for about 9km. The road reaches a junction (the right branch goes to Die Dam on the coast). Bear left for another 3km. At the next junction bear left again in a north-easterly direction to Bredasdorp. The surrounding flat countryside is characterised by low growing shrubs, grass, bush and wheat. Sheep and cattle seem to thrive in these flat lands.

sheep

and cattle

Finally, relief from dust is at hand: the gravel road turns to tarmac and soon the R319 enters

BREDASDORP

founded by Michiel van Breda in the 1830s, though the town's story reaches further back into history.

In 1708 several pioneering farmers had received loan farms at Langsfontein on which, later, the town was laid out when increasing numbers of settlers arrived in the area. The need for a church was felt acutely by the community, led by Michiel van Breda in the eastern, and Pieter Voltelyn van der Byl in the western part of the area. The numerous meetings failed to produce an agreement as to where the church should be built. As a result, two villages were born: Bredasdorp, named after its leader, and Napier (see page...), bearing the governor's name, Sir George Napier.

Shipwreck Museum

All Saints Anglican Church

Michiel van Breda, the farmer, laid the foundation of the merino sheep industry on his own farm Zoetendalsvlei. Van Breda, the businessman and politician, became the first mayor of Cape Town and a member of the Cape Legislative Assembly.

As van Breda spent considerable time at his residence in Oranjezicht (Cape Town), he set out detailed management instructions for the farm in his journal *Groot Boek,* (Great Book). Apparently he visited Zoetendalsvallei only once a year to supervise the washing and shearing of the sheep, and then accompanied the wool wagons on their journey to Cape Town.

Dutch Reformed Church Bredasdorp

Bredasdorp attained municipal status in 1917. Today it forms the economic hub of the dairy, wheat and wool farming region. It is a clean, neat town with a first class **Shipwreck Museum** - a major attraction of the town about which the author Audrey Blignaut wrote so lovingly. At the tourism information bureau the **Audrey Blignaut Room** honours the well known writer of the region.
The Dutch Reformed Church with its beautiful oak pulpit was built in 1911 in the Cape Gothic style. The Anglican Church, All Saints, dates back to 1861, attractively built of sandstone and designed by Sophie Gray.

The Merino sheep which brought so much wealth to the region is honoured through a statue at the entrance to BNK Landbou building in Swellendam Road.

The forebears of the Merino sheep came to South Africa from the Netherlands in 1789. Four ewes and two rams, a present to the Dutch Government from the Spanish king, were shipped out as the northern European climate was thought unsuitable for the animals. They were entrusted into the care of Colonel Jacob Gordon, Garrison Commander at the Cape. His ambition was to cross-breed the merino with the indigenous woolled sheep, a project that started several years later. By the time of his death in 1795, the merino sheep had increased substantially, and 29 were shipped to Australia. Two enterprising farming brothers, the Van Reenens, bought several pure bred rams from the Gordon stud and crossbred them with their selected Cape ewes. The cross-breeding proved so successful that by 1804 the landdrost of Swellendam already kept a flock of 1000 crossbred sheep on his own farm. The Overberg had become the cradle of merino farming. In 1812, Jan Frederik Reitz of Cape Town, bought land north of Cape Agulhas and began crossbreeding here, using 25 rams and Cape ewes from the van Reenen stock. Three years later, he marketed the first wool clip from his farm Zoetendalsvallei. Subsequently, Reitz formed a business partnership with his brother-in-law, Michiel van Breda, and then retired. Michiel took over farming operations which signalled the beginning of systematic merino farming in 1817.

At the foot of the Bredasdorp mountains lies the **Heuningberg Nature Reserve,** criss-crossed by numerous hiking trails.

Every year in October, the **Foot of Africa Marathon** attracts runners like a magnet. The gruelling route leads over the mountains from Bredasdorp to Napier.

Excursions from Bredasdorp
On the town's southern doorsteps lie attractions like **Cape Agulhas, Waenhuiskrans/Arniston** and **De Mond Nature Reserve.**

No traveller will want to miss the opportunity of standing on the most southerly edge of Africa, **Cape Agulhas,** only 38km away. Take the R319 towards the coast.which first reaches **Struisbaai,** an idyllic holiday resort and fishing village. The name arises probably from the vast bay of the same name, and is a short form for 'Vogelstruisbaai', the 'Ostrich Bay'. Its growing popularity may be ascribed to its 14km-long uninterrupted beach. Water sports dominate. The historical fisherman's cottages at **Hotagterklip** warrant a visit, as does also the thatch roof church, a National Monument.

The road winds along the coast for a few kilometres and then reaches

CAPE AGULHAS – THE NEEDLE CAPE
Portuguese seafarers named the southernmost tip of Africa 'Agulhas' at the end of the 15th century, because here the compass needle shows no deviation between true and magnetic north. The official position of the continent's southernmost tip is **34°49'58" south** and **20°00'12" east**. A simple stone cairn, about 1km west of the lighthouse, marks the spot. The cairn was erected in 1986.

How disappointing it had to be for Capetonians who believed, and still cling quite passionately to the conviction that the Indian and Atlantic oceans meet at the Cape of Good Hope!

But whereas the Cape of Good Hope and Cape Point majestically rise from the ocean's depth, the tip of Africa is altogether unimpressive. The land seemingly runs into the sea, onto a flat, rocky protrusion, the Agulhas Bank. The Agulhas Bank continues underneath the curling sea for another 250km at a depth of 60 fathom (about 110m) before it drops dramatically to 1800 fathom (3292m) onto the continental shelf. Low hills separate the flat inland from the ocean watched over by the lighthouse.

The desolate, barren surroundings call to mind the hazardous sea voyages, the hardships and deprivations endured by many sailors. Not without reason is this coastal stretch known as a ships' graveyard: merciless gale-force winds, rapidly changing weather conditions and mountainous swells have claimed more than 125 ships from the nearly 2130 ships that have been wrecked along the entire South African coast. Many items from these shipwrecks, such as anchors, figureheads, cannons and coins are exhibited in the Shipwreck Museum at Bredasdorp.

The **Agulhas Lighthouse**, inspired by Egyptian architecture, was built in 1848. Today it houses the Lighthouse Museum which opened in 1994. Exhibited are detailed accounts of the development of lighthouses throughout the ages and photographs of all 56 South African lighthouses, together with a map showing their exact position. The history of the Cape Agulhas Lighthouse is shown in detail. The energetic visitor can climb the 71 steps to the top. If disinclined, climb the hill behind the Lighthouse for a splendid panoramic view.

The International Hydrographic Organisation determined that the Indian and Atlantic oceans meet at the southernmost tip of Africa, Cape Agulhas. But this must not be confused with the meeting of two ocean currents, the warm

Agulhas and the cold Benguela current. The meeting place of these two varies greatly, for individual branches of the currents continually move along the southern and southwestern Cape coast, and intermingle somewhere between the Cape of Good Hope and Cape Agulhas.

Arniston/Waenhuiskrans(25km)

The most direct link from **Bredasdorp** to **Arniston** is the tarred R316.

Alternatively, from **Struisbaai** retrace the drive northerly, take an easterly turn after 12km towards Prinskraal (gravel road). Here turn east (right) to connect with the R316. Once back on the tarmac road, another 7km past massive sand dunes and you reach Arniston and the sea.

Fishermen's cottage

ARNISTON (WAENHUISKRANS)

Arniston is named after a transport ship which was wrecked in the bay in May 1815.
The East Indiaman 'Arniston', coming from Ceylon (Sri Lanka) and heading for home when she ran onto the shore, driven there by forceful winds and a powerful current. Help never came and of the 378 people aboard, including passengers and crew, only five sailors and a carpenter survived. A monument was erected to commemorate the tragic loss of life.

Waenhuiskrans is best known for its 200-year old restored fishermen's cottages at Kassiesbaai. The entire village is a national monument. The white-washed, crooked walls and thatched roofs have captured the hearts of countless visitors – sadly, urban sprawl is leaving nasty marks on the tranquility of Waenhuiskrans.

South of the village, the sea has gnawed a huge cave into the cliffs which gave the village its original name Waenhuiskrans, the 'Wagon-house Cliff'. Older inhabitants claim that the massive cave is big enough for a complete oxwagon to turn in it.

Arches, caverns and bizarre rock formations dominate the coastline here, formed by marine erosion. The great Waenhuiskrans cavern, situated in the 267 hectare Waenhuiskrans Reserve west of Arniston, is only accessible at low tide. Be careful on the way to the cave as the path leading to it may be covered by dune sand and dangerous.

WAENHUISKRANS.

The area's original inhabitants left behind large shell middens and other objects of archaeological importance which allow a glimpse into their lifestyle.

In the shallow waters of the intertidal zone fish traps are visible. They are also known as 'vywers'. Fish swim into the flooded ponds during high tide and are trapped by the receding waters, an easy catch either using a net or a spear-like instrument. The local community has maintained these stone retaining walls over the years, which still provide the food, especially in winter when boats are unable to go to sea because of inclement weather.

Cape Cormorant

The beacon on the shore is also of historical interest. It is probably the only one ever built of its kind. The purpose of the large copper ball on top was to reflect the sun's rays as a warning to ships. Time and again ships had struck the Saxon Reef outside Struis Point because they could not see the light from the Agulhas Lighthouse. Built in 1871, it commemorates the sinking of the 'Queen of the Thames', the Australian Royal Mail steamer.

The modern visitor may fish, swim and picnic, but neither fires nor overnight camping are permitted. Visitors are also requested to park only at demarcated spots and to stay on the defined roads.

In the strandveld vegetation, limestone and dune fynbos you may spot grysbok, steenbok and grey duiker. Perhaps your path is blocked by a puff adder, Cape cobra or angulate tortoises. The birdlover may spot the crowned cormorant: the reserve is the most easterly area where it breeds in South Africa.

Between Struisbaai and Arniston, at the mouth of the Heuningsnes River, (Honey Nest River), stretches the magic De Mond Nature Reserve (The Mouth), proclaimed in 1986.

Crowned Plover

DE MOND NATURE RESERVE

From Cape Agulhas: travel via Struisbaai and Molshoop along the R319. After about 22km a gravel road turns off to the right (east). Another 7km across level farming countryside leads to Prinskraal. Here go south to reach the reserve.

From Bredasdorp: follow the R316 towards Arniston. After 10km turn off for Prinskraal, 5km away on a gravel road and continue for another 9km to reach De Mond.

The attraction of De Mond is the lack of human encroachment. Grysbok, steenbok and grey duiker may be spotted as well as the only predator of note, the caracal – gone are the days when elephants roamed these dunes, when the entire Agulhas plain was mostly a milkwood forest.

Black Oystercatchers

A rich and varied bird life distinguishes the reserve. In fact, the endangered Damara tern, first scientifically described from a specimen found on the Namibian coast in the 1850s, has adopted it as its home by establishing a breeding colony here. The endangered African black oyster catchers were also not slow to discover the lack of human interference.

The 7km-long Sterna hiking trail, named after the diminutive tern, is a 2 to 3 hour circular walk. It traverses riverine vegetation, dune forest and stabilised dunes before following the coast to the river mouth and saltmarshes.
Another hike, just a little longer, is the 4-hour walk from De Mond to Arniston,

along the coast, past Waenhuiskrans Cave, fish traps and ancient middens. Make sure you have transport at the other end!

Presently, there are no overnight facilities. The reserve is open daily from 07h00 to 16h00. Picnic sites are available. Gas braais are permitted, but no open fires.

A fresh water angling licence can be obtained form Cape Nature Conservation and a licence for fishing in the estuary from the Marine and Coastal Management (tel. 021 402 3911).

'Hunting and horseracing in the Overberg' – memories of an Overberger, Johan Albertyn. Translated from Afrikaans:

In the early 1900s there was very little enter-tainment for people. Hunting and horse racing were top of the list for wealthy Capetonians vis-iting Bredasdorp.

Them, the Overberg coastal stretch still teemed with wildlife. Duikers, greysbokkie and steen-bokkie abounded.

There were farms such as Potberg and

Caracal

Ratelriver as well as others owned by the Ohlsens and the Fletchers, with magnificent stables built of rock where horses looked out over the stable door. Grazing was plentiful as the fynbos was regularly burnt because of the sheep farming in the area. It was rumoured that the farmer caused the fires as he lit his pipe and then dropped the burning match into the fynbos vege-tation. This way, 'tortoise paths' were created, which prevented larger fires. The young fynbos shoots then became a feast for the tortoises, small buck and sheep. The rocky coast was the favourite haunt for the dassies which which later succumbed to the caracal.

Hunting trips occurred regularly. During the hunting season from May to July, my father organised on our farm Rietfontein two shoots annually: one hunt for his friends and the other for his labourers/employees – white shepherds and workers. At the time, were very few coloured workers on the farm. The hunters used shotguns with very rough shots. A good hunter could shoot a buck which jumped out of the bush at a distance of 40 to 50 paces.

The hunt began towards ten in the morning. Eight to ten hunters rode out in a long row through the veld. They would only shoot ahead so that they would not shoot each other! Later two horse carts came bringing everything neces-sary for the midday braai, and also to load the buck. Each hunter was allowed to shoot for himself three buck. Most of the buck roamed in the dune area. Towards braai time, at about two in the afternoon, when the hunters had more or less shot the permitted number of buck, the hunt finished.

At fifteen I bought my first shotgun for £ 15 at Rothman's shop in Bredasdorp. It was the German Walther type.

Hunting was popular throughout the Overberg. One day in 1933 the first rooikat was caught in a trap at Potberg. All the farmers came to look at the animal which they had heard of, but never seen. Somehow, the rooikatte must have found their way into the area from elsewhere. Farmers began los-ing sheep because of the rooikat, and towards 1039 even smaller wild ani-mals became scarcer. During the war everybody had to hand over his rifle to the police and for at least five years no hunting took place. After the war when our rifles were handed back to us, we went hunting on Rietfontein. Where before the animals had abounded, we were able to shoot with great difficulty a mere six buck. After that devastating experience we never hunted again, as buck numbers decreased steadily.

Flower farming also brought about changes as the veld was only burnt every ten to fifteen years. Rooikrans and Port Jackson, invasive plants, started to wreak havoc with the fynbos, destroying the grazing for sheep , buck and tor-toises. Today when you walk through the veld at Rietfontein you are unlikely to encounter a single buck. Rooikatte are caught in traps, twenty to thirty per year and a small area of Rietfontein has been claimed back. This is the case all over the Overberg, where somewhat dense veld occurs. Only on farms where fynbos is ploughed and animal fodder is sown with grain alternating and the veld is not dense, can one see occa-sionally steenbock and greysbok.

Horse racing also became something of the past in the region. The last

Overberg Horses

race I attended was as a young man. The racecourse was just outside Bredasdorp in the Bontebok Camp on the farm Nacht-Wacht. There was even a small stand from where spectators could watch the races. That was around 1928. Over time the wealthy 'Kapenaars' (People of the Cape) sold their magnificent farms to local farmers. Times were changing. These were the years of the Depression, and it became a luxury indeed to keep race-horses just for the pleasure of looking at them! The magnificent stone buildings still stand on Potberg and Ratel Rivier, nostalgic reminders of the 'Good Old Days'.

Overberg fields

Deviation for the traveller wishing to rejoin the national road:
BREDASDORP – SWELLENDAM (R319) connecting to N2 (56km)

*Driving north for Swellendam you traverse the lovely Rûens region (The Backs) characterised by seemingly endless rolling wheatfields which, after the winter rains, are clad in indescribably beautiful colours. Red, green, yellow, even bluish tints paint a work of natural art. Occasional gravel roads lead off to lone farms and villages, a couple of rivers are crossed, like the Soesrivier. Aloes are sprinkled along the side of the road and then, about 30km outside Bredasdorp the mighty **Langeberg Mountains** loom on the horizon.*

*The rush of the national road is not far away now. You join it 14km outside Swellendam.**(see page 29)*

Farm enfolded by the Langeberg Mountains

ROUTE THREE

CALEDON–NAPIER-BREDASDORP–MALGAS–WITSAND-PORT BEAU-FORT–VERMAAKLIKHEID–STILBAAI–GOURITSMOND–VLEESBAAI-MOSSEL BAY

The total distance of this route is about 385km, without any deviations.

Caledon via Napier to Bredasdorp (75km)

From Caledon the R316 leads south-easterly via Napier to Bredasdorp.

Immediately outside Caledon the R320, a link road to the coastal town of Onrus, is encountered. It follows **Shaw's Mountain Pass** which has untarred sections of about 20km before it reaches Onrus, 14km away from Hermanus. (see page 45)

Our scenic route towards Napier weaves through gentle hills and fields. The pastures roll by, flocks of blue cranes wing their way into the blue sky to forage in the fields. Sheep gently nudge their young and small farm buildings dot the countryside. After about 32km, near Springerskuil, the R326 branches off northerly to link with the national road, a few kilometres outside Riviersonderend (see page 25); in the coastal direction it leads to Stanford (see page 52).

A vast loneliness seemingly envelopes the countryside outside the small town of

NAPIER
which offers a quiet charm that extends a warm welcome in ever increasing numbers to city dwellers, tired of the haste of urban life. Donkey and horse carts still manage to bring traffic to a standstill, particularly in April during the **Horse & Cart Festival.**

If horse and cart do not appeal, maybe the annual **'Patats' Festival** could be of interest. Patats are sweet potatoes or yams which grow extremely well in the district.

The town's Dutch Reformed Church which fronts the main street, and its neighbour, the 'Feeshuis', are worth a visit. Built in the form of a Greek Cross, it was declared a National Monument in 1978. The darker teak wood of the pews, pulpit and galleries contrasts with the solid yellow copper of the splendid pipe organ. The 'Feeshuis' or 'Festival House' served once as a wine cellar and even as slave quarters from about 1810 to 1820. It is one of the oldest buildings in town.

In Sarel Cilliers Street the **Ox Wagon Monument** commemorates the Great Trek of the 1830s when thousands of Boers trekked from the Cape, now under British rule, to look for a land to settle where they could organise their own affairs.

In the same street one finds the Overberg's only **Toy Museum** and the **Vindigo Wine Shop** which offers a delectable range of Overberg wines.

NG Church Napier

Almost as if to remind us that beauty is not everlasting, one passes brickfields outside Napier and the landscape along the last 15km towards Bredasdorp takes on a less picturesque mantle. Another tarred link road to the N2 is reached just outside Bredasdorp, the R317. It leads to Stormsvlei (55km.) Soon **Bredasdorp** spreads out on the hills ahead. For its story see page 61

Bredasdorp – Malgas - Port Beaufort/Witsand (about 92km)

Diversions and deviations add a little spice to travel. The continuation of the route touches tarmac only for a few kilometres at the start and at the end, 35km outside Mossel Bay. It should not be undertaken in wet conditions, during, before or after rains.

If you wish to return to the national road, take the R319 to Swellendam.

Proceed from Bredasdorp on the R319, momentarily heading north for Swellendam. The luxury of a tarred road is brief, as after 6km one re-enters the world of dust and gravel roads for '**Malgas/Infante**'. Malgas is situated on the western bank of the Breede River which has to be crossed by ferry to reach Port Beaufort. Ostriches usher the visitor into a landscape of bulging hills and rolling fields. The odd farmhouse stands lonely in the vast expanse. Ignore several gravel roads pointing towards Swellendam. Instead, time allowing, explore a genuine treasure, the magic **De Hoop Nature Reserve.** Look for the clearly marked route near **Ouplaas.**

DE HOOP NATURE RESERVE

The original De Hoop land was a loan farm of the Dutch East India Company. Grazing rights were leased to Fredrick de Jager in 1739. The earliest recorded owner of the 'Hope Farm' was Pieter Lourens Cloete who established a successful horse stud.

Pieter Cloete built the homestead, horse-mill, sheep shearing shed and schoolroom. Above the front door of the homestead one can see the shell of a large oyster which apparently caused the death of his wife. Stories of her ghost, said to haunt the house at night, are told.

It was proclaimed a reserve in 1957 and used for the breeding of animals such as the bontebok, and rare Cape mountain zebra. Today, the reserve controls over 36 000ha of indigenous lowland and coastal fynbos.

In 1986 a marine protected area was proclaimed which covers the reserve's coast and extends 5km out to sea.

Wind and waves have sculpted at times bizarre shapes out of the limestone and sandstone cliffs along the rocky part of the 45km-long coastline – in stark

Cape Mountain Zebra

contrast with the endless white dunes. The shifting dunes at 'Koppie Alleen' cover a vast area and climb up to 100 metres.

The landlocked De Hoop Vlei stretches for 15km from Die Mond in the south-east to Windhoek in the north-west. Its main feeder is the Sout River (Salt River) which drains the farming lands south-east of Caledon. The north is drained by the Potteberg River which rises in the Potberg mountains. Throughout the year the vlei is popular with birds, particularly waterfowl and waders. Its salinity, water and temperature levels vary.

White breasted and Cape cormorants, sanderlings, grey and whitefronted plovers, several kinds of terns, small egrets or grey herons, kelp gulls entertain the bird enthusiast near the coast,and further out to see, one may spot the Cape gannet. Be careful not disturb the African black oystercatcher, particularly during the breeding season. They are known to be shoddy nest-builders.

the white dunes at De Hoop

In the essentially limestone coastal plain, broad-leaved evergreen shrubs are found closer to the coast, whereas further away, dune fynbos, the typical fynbos families of *Proteaceae*, *Ericaceae* and *Restionaceae*. Other scrub thickets flourish amongst these, such as blombos, Christmas berry, bietou, cancer bush, milkwood trees and the wag-n'bietjie ('Wait a while'). Sunbirds, pied and redwing starlings and many other winged beauties are attracted to this vegetation.

Away from the shrublands, one can observe larks, black korhaans, crowned plovers, Steppe buzzards, secretary birds, blue cranes and others. Ostriches too stalk about in the open grass land.

Small antelope species dart about in the low limestone hills. A very special treat will be to spot the Cape mountain zebra (*Equus zebra zebra)* which was threatened with extinction in the 1920s. The population had dropped to a scant 90 animals. They have adapted to this terrain and their numbers are increasing again. The diurnal Cape mountain zebra is identifiable by its unique stripe pattern – it sports a distinctive dewlap 'grid-iron' pattern on the rump above the tail and lacks shadow stripes. The belly is white and strong stripes encircle the legs. (Burchell's Zebra has stripes which encircle the entire belly and has brown shadow stripes)

In the north-eastern part, closer to the Potberg, live the threatened Cape vultures, once common throughout the region and southern Africa. Their drastically decreasing numbers can be ascribed largely to the farmers' ignorance of their importance within the ecosystem: poisoning reduced their numbers to a mere 40 birds in the mid-1980s. Since the launch of an educational awareness campaign and a feeding programme, the numbers of this breeding colony have grown steadily to about 120.

Within the Reserve several shorter walking trails and two drives can be undertaken. The trails are laid out at the vlei, along the coast and at Potberg (611m). One of the drives leads to Potberg, the other to the coast at Koppie Alleen with game viewing and birding abounding.

General tips:
Motorists beware: fuel is only available at Ouplaas. Hikers need insect repellents in summer to ward off horse flies. There are no water points along either the Whale Hiking Route nor the Mountain Bike trail.

The Whale Trail

The 55km-long popular five-day trail meanders through the awesome De Hoop Nature Reserve. Hikers should be reasonably fit. Overnighting is in comfortable cottages that accommodate a maximum of 12 hikers. All cottages, except the one at Noetsie (day 2) have a built-in braai. Warm water, mattresses, firewood and solar power batteries for lights only, are available.
The trail is suitable for children eight years and older.
Rucksacks and bags can be transported to the cottages- this luxury comes at an extra charge, however.
Bird enthusiasts will want to walk between September and April
Whale watchers should book between July and December
Flower lovers will enjoy the hike during August and September.
The trail is so popular that hikers' permits will be auctioned off on the internet as from 2004.

Hikers at rest

After De Hoop, the drive heads north-easterly towards **Malgas**. En route, spot the steep hills of the Potberg (811m), on the northerly edge of the De Hoop Reserve. Quite suddenly the see-saw road chances upon a T-junction: another turn-off to Swellendam, but also to Malgas. The tranquil hamlet lies a mere 1km away. Be careful not to turn down towards Infanta on the coast! The road descends gently towards the Breede River.

MALGAS

once the main inland port, was named after the gannet sea bird. The Khoi people knew it as *Malagas*, but postal confusion in the end led to the re-naming as mail addressed to Malagas landed up in Malaga, Spain!

A major attraction, apart from the rural tranquility, is the hand-operated pontoon ferry, the last one of its kind in the country. The earliest ferry to ford the river was probably installed in the first half of the 19th century. The much later vehicle ferry was pulled for years by 'Oom' Moxie Dunn who harnessed himself to the standing cable and literally 'walked' the ferry and its load across the water. Nowadays, two men do 'Oom' Moxie's job and haul the load 120 metres across the river. The ferry can comfortably take 3 small cars, or one medium sized lorry (max. weight 10t). The tidal influence is marginally noticeable at Malgas: according to the ferrymen, the Breede River widens by about 2 metres at high tide.

The story was told how the enterprising Joseph Barry had been awarded the government tender for the conveyance of food emergency supplies to the

The Malgas Ferry

The Ferrymen

region: he would ship goods to the Breede River mouth, the widest river estuary in South Africa, and from there up-river to Malgas, a distance of about 33km.

From Malgas, where the cutter could go no further, some 500 oxen took over and hauled the cargo to Swellendam.

Joseph Barry built the 158-ton Kadie which plied the river, carrying agricultural produce for the Cape and returning with trade goods such as aloe sap, wool and hides for the flourishing Barry enterprise. After more than 200 successful river runs the *Kadie* journeys ended abruptly in 1865 when she stranded on a rock.

Inevitably the river mouth in St. Sebastian Bay with Cape Infanta on its south side developed into a busy port. This is

PORT BEAUFORT/WITSAND
on the northern river bank. To reach it, after ferrying across the river, drive easterly to join the R324 which then heads south towards the coast. In the flowering season, early winter, one travels through aloe wonderland.

The town is named after the Duke of Beaufort, father of Lord Charles Somerset (see page7).

Port Beaufort/Witsand Harbour

Pioneering the port development was Benjamin Moodie, owner of the Grootvadersbosch farm (Grandfather's Farm) near Swellendam who also had keen shipping interests. In 1817 Moodie built the first stone warehouse on the shore. When Joseph Barry became involved in 1822, maritime activities at Port Beaufort surged. In 1841 it became an official port of entry, when also a customs house was built. In 1859 Thomas Barry built a little church, today a National Monument and still in use for services. Fortune and misfortune went hand in hand. The port was inextricably linked to the fortunes of the Barry empire. When this folded in 1866, Port Beaufort ceased to be a port.

The Barry Church

Today, Port Beaufort is a pleasant sea-side resort, as is the near-by **Witsand** with its beautiful beach and small fishing harbour. A multitude of whales visit Witsand from June to November. Indeed, Witsand claims the largest concentration of Southern Right whales on the South African coast, growing at an annual rate of 7%. An official whale count carried out by helicopter in 2002, established an adult whale population of 117 and 49 calves in St. Sebastian Bay.

Witsand/Port Beaufort – Vermaaklikheid

Drive out of Witsand on the tarred R322 towards Heidelberg (see page 83). After about 12km turn onto a gravel road marked '**Vermaaklikheid**', which means 'Amusement'.

Embraced by canola fields, greeted by curious ostriches and grazing cows the route traverses the peaceful countryside for a good dozen kilometres. Then another sign directs to Vermaaklikheid. Though the road now narrows,

Vermaaklikheid cottage

it is well maintained. Downhill it slopes, aloes peep up from the hills and quite soon the Duiwehoeks River is reached, spanned by a narrow drift. (After heavy rains one may not be able to drive across the drift). A short, uphill drive out of the riverbed is followed by a right turn to Vemaaklikheid.

Though the countryside over the last couple of kilometres has shed its loveliness and put on a rather plain covering, the hamlet of Vermaaklikheid is endearing indeed. Modest cottages, some a little derelict, others spruced up, are tucked away in the low hills. Artists have been lured to this village lost in time.

Smiling people wave you on to

Puntjie, on the coast. Here stand the famous Kapstyl houses; unfortunately entry to this privately owned property is barred by a locked gate – yet, it is nonetheless a worthwhile detour of only a few kilometres, simply to marvel at the spectacular Duiwehoek River mouth.

Kapstylhuisies

Over the years, fishermen and holidaymakers built their kapstylhuisies, or 'truss style houses' on coastal farmland without the owners' consent and much to their annoyance. Yet, the owner of Kleinfontein Farm accepted the inevitable:on a portion of his land he permitted them to build their kapstylhuisies at an annual rental of 50 cents. The designer / builder of most of the houses subsequently built was Mr F.J. de Jager of Vermaaklikheid.

These 1920s houses consist of a roof resting on about eight poles, that reach right down to the ground. The poles or pair of poles are spaced at regular intervals. At the top they are joined by a tie-beam and fastened with wooden pegs. Battens are then secured across the couples to which bundles of reed and thatch are sewn wirh twine, grass rope or rimpie. The most primitive form of this type of house has no walls and resembles a thatched roof built at ground level. To make the house watertight, cow dung mixed with sand was smeared on to the ridge. Later, this mixture was coated with tar.

Two small windows allowed light into the interior. One was normally positioned opposite the entrance. Sleeping areas were divisioned off and cooking was done outside.

Return to Vermaaklikheid. A short distance outside the village, watch for directions to **Stilbaai/Jongensfontein.**

Low growing vegetation characterises this particular coastal stretch. The road see-saws parallel with the invisible coast. Occasionally one catches a glimpse of the ocean and some massive sand dunes. Harvested thatch is piled up along the road verge – reminding the traveller that he is indeed in 'thatch country'.

Dakriet - thatch drying in the sun

At the next T-junction, the right arm leads to Jongensfontein, the left to Stilbaai.

Jongensfontein (Young Man's Fountain) is an amazingly extended holiday resort where modern homes overlook Cape Barracuta. The rocky coastline lures the angler, whilst the keen surfer is spoilt by rolling waves. Particularly interesting are the fish traps, clearly visible at low tide. These traps, once known as *vywer*, meaning 'pond', consist of rocks and stones that the native Strandlopers built ages ago. Some of these *vywers* are still in use.

The historic 'White House' is the a local museum and information centre.

Jongensfontein is only 11km away from the ever expanding

STILBAAI
The first houses of this popular holiday town are glimpsed, and the bridge spanning the Goukou River is reached. Goukou was a chief of the Hessequa Khoi whom Izak Schrijver (see page36) met on the riverbanks in 1689.

The Goukou provides the tranquility the canoeist might seek, whilst the pure white sandy beaches attract bathers and sunseekers alike.

Tourism forms the backbone of Stilbaai's economy. Allow the information offices to suggest the right activity and to direct you to places of interest.

On the eastern riverbank, follow the R305 for about 4km. Then a gravel road

branches off to the right for **Gouritsmond, via Melkhoutfontein and Reins**

Nature Reserve (approx. 36km).

The many stone-walled thatched cottages lend **Melkhoutfontein** particular charm. Its churchyard with the shell decorated graves is a stark reminder of the unrelenting power of the sea – these are mostly the graves of fishermen who perished at sea.

From Melkhoutfontein the countryside opens up. The quite badly corrugated road bumps the driver awake as he heads east. Francolins are spotted, foraging in the fynbos vegetation and, alarmed, scatter in the bush.

After about 22km ignore the turn-off to Albertinia. It connects to the national road N2. From this point onward, the countryside takes on a far more pleasing character. Erica and protea species paint the low, rolling hills in bright hues. The loveliness is soon explained: the gates to the private **Rein's Nature Reserve Gouritsmond** bid you welcome.

Rein's Nature Reserve extends over 2550ha of exquisite fynbos along a coastline of undulating rocks and reefs that reach far out to sea. It is home to some very rare plant species.

Protea speciosa

Restio

Beyond Rein's Nature Reserve, the road swings happily through this lovely, flowery world and then joins a tarred road. Here you have a choice: to the north it ties with the national road (29km away), to the coast it goes to **Gouritsmond** (9km), the pleasant seaside resort on the Gourits River mouth which has as its main contributaries the Groot, Gamka, Olifants and Kamanassie rivers.

Why not accompany the river over the last few kilometres before it joins the sea in an enticing sandy bay? The beach west of the river is rather rocky.

It is believed that Bartholomeu Dias, the Portuguese circumnavigator of the Cape in 1488, made landfall at Gouritsmond after having been blown off-course by a storm. When the storm subsided and he steered north, he sighted land to the west realising that he had rounded the Cape.

Return from Gouritsmond and continue towards **Vleesbaai.** On the way, after crossing the Gourits River over a single-lane bridge, another coastal road leads to **Kanonpunt/Fransmanshoek**. Here, a storm whipped and wrecked a French ship in 1763. Several cannons washed up on the beach. Some of these, the Rev. Johnson of Riversdale, owner of a cottage nearby, collected and placed close to his home – unavoidably the place became known as Kanonpunt. Another version of the origin of the place name is that its headland resembles a cannon.

Vleesbaai (Fleshy Bay) is reached by backtracking the Kanonpunt gravel road for a 3km stretch and then travelling easterly for about 4km.

This popular holiday resort offers a fine sandy beach. Its curious name goes back to the early 17th century when two Dutch vessels under the command of Paulus van Caerdon, scoured the coast in search of a pastoral tribe with whom to barter for cattle. One of the ships finally spotted cattle herders and, after some very successful cattle bartering, named the bay 'vleesbaai'.

Maybe visit also **Boggomsbaai.** (boggom is a small, sun-dried fish). The rising and falling road weaves towards this small resort and rewards you with lovely views of Visbaai (Fish Bay).

Finds of clay pots, kitchen middens of sea shells and other artefacts indicate that fishing played a major role even in far distant times.

Returning from Vleesbaai, ignore the gravel road north, and turn onto the last stretch of this route towards **Mossel Bay**, only 25km away.

Country charm is swiftly left behind. Intense farming points to civilisation close at hand. Indeed, it almost comes as a shock to come upon the smoke belching towers of **PetroSA,** formerly known as 'Mossgas' and the busy N2.

At this point there is no escape: you have to use the national road to reach Mossel Bay. (see Route Four)

ROUTE FOUR

SWELLENDAM/N2 – HEIDELBERG – RIVERSDALE(GARCIAS PASS) – MOSSEL BAY - GEORGE

The distance from Swellendam to George is 216km, excluding deviations.

Outside Swellendam and beyond the Barrydale turn-off (R324), the N2 continues its polka dance-like swing for another 40km, past another turn-off (R322) to the coastal resorts Witsand/Fort Beaufort/Malgas and a couple of gravel roads branching off for Suurbraak. It then reaches the farming town of

HEIDELBERG
The town is situated on the Duiwenhoks Rivier, (see page 79) the Dove Cote River. Time and again one encounters the fearless explorer Izak Schrijver. Apparently he camped on these riverbanks in 1689 where his only company was a multitude of wild doves – hence the river's name.

In time, pioneer farmers settled but soon tired of the tedious ride to Riversdale or Swellendam to attend church. The Doornboom (Thornbush) farm was purchased from a Louis Fourie as a church farm, a church built and a congregation established in 1855. The growing village took the name of the German city where the Heidelberg Catechism originated. The original church no longer stands, it has been replaced by a fine neo-gothic Dutch Reformed church building around which the busy little town huddles.

As the journey continues, ostriches in the fields keep a keen eye on the traffic and delight the motorists. The Duiwenhoks and Krombeeks rivers flash by, the vegetation changes distinctively to more ericoid, and after about 30km you arrive at

RIVERSDALE
on the banks of the Goukou River. The lively farming town is named after a former commissioner and magistrate at Swellendam, Harry *Rivers*. The town's first homestead, *Zeekoegat* dates back to 1796.

Art and antique connoisseurs will enjoy the Julius Gordon Africana Centre, built in 1880, with its fine Julius Gordon collection.

The churches tell their own stories: visit quaint St. Matthews (Anglican) 1859, the Lutheran and Dutch Reformed Churches which were both built in 1907.

The wealth of wild flowers and aloes contribute to the enjoyment of a visit.

Aloe arborescens   *Aloe ferox*

ALOE FEROX

The aloe ferox has been captured in many San rock paintings. The nomadic San used the plant for ritual and medicinal purposes. Khoikhoi herders added the sap to the drinking water of sheep to rid them of intestinal parasites.

By the end of the 17th century, aloe crystals were used as a purgative and laxative. Today the main use is for skin and hair treatment, insect bites, blue bottle stings, sunburn, and many others.

There are two main components of the aloe ferox:
1.   the bitter sap which comes from the peel
2.   the juice/jelly from the inner part of the plant.

The Khoikhoi probably used a mixture of both for the treatment of wounds, skin ailments and gynaecological problems.

The bitter sap from the peel, which forms dark brown crystals when it is boiled, reduced and allowed to dry, is still extracted in the same way as hundreds of years ago. The leaves are harvested from plants growing in their natural habitat, requiring no treatment with pesticides, fungicides or fertilisers. At no stage of the extraction process is the gel exposed to methanol or other solvents, it is a pure product.

Aloe ferox differs from other aloe species in its exceptionally high calcium content, as well as its high content of total amino acids. It also contains low levels of iron, magnesium, sodium, manganese and potassium, as well as trace elements of copper.

The radiation burns of victims of the Hiroshima and Nagasaki nuclear bomb attacks were treated with the leaves and juices of the South African aloe arborescens.

Take a stroll through the town's botanical garden, Jurisch Park, created by the late Werner Frehse, acting town engineer from 1950 to 1972. It lies on the eastern edge (Mossel Bay side) of Riversdale. Here, exotic and indigenous plants grow harmoniously side by side.

Explore the fynbos covered mountains, dominated by the Sleeping Beauty Mountain Peak, fish in the rivers, water ski or canoe on the dam – Riversdale offers many thrilling outdoor activities.

Mimetes cucullattus

Cape Honeysuckle

Likewise, Riversdale is the starting point for the **GARCIAS PASS (R323)**

Deviation: Riversdale – Garcias Pass:

Riversdale rests comfortably in the shade of the 'Sleeping Beauty Peak'. This mountain silhouette requires a little imagination, but the dreamer can make out the contours of a sleeping maiden, the peak formed by her upright feet. Good luck in spotting her. (clue: she stretches from west to east)

*The **Garcia Pass** is one of several passes that link the coastal plateau to the Little Karoo. On the way, the Sleeping Beauty Peak always ahead, you cross the Klein Vette and Vette Rivier (Fat River) coursing through green farmland. The road rises gently, past smallholdings dotted on the hills and the Garcia Forestry Station, the actual start of the mountain pass. This impressive mountain route over the Langeberg Mountain started off as a narrow bridle pass*

built in 1868 by the Civil Commissioner of Riversdale, Maurice Garcia. The bridle pass through the deep gorge chiselled out by the Goukou River was improved and completed between 1874 and 1877 by the well-known road builder Thomas Baines.
In the lower ascent, trees and ferns line up along the route which penetrates into an ever narrowing valley. Dense vegetation bedecks the slopes, a gay display of colour in late winter and early spring when the flowers are in full bloom.

The Old Toll House is passed. Nearby the 'Sleeping Beauty Hiking Trail' starts and shortly afterwards, the mighty Swartberg mountain range rises on the far horizon. Cannaland, the Little Karoo, lies ahead. Several gravel roads branch off, such as to Barrydale (see page 115) and Herbertsdale, but you stay on a northerly course and enjoy a change in vegetation which becomes typical Karoo shrub. At Miertjieskraal, the Brandrivier is crossed. Once more the road ascends into a narrower valley of low hills where goats seem very much at home. After the Zee River a dry but broader valley stretches out - one wonders how people can live off this arid land. Ignore the sign-post to Van Wyksdorp, cross three more rivers, the Groot, Doornkloof and Knuy and travel on through a particularly parched plain. Suddenly a T-junction appears: you have joined the R62 which comes from Barrydale and leads to **Ladismith. The onward journey is described in Route Five.**

From the Riversdale town centre, return to the national road. Once over the Goukou River, it comes to the R305 turn-off marked **Stilbaai.** The distance to this coastal resort is about 30km. At Stilbaai, **Route Three** may be joined which explores, on mainly gravel roads, Melkhoutfontein, Gouritsmond, Vleesbaai and exits near Mossel Bay.

Ignoring this turn-off to Stilbaai, continue on the national road eastward and after 27km travel, one passes the town of

ALBERTINIA
For its existence, Albertinia is indebted to a Dutch Reformed Church minister, the Rev. J. *Albertyn* of Riversdale. To reach all his parishioners scattered over vast distances, he regularly travelled by ox-cart from Riversdale (27km) to conduct services on Grootfontein Farm, until 1882. The farm was to eventually bear his name.

Though essentially a farming centre, Albertinia's economy is backed by the exploitation of ochre. As early as 1797, extensive beds of yellow and red ochre were discovered. Ochre is a mineral of clay and hydrated ferric oxide and used in the manufacture of paints and for imparting colour to cement and linoleum. Mining activities began in 1925 and continue to date.

Another major contribution to the economy is made by the aloe sap gathered here from the aloe ferox. Take the time to visit one of the aloe factories.
Throughout the area, but particularly in the Albertinia district, *dekriet* or thatching reed, abounds - yet another major contributor to the economy. It lines the roads, sprouts in the *veld* and on the hills. Dekriet, *Chondropetalum tectorum* is the most popular reed for thatching in the Cape.

Should you feel like savouring the thrills of wild Africa, visit the **Garden Route Game Lodge** on the doorsteps of Albertinia. Experienced game rangers drive you through this malaria-free reserve which hosts the 'Big Five' and, of course, countless smaller creatures.

The King of Beasts

On the onward journey, you pass two further turn-off to the coast. One will link with the tarred R305 to Stilbaai; the other with Gouritsmond.

Continue on the national road. Soon it leads across the deep gorge forged by the Gourits River as it forces its way through the mountains to the coast. The Gourikwa Khoi once lived on its banks, hence the name. A striking twin rail and road bridge spans the Gourits, 75m above the riverbed. The bridge is 270m long and favoured by dare-devil bungy-jumpers. If you want to join in the adrenaline-pumping fun, turn up between 0900 and 1700 daily, weather permitting, have your money ready (presently a jump costs R 170), steel your nerves and plunge towards the river bed.

Near Cooper, a minor road branches off to the north. It leads to

Herbertsdale, set in amazingly beautiful countryside. It is a former mission station established by the Rev. James Herbert. Fynbos is abundant in the Herbertsdale area.

Herbertsdale countryside

As the national road finds its way to Mossel Bay another turn-off for Herbertsdale is passed, and shortly afterwards the massive **Petro SA installations (Mossgas)** appear on the left.

PETRO SA

The project for the production of synthetic fuels was launched in 1987. It was designed to extract natural gas and associated condensate (unrefined petrol and diesel) from two larger off-shore fields, as well as some smaller satellite fields in the Bredasdorp Basin. The gas and condensate are piped in separate pipelines from an offshore production platform to an onshore plant for conversion to petrol, diesel, liquid petroleum gas, kerosene and alcohol.

Gas and condensate are recovered from a fixed steel platform, standing in 105 m depth. The total height of the platform is 220 . It is constructed to withstand storm waves of up to 24m , and gales of up to 170 km/h.

To explore the exciting attractions of **MOSSEL BAY exit at No 387 and follow the R102.** It dips towards the ocean past the Garden Route Casino, with spectacular views of the immense bay into which Bartholomeu Dias sailed in 1488.

Holiday-makers are drawn to the shores of Mossel Bay which enjoys a pleasant, dry climate. The general boast is that it only rains on five days a year – maybe it is true, as the annual rainfall reads about 375mm.

Mossel Bay Harbour

We enter a busy town with numerous beautiful older sandstone buildings. To discover its history, follow the signposting for the **'Postal Tree/Posboom'** and **Museum**.

What motivated the voyages of discovery?

In 1453 Constantinople fell into Turkish hands which effectively blocked the overland route to the riches of the east, forcing the European nations into the discovery of an alternative sea route. Portugal emerged as the leading sea power under King Henry the Navigator and his successors. From his naval school at Sagres, King Henry dispatched his caravelles on their exploratory journeys. His ambition was perpetuated by his successor Joao II whom, in 1481, Pope Sixtus V favoured with the title of 'Lord of all African possessions'. To mark these possessions, explorers were ordered to erect 'padraoes' or landing crosses, which bore his Coat of Arms with a Latin - Portuguese inscription.

In 1482, King Joao sent Diego Cao to survey Africa's west coast. Cao reached the Namibian shore, about 130km north of Swakopmund, and marked the landing by a padrao: today's Cape Cross.

Bartholomeu Dias left Sagres in 1487. He reached Lüderitz on the Namibian coast, and called it 'Angra Pequena' or 'Little Bay'. Finally, during a devastating storm, he unwittingly rounded the Cape and reached today's Port Elizabeth. Here, a mutiny on board forced him to turn back. On this return voyage, on the feast day of St. Bras, 3 February 1488, he stepped ashore in a protected cove where he discovered a fresh water spring and named it 'Aguada de Sao Bras', the 'Watering Place of Saint Blaize' where modern archeologists have found Khoi-San artefacts dating back more than 80 000 years. This was at Mossel Bay.

The Caravelle

The caravelle was developed between the 14th and 17th centuries in the Mediterranean for the specific purposes of exploring the African coast. Both Portuguese and Spanish seafarers sailed in them. The replica was built near Oporto in 1986 in the shipyards of Samuel & Silhos, at Vila do Condo, near Oporto. The hull of pine and oak measures 23,5m in length and is 6,2m wide at its broadest point. The vessel has a displacement of about 130 tons, of which 37 tons are ballast of cement, granite blocks from Lisbon, and lead. The grandsail measures 147 square metres and weighs 1.5 tons! The smaller mizzen sail measures 73 square metres.

Dias established little contact with the Khoi, but after Vasco da Gama finally reached India in 1497, increasing numbers of ships dropped anchor in the sheltered bay where sailors hid messages in a sailor's boot hanging in a Milkwood tree (*sideroxylon inerme),* or left messages beneath it. Best known of these messages is the one written by a captains in Pedro Cabral's fleet, dispatched in 1500. Bartholomeu Dias accompanied Cabral to organise the gold trade with the East coast of Africa at Sofala. A storm in the South

Atlantic wrecked many ships in Cabral's fleet, amongst them that of Dias. His drowning was recorded and the letter left behind in a seaman's boot. This was discovered by Joao da Nova, commander of another Portuguese fleet.

Dias Statue and Melkhout Tree

The Postal Stone

Da Nova built a small church in 1501, near the ancient milkwood tree. A simple cross indicates the site.

A cast of the 'Post Stone' on which he engraved an inscription is exhibited in the Mossel Bay Maritime Museum.

Nearly a century later, the Dutch mariner Paulus van Caerden put into the bay. Exploring the area he came across a huge cave, today's Bat Cave near the lighthouse. Thick layers of shells covered the cave floor which were to give the future settlement its name:*mossel bay* - Bay of Shells.

Mossel Bay remained a trading post until the late 18th century. The first permanent settlement was established in 1787. To increase trade, a granary was built, which in turn encouraged development of the village into a major port. Agricultural products, particularly during the ostrich boom, were shipped from here and of course, the port provided for the fishing industry. Growth accelerated after 1905, when the railway reached the town.

An absolute 'must' on the visitor's agenda is a visit to the **Maritime Museum**. A replica of Dias's caravelle is the main exhibit. It reached the bay after three months voyage from Portugal on 3 February 1988. The modern voyage celebrated the quincentenary of Dias's achievement who himself had taken six months for his epic journey.

The museum's information centre is housed in the replica of the original granary on the foundations of which it was built. Visitors interested in shells will spend hours in the South Africa's largest **Shell Museum** which forms part of the museum complex.

On the grassy slopes below the Maritime Museum stand possibly the town's first homes: the Munrohoek cottages, were built in 1830 by Alexander Munro. Not far from these are Muslim graves, believed to be the resting place of an influential Muslim who died at sea in the 19th century.

St. Blaize Trail - Dana Bay Walk

It is time to survey the ocean from the rugged cliffs between Mossel Bay and Dana Bay:

The trail takes its name from **Cape St. Blaize***, the promontory on which stands the lighthouse. Directly below the lighthouse is the cave which gave the settlement its name. This is the starting point. A boardwalk allows one to explore the cave before embarking on the scenic coastal trail with its dramatic rock formations and a remarkable diversity of plant life.*

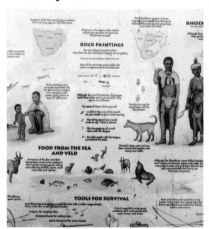

The People of St. Blaize

The total distance of about 16km can be walked in 5 hours (one way) with relatively little exertion. Make sure that transport has been arranged at Dana Bay for the return. There are sheer drops at numerous places, care must be taken by vertigo sufferers. But there are no steep climbs along the route, once the level of the Lighthouse has been reached.

When you wave good-bye to Mossel Bay, the R102 will reconnect with the national road N2, and pass

HARTENBOS

In the early 18th century one Sias Meyer ventured this far, probably hoping to be granted a loan farm. His hope was soon rewarded: the treacherous coast had claimed yet another victim. In 1734 a badly damaged ship sought shelter in Mossel Bay. Though fourteen lives had already been lost, Sias

Meyer managed to save the remaining sailors. He reported the incident and was rewarded with a land grant from the government in recognition of his valiant deed.

Today, Hartenbos is home to the *Afrikaanse Taal en Kultuurvereeniging*, a cultural association which was formed in 1930 during the great economic depression. Its aim was to restore awareness of his language and culture in the Afrikaaner community. Today the A.T.K.V. manages most of the resort area of Hartenbos.

During the summer holiday season the tranquility of the village is shattered when tens of thousands of visitors flock here to enjoy the sea.

Many guests will be drawn to the fascinating **Voortrekker exhibition,** the focal point of the **Hartenbos Museum,** an outstanding local history museum.

In minutest detail one learns about the preparations for the Great Trek, the Trek itself, the experiences of the *trekkers* and their living conditions. There is also a commemoration hall for the 1938 Symbolic Ox Wagon Trek, together with a complete display of the history of Hartenbos. The contents were donated by South Africans throughout the country in 1938..

Deviation: if you wish to visit Oudtshoorn, take the R328 from Mossel Bay. It is also known as the **Robinson Pass.**

The Robinson Pass

Early adventures along the coast eager to venture into the interior, found their passage blocked by the seemingly impregnable Outeniqua mountains. Assisted by local Khoikhoi they finally forged a way across in 1690, a path that became known as the **Attaqua Kloof***, named after the Khoi tribe living here.*

As settlements along the coast moved eastward, the pioneering settlers in the Knysna and Plettenberg region soon wearied of the long and tedious journey westwards to cross the Attaqua Kloof to gain access to the interior. Consequently a pass route was built between George and Knysna, the Cradock Pass which proved to be as hazardous and arduous as the Attaqua Kloof route and was soon replaced by the Montagu Pass. The people of Mossel Bay now had to choose between the degenerating Attaqua Kloof route or the Montagu Pass in the east – a good 80km away! To compromise, Thomas Bain was commissioned in 1867 to construct a new pass east of the Attaqua Kloof which he completed in 1869. It was named Robinson Pass, after the Commissioner of Roads, M.R. Robinson, whose efforts had brought about the construction of the new pass.

*The Robinson Pass leads through magnificent countryside across the Outeniqua Mountains. This is a particularly scenic route via the Eight Bells Hotel and past two well known and popular ostrich farms, **High Gate** and **Safari** (see page 128). The total distance to Oudtshoorn from Hartenbos is about 75km, easily achieved in one hour, barring photo stops.*

Gentle curves and gradients lead to the 860m-high summit. And one should have leisure to enjoy the scenery: there is the majestic 1363m-high Ruitersberg and the 1263m-high Skurweberg. At the summit the sharp peaks of the Outeniqua Mountains stretch to the west blending in the far distance with the Langeberg Mountain near Swellendam.

Ignoring the Robinson Pass option, carry on towards **George**, 41km away.

The visitor pressed for time should rejoin the N2. The R102 is the better option for the unhurried traveller. Both weave their course gently uphill, in broad bends, cross the Little Brak River and after 4km reach the tranquil **Little Brak Rivier** (exit 401), a popular holiday resort. Ever changing views of ocean and undulating hills accompany the driver for the next 10 kilometres, whether on the national road or the minor road. Aloes peep down from the hills, rising mist plays hide and seek with views of the ocean and the Outeniqua Mountains loom higher to the north.

GREAT BRAK RIVER (exit 409)
offers the holiday-maker a river, lagoon and unspoilt beaches. It even boasts the biggest known pepper tree in South Africa, a proud 11.2m in diameter.

Great Brak River

You find it behind the art gallery in Mossienes Avenue.

The Searle Church

The Searle family name is intimately linked to the history of Great Brak River.

The river crossing was a hazardous affair, particularly when leopard, buffalo and elephants still roamed free. Plans were made for a bridge, and Richard Searle from Cape Town was sent for to supervise its construction. On completion he became its first toll keeper. Richard Searle's desire was, however, to move to a farm he had acquired at Blanco near George. To find a replacement tollkeeper, he sent for his brother Charles. Soon afterwards, Brother Charles and his family arrived from England on the 'Vocalist'. He operated not only the toll, but also built a water-mill, acted as postmaster, established temperance accommodation, conveyed passengers from Great Brak River to Mossel Bay and George, and acquired large tracts of prime land. In 1877 he started a wool-washery and a cornmill. This commercial empire on the banks of the Great Brak River he sold to his sons Charles jnr, Willie and Thomas. They in turn established a boot and shoe factory, and a tannery in 1886/87. A village developed around these activities. Its inhabitants were mostly employees of the various Searle enterprises.

A walk to the Wolwedans Dam
(The Wolves' Dance)

The total distance is 6km. Allow about 2 hours.
The trail follows the Great Brak River to the lookout point of the Wolwedans Dam.

From Charles Street in town, walk northerly past the two churches on the right side of the road. As the road goes uphill, turn left on to the gravel road. You reach a farm gate. About 40from the gate, follow the path up the slope on the right, then the path along the old water furrow which brought irrigation water to Great Brak River. It crosses the river over a cement block that protects the pipeline to PetroSA. Not far away, two yellowwood trees offer some shade and rest before you continue the walk laong the riverbank. For a short while you actually walk in the riverbed. Finally you have to climb some stairs to the viewing platform. Return the way you came.

Willie Searle's ingenuity led to the building of the hydro-electric power station which supplied the village with electricity for the first time in 1924. The power station is in use again today.

The nearby Wolwedans Dam was built in 1989. It supplies cooling water to PetroSA in Mossel Bay, and helps to control floods.

The enthusiastic staff at the information offices in Amy Searle Street, housed in what used to be the Old Schoolhouse, will happily advise you of activities and events in the town.

*From Groot Brak Rivier the scenic R102 continues in a north-easterly direction towards George. It swings more inland. After approx. 18km it reaches the R404. This goes south to **Herold's Bay,** set in steep cliffs on the coast (named after the Rev. Tobias Herold of George), and north to **Blanco** situated close to the stunning Outeniqua Pass. The R102 itself leads directly into **George**.*

The N2 continues in gentle ups and downs through the green foothills of the Outeniqua Mountains and passes exit 419 for Glentana, a coastal hamlet.

Once across the Malgate River, **exit 425** leads to **'George Airport'** and, via **Blanco** links up with the **N12** to **Oudtshoorn** (see page 128).

The southern exit leads to **Herold's Bay** (see above). Watch for **exit 431. As the national road by-passes George, you must exit here if you wish to visit this spirited town.** To the south and coast it heads for

PACALTSDORP
a village first known as Hoogekraal (High Corral). In 1812, descendants of the Outeniqua Khoi lived here under captain Dikkop ('Stubborn'), sometimes also called 'Het Kop', ('The Head'). The chief had requested a minister for his people in 1813 when the Rev. Campbell of the London Missionary Society visited his kraal. As it so happened, the Rev. Carolus Pacalt of the Moravian Church was available at the time. Captain Dikkop personally travelled by ox wagon to Swellendam to fetch Rev. Pacalt and asked him to become his minister, promising him his best and biggest hut until a house could be built. The Rev. Pacalt died after five years of missionary work and the village was renamed from Hoogekraal to Pacaltsdorp.

GETTING TO KNOW GEORGE

The town stretches in the shade of the two highest peaks of the Outeniqua Mountains. Cradock Peak climbs steeply to 1583 metres and George Peak reaches 1372 metres.

George, named after King George III of England, is the commercial and agricultural centre of the Garden Route. It is situated on the coastal belt about 226m above sea level, and nearly 8km away from the sea. Climatically the town's old motto best expresses it 'Semper amabile' – always pleasant. Wicked tongues though, think of George as '**C**old **A**nd **W**et' as it is displayed by George-registered motorcars! (CAW).

Insatiable demand for timber attracted settlers as early as the mid-18th century to the heavily wooded region, home to the Attaqwa and Outeniqwa Khoi. The latter means 'A man laden with honey'. Governor de la Fontaine established a timber post and granted woodcutters the first six plots on condition they provided the timber necessary for the official government buildings.

The George Beacon

In 1785, an English East India Company vessel ran into trouble and sought the safety of Francis Bay, some fair distance east of George. Some of the officers decided to head for Cape Town, either by wagon or on foot. On their southward bound journey they recorded their findings. Somehow the VOC was alerted to the presence of British soldiers. Highly alarmed, Governor van der Graaff and the Council of Policy decided to spirit some 100 soldiers off the first ships that called in Table Bay with troops on board, and to station them along the coast, at Mossel Bay, Plettenberg Bay, St Francis and Algoa Bay. This well intended strategy failed: no ships with soldiers arrived in Table Bay! Instead, stone beacons, bearing the arms of the Netherland and the VOC were erected at important points to enforce the Dutch East India Company claim over the land. One of these was allocated to George.

It had not escaped the notice of the VOC that it was almost impossible to exercise any form of control over the vast region from the Swellendam magistracy. An additional magisterial district had to be established, if governance was to be effective. The British authorities who took over from the Dutch in 1806 concurred with this view. The new British governor, the Earl of Caledon, dispatched Lieutenant Collins to investigate the matter. The result was the proclamation of a new magistracy in the Outeniqua region in 1809. Two years later, on 23 April (St. George's Day) the new district was proclaimed and

Adrianus van Kervel became its first landdrost. The town grew at a leisurely pace. It became a municipality in 1837. In 1907, George was connected by rail to Cape Town. This railway line continued its path towards Oudtshoorn via seven tunnels cut into the steep slopes of the Outeniqua mountains. (The line can be seen from the Outeniqua and Montagu Passes (see page 109).

Today, as George is home to the smallest Anglican cathedral in the country, if not the southern hemisphere, it is no longer a town, but a city!

WHAT TO DO IN AND AROUND GEORGE

Let's look at some historical buildings.

At the top end of York Street, one finds the

George Museum
This was the old Drostdy building, or magistrate's court built in 1811, first occupied by Adrian van Kervel. The building succumbed to a fire in 1826, was rebuilt and became first a private residence, then the Victoria Hotel.

The museum is also home to the original 'George Beacon' erected by the VOC in 1785 to deter the British from trying to stake a claim in Outeniqualand. Other impressive exhibits include a gemstone collection and a unique collection of mechanical musical instruments - probably the biggest in the country.

The Information Centre in York Street
is housed in the old King Edward VII Library on the site of George's original gaol. It was designed in 1905 by Charles Bullock in the neo-Renaissance style.

In front of the building grows a massive **Oak Tree**, reputedly a former slave tree.

Further down York Street appears
St. Mark's Cathedral
the smallest cathedral in the southern hemisphere, consecrated in 1850. It is built along the lines of the church of Littlemore near Oxford, from designs prepared by Sophie Gray, wife of the first Anglican Bishop Robert Gray.
The Anglican Diocese of George was formally constituted on 23 April 1911.

The treasured Cathedral Bible bears the signatures of King George VI, the late Queen Mother, and of the Princesses Margret and Elisabeth, today's Queen Elisabeth II, and the Duke of Kent. It was signed in 1947 when the royal family visited South Africa.

In the grounds are the graves of the first South African born and first bishop of George, Bishop Sidwell, and of Henry Fancourt White, the engineer responsible for the Montagu Pass .

St Marks Cathedral, George   *interior of St Marks Cathedral*

The Roman Catholic church one discovers to the back of St. Marks Cathedral, off Cathedral Street:

St. Peter & St. Paul
This is the oldest original church, except for a small entrance, of the Roman Catholic faith in South Africa, going back to 1842. The altar is of Italian marble.

The first priest, Father A. Devereux from Ireland, went on to become the Bishop of Grahamstown.

The Old Townhall

stands near the corner of Market and York Streets. It was a simple brick and mud construction built in 1848-50. Its neighbour is the **Centenary Town Hall** built in 1911 in the neo-baroque style.

Today's municipal administration is accommodated in the Civic Centre across York Street.

Walk up **Meade Street** towards the mountains to visit the

Dutch Reformed Church

unmistakable with its huge church tower.

NG Church, George

The original church was consecrated in 1817. Its first minister was Dr Tobias Herold after whom Herold's Bay is named (see page 96) Disaster struck soon when lightening damaged the building so badly that it had to be demolished. Financial constraints prevented immediate re-building. The corner stone for the new church was only laid in 1832. Three highly skilled slaves were brought from Cape Town to assist in the construction of the cross-designed building. Imagine the labour involved: apparently 18 000 wagon loads were used for the foundation of paving and flat stones; nearly 2 million bricks were laid. The Outeniqua forests delivered vast amounts of yellowwood which was used for the vaulted ceiling and the pillars supporting the galleries. The massive teak entrance door was brought by ox wagon from Cape Town. Construction lasted a full 12 years.

Another highly prized indigenous wood, stinkwood (ocutea *bullata),* was used for the carving of the pulpit which is modeled on Anton Anreith's famous Lion Pulpit in the *Groote Kerk* church of Cape Town.

The original reed roof, with reeds from Riversdale, was replaced in 1880.

A second disaster struck after torrential rains in 1905 which collapsed the tower. The timber had weakened considerably and could not withstand the force of rain. The tower was subsequently rebuilt in a grandiose style, adorned by a clock donated by a London firm. During the repair work, valuable coins were discovered, now exhibited in the George Museum.

As one strolls through the town, beautiful furniture catches the eye, crafted from rare woods such as stinkwood, blackwood, yellowwood, ironwood and wild olive, in traditional or rustic designs.

Outeniqua Mountains

Indeed, nature has spoilt the Garden Route region. The high annual rainfall and mild climate are conducive to the formation of forests. Man's destructive intrusion has destroyed vast areas of indigenous forests country-wide. The old tools used for the different woods, the implements, boats and wooden wagons built from local timber, are on display at the timber section of the George Museum.

The Garden Route, thankfully, can still boast some 65 000 hectare of continuous, natural forests which for centuries formed an almost impenetrable barrier to travellers. Most popular and highly prized woods were the stinkwood, and the Outeniqua yellowwood.

Walking in the Outeniqua Nature Reserve

The Outeniqua Nature Reserve stretches over 38 000 hectare across the sometimes steep and rugged mountain ranges. It lies between the high-rainfall coastal region and the dry Little Karoo and boasts a very diverse vegetation. The moist southern slopes are mostly covered with mountain fynbos, whilst the drier northern slopes are quite sparsely vegetated.

Throughout the reserve rock paintings of animals, hunters and honeycombs drawn by the Outeniqua Khoi have been found on secluded rockfaces.

Numerous hiking trails of varying length and difficulty have been laid out. Some suggestions are:

Tierkop Hiking Trail

with spectacular views of George and surroundings. This is a two-day walk with an overnight hut at Tierkop. It covers approx. 30 km.

Attaqwaskloof Hiking Trail

Another two-day hike of about 35km of steep but breathtaking (literally and metaphorically) views.

The Cradock Pass Trail

a moderate walk of 17.2km with a few steep hauls. Allow 8 hours.

> ### Sir John Francis Cradock
> *He was born in Dublin, Ireland, in 1762. He enjoyed a successful army career in Ireland, after which he was appointed Governor of the Cape Colony from 1811-1814.*
> *During his term of office he conscripted local burghers and used the British army to drive the Xhosa over the Fish River (Eastern Cape) in 1811-1812; he ordered the circuit court to investigate allegations of settler ill-treatment of the Khoikhoi people and replaced the loan farm with a perpetual quitrent system; he sought to limit the farm size and that farms were properly surveyed; he promoted education for white children and created new magisterial districts. Sir John Cradock died in Grimston, Ireland.*

The Cradock Pass was constructed by Adrianus van Kervel, the first landdrost of George. Governor Cradock made funds available and the pass was built in the record time of two months! The haste may well explain its steep gradient, never well thought out nor ever popular: – up to three days man and beast toiled to haul ox-wagons to the top, and then down into the Little Karoo. Grooves gouged by wagons wheels as they braked down the steep northern ridge are still visible on rocks. The Montagu Pass, (see page 108) built in 1847, later replaced the Cradock Pass.

The walk ends at the 'Old Hotel' on the Montagu Pass. Plan transport for the return!

Yellowwoods – Podocarpaceae

The tree is a cone-bearing member of the conifer family, but bears its seeds in round shells with a fleshy skin, and not in the usual cones associated with conifers. The trees are male or female. Male trees bear small catkin-like cones which consist of scales, each of which bear two tiny pollen sacs which open to release the winged pollen grains. These fertilize the female cones. In some species, these seeds are perched on a swollen, red base which is the enlarged stalk. This fleshy stalk has given the genus its name the Greek podo for foot and carpus for fruit.

The yellowwoods are the giants in the moist forests: the **Outeniqua Yellowwood/Kalander (Podocarpus falcatus)** *grows up to 60 m high.*

The early settlers were fond of the well-wearing **Real Yellowwood (Podocarpus latifolius)** *from which they manufactured mainly furniture. But floor and ceiling boards, door panels, roof rafters and railway sleepers were made from it. Of the four known yellowwood species in South Africa,, Real Yellowwood is the most widely spread. It grows to 20 to 30 m high. It prefers dark, moist forests. It has yielded more timber than any other indigenous tree in South Africa.*
The timber is a pale yellow, with a mostly straight, even grain . It is a light wood, but fairly hard and strong.

Stinkwood – ocotea bullata

The indigenous black stinkwood is a large evergreen tree. Under ideal conditions it reaches a height of 30 metres. It belongs to the laurel family (Lauraceae) and gained its common name from the pungent smell the bark emits when freshly felled.

The tall, straight tree has a clean trunk and a smooth, light-grey bark, frequently marked with salmon-pink and mauve, when it is young. With age, the bark becomes rugged, scaley and dark-brown.

The dark green leaves have a wavy margin and are tapered at the base and tip. The bullata are prominent bubbles or swellings on either side of the midrib towards the base of the leaf.

In the summer months, from December to February, the tree bears small pale yellow-green flowers. These are followed by the small acorn shaped fruit. The fruit ripens in autumn and is eaten by most fruit-eating birds, such as hornbills and loeries; but also by monkeys, baboons, elephants and wild pigs.

The Stinkwood timber darkens to a golden-brown and black. It is moderately hard and the timber works well by machine and hand, saws easily but is hard on tools.

The **George Peak Walk** (17km) and **Cradock Peak Walk** (19km) are both arduous and long. Allow about 9 hours to complete either walk.

Both hikes start at the Outeniqua Nature Reserve office at the foot of the Outeniqua Pass. They start as a single trail but split into two routes in the summit area. From the summit of Cradock's Peak in particular, the views are astounding and certainly rewarding for the immense energy expended by the hiker to reach the mountain top.

Pass To Pass Trail
This moderate trail of about 4.7km connects the Outeniqua Pass with the Montagu Pass and can be started at the top of either Pass. It crosses beautiful mountain streams, runs through indigenous forests and fynbos vegetation. Allow about 4 hours for the traverse. Unless you return the same way, arrange for transport at the other end.

Not everybody has the time nor energy to walk the mountains. Don't despair, the **OUTENIQUA CHOO-TJOE** will rattle and shake travellers along a picturesque route that links George with Knysna.

Depart from George Station (at end of Market Street) on the heritage line and travel fern-covered hills, through forests, past Victoria Bay, over the railway bridge that crosses the mouth of the Kaaimans River, along the spectacular lakes and coastal dunes, through the estuary of the Goukamma River and

The Choo-Tjoe on the turntable in Knysna

finally across the long lagoon bridge in Knysna to puff and huff into the Knysna Station. During the winter months, the train service is reduced.

The Outeniqua Choo-Tjoe is South Africa's last scheduled steam train service. The train service started in 1928.

Outeniqua Railway Museum

This fascinating museum opened in 1998 and is the only National Railway Museum in the country. It is housed in a huge shed in Mission Street (turn-off from Courtenay Road on the way to Knysna at Mission Road). Four railway lines run into the museum which exhibits locomotives, coaches, road transportation vehicles, replica of a station and signal cabin, uniforms, crockery, silverware, model trains and furniture.

George Crocodile Farm

Tired of walking the forests or clattering along on the train? In that case, George offers an encounter with over 4000 crocodiles at the Crocodile Farm in York Street. Feeding takes place daily at 1500.

Deviation: N12/N9 route George to Oudtshoorn via the

OUTENIQUA PASS

The Outeniqua Pass was designed by the wartime Chief Engineer of National Roads, P.A. de Villiers. Construction started in 1943 with Italian prisoners of war providing the skills and labour. The pass was completed in 1951.

Finding its way out of town from the traffic circle where York and Courtenay Streets meet, the road passes the Hospital and comes to a turn-off for **Blanco.** *This colourful village was once the postal centre from where Henry Fancourt White, an Australian engineer operated during the construction of the Montagu Pass (1842-1849). In recognition for his services, the Colonial Secretary, the Honorable John Montagu, renamed the postal centre after him. Initially known as Whitesville, it was later latinised into 'Blanco'.*

Henry Fancourt White and his two sisters died of mushroom poisoning in his home which today is the internationally known luxury **Fancourt Hotel** *and* **Golf Course***.*

Nearby, to the right of the route, lies **Witfontein Forestry Station** *from where the many hiking routes through the Outeniqua Nature Reserve start (see above).*

The alternative **Montagu Pass to Oudtshoorn** *route turns off soon afterwards. (see below).*

The road dips across the Malgas River, then rises in broad leisurely bends. Grand views of George and the coastline alternate with equally grand views of the mountain through which it snakes.

*Fynbos covered hills, treed and bushy sections alternate; closer to the summit stop at a lay-bye to savour the majestic view towards the coastal plain, across the valley to the mountains. Look out carefully for the railway line cutting into the slopes above and disappearing into one of the seven tunnels, a thrilling train ride indeed! Deep down in the wooded valley the **Montagu Pass** toils uphill. At 16 kilometres outside George, the summit (800m) of the Outeniqua Pass is reached.*

Splendour of the Outeniqua Mountains

*From its highest point, the Pass descends unhurriedly into the basin of the Little Karoo. Did you spot an unusual crop climbing up high frames? This is **hops**. George is the only only area in South Africa where hops is cultivated. As the Pass reaches the valley below and enters the Little Karoo, a turn-off leads **westwards** to **Oudtshoorn**. (The easterly direction, marked **Uniondale N9/N12** leads through a long fertile valley known as the Kammanassie, the Place of Perennial Water, or Longkloof, see page 220)*

Red soil glistens in the morning sun, the railway line keeps the road some company, and 10km outside the town, one has the first glimpse of Oudtshoorn. Eventually the Olifants River is crossed and a light industrial area passed. Then we enter the town of Oudtshoorn whose story is told elsewhere. (See page 128)

Hops farming

began in the 1820s when it was recognised that the mild climate and year-round rains, little or no hail and wind during the growing period would be the ideal conditions for hops cultivation. About 500ha are under cultivation and 40% to 70% of the harvest is used in beer brewing. To mature, the plant needs a certain number of daylight hours. Because the days are too short, artificial lights are switched on for 3 to 4 hours a night, this way increasing the required light and making the traveller feel like a journey through wonderland.

Hops is a perennial climber. From flowering to fruit forming and ripening the plant needs a mere three and a half months. Under perfect conditions, hops grows by 10cm daily.

The thin shoots reach the top of the frame normally by mid-December when the side shoots begin to form. A month later the plants flower and then develop a cone which consists of overlapping bracts.

Small balloon-shaped sacs are at the base of each bract which contain acids and oils. It is the acid solution which gives the bitter taste to beer, its aroma and head, but has nothing to do with the alcohol content of beer.

Hops is harvested in February/ March. The plants are cut at ground level, fed into a picker which strips the leaves and cones. The cones are taken to a drying kiln for 6 to 8 hours, ground and processed into pill-form and finally dispatched to the breweries.

Deviation: George to Oudtshoorn via the

MONTAGU PASS
A word of caution: the Pass is untarred, narrow, steep and not suitable for caravans or cars with trailers. Avoid it in wet conditions.

From the traffic circle near the Museum where Courtenay and York Streets meet, leave George town on the N12/N9 in the direction of Oudtshoorn.

Shortly after passing **Blanco,** *at about 6km away from George, the turn-off for the scenic Montagu Pass is reached. (Just in case you miss this turn-off, do not worry, a second one is reached a couple of kilometres further on).*

The old, torturous Cradock Pass (see above) which ascended for 9km the steep slopes of George Peak, Skurwekop and Cradock Peak proved almost insurmountable for man and beast. Probably one of the last larger groups to brave its steep inclines were Voortrekkers from the George region on their northward bound journey in the 1830s. An alternative route was sorely needed. Charles Michell, the Surveyor-General of the Cape, strongly supported the idea and work on a new route began in 1844 under the supervision of the Australian engineer Henry Fancourt White. The new pass, blasted out of the rocks and retained by massive dry-stone walls, tracks the contours of the

Montagu Pass rock wall

mountain very closely. In sharp bends the narrow road climbs steadily uphill. On completion it meant that travelling time for ox wagons was shortened from the customary three days trek via the Cradock Pass to a mere three hours. Different toll fees applied for vehicles with or without brakes, draught animals or bigger animals.

After about 8km, a stop sign arrests the steady climb. Here one also finds a plaque in honour of the construction of the pass. Look behind occasionally, as the coastal plateau still gleams in the distance. The Keur River bridge is crossed and as you wind uphill, the Outeniqua Pass can be seen to the left. Relax, take time to enjoy the mountain splendour. But also watch for possible oncoming traffic: there are no turning points. At about 12.5 km after the begin of the ascent, the 'Old Smithy' remains invite you to a stop. Just to remind today's traveller of the torturous, ox-wagon travel, many a bend is aptly named, such as 'Haarkantdraai' (Hairpin Bend), the 'Remskoendraai' (Brakeshoe) and the 'Regop Draai' (Straight Up). Then the amazing railway lines come into view. Though there is no longer a regular rail service from George or Mossel Bay to Oudtshoorn, excursions in a specially adapted 'Outeniqua Power Van' can be organised.

Outeniqua (top) and Montagu Passes

Relentlessly the road rises, surrounded by unbelievable mountain splendour. Then one drives under the railway bridge at 'Stinkhoutdraai'. Here the rails disappear into yet another tunnel.

Eventually the route begins to descend into a widening valley. A few bridges are crossed, hops farming re-appears (see above) and, after about 28km the church at Herold greets the traveller. Three more kilometres, and the sign: **Uniondale/N9 – N12/Oudtshoorn** welcomes you to the Little Karoo and the Longkloof (see page 220).

Leather in George
During the construction of the Montagu Pass, a tollhouse was built on the George side of the mountain. John Kirk Smith was the first tollkeeper, succeeded by his son William.

Father and his son, in true entrepreneurial spirit, made 'veldschoens/veldskoene', simple, comfortable leather shoes which they sold to travellers from the tollhouse. Business flourished and the first tollkeeper's grandson, J.K. Smith, opened a store in Market Street, George – the forerunner of a thriving leather industry in the region.

Rail and road meet on the Montagu Pass

Railway Bridge on the Montagu Pass

Lichen coloured rocks on the Montagu Pass

Tree Ferns

The Khoikoi and San

Numerous theories exits as to the origin of both, the Khoikhoi and the San, the indigenous peoples of the Cape. One of them believes that hamitic cattle herders moved south from the Nile region, imposing their culture on the conquered peoples. Intermarriage took place and in time a new race evolved which maintained many of the customs and linguistic peculiarities of the original inhabitants.

Renewed splintering occurred at a later stage from which the nomadic hunter, the San and the pastoralist Khoikhoi emerged.
Both races are of small physique, reaching an average body height of about 150cm.

The pastoralist Khoikhoi, 'The Brave Men', excelled in many crafts: they twirled sticks to produce fire; cured animal skins for clothing,blankets and bags; with clay they shaped pottery, and from shells, copper, ivory, later brass, they created artistic ornaments.

The Khoikhoi were organised into different groups, each led by a chief. Each group possessed its own pastural land which led to frequent cattle raids amongst them, and was also the cause of friction between them and the Europeans who failed to understand the importance of the Khoikhois' right to water and pasture.

Their numbers dwindled drastically in 1713 when thousands succumbed to a devastating smallpox epidemic.

The nomadic San, often called the bushman, is probably a descendant of the Late Stone Age hunter-gatherers.

The San were organised in small bands from 50 to 100, togehter they roamed the countryside for food. In huge rock overhangs they found shelter from the elements; here they depicted their life in graceful murals. The bushman's survivial depended on the availability of water, game and his own hunting skills. 'Naua', or Fate, had given him the desert, veld, game and mountains. This fundamental belief led to fierce fighting against those who poached on his preserves.

The coming of the Europeans aggravated the San's situation. Agains the powerful rifle which thinned out the game, he was helpless. In retaliation he now stole the white man's cattle. Soon the Europeans thought of the bushmen as marauding, stealing hordes, and organised hoffific punitive raids agains them. Thousands of men were killed towards the end of the 18th century, whilst their women and children were sold into slavery. The surviving bushmen sought safety in the dry desert of the hinterland. Their fate intermingled with that of other races, and today few pure blooded San survive, mainly in Botswana and remote parts of Namibia. Their culture, their language is threatened by extinction.

ROUTE FIVE

SWELLENDAM – R324/TRADOUW PASS – BARRYDALE

ROUTE 62 – LADISMITH - CALITZDORP - OUDTSHOORN

The total distance of this route is about 208km, without deviations.

25km outside Swellendam, on the N2 national road, the R324 turn-off marked **Barrydale** lures you off into the countryside. The R324 changes its name to **Tradouw Pass**.

At first the road fringes the foothills of the Langeberg Mountains. In spring, the valley below the gently climbing route is filled with the white blossoms of the **youngberry**, a delight to the eye. This tasty berry prospers in the black alluvial soil deposited by the streams cascading down the Langeberg Mountain kloofs.

Youngberries hail originally from America. The fragile fruit is handpicked in the months of November/December. The bulk of the crop is destined for the export market.

After a few kilometres you enter the village of

SUURBRAAK

founded by the interdenominational London Missionary Society in 1812. In 1875 it was taken over by the *Algemeende Sending Kerk* (General Mission Church). The Anglican church and school were built in 1880 because of a split in the congregation.

Suurbraak

The historic church, parsonage, old school, bakery and older homes dress the centrally located village square in an atmosphere of yesteryear.

Children play noisily in the main road, chicken cackle loudly, horse and donkey carts rumble by –

drive carefully through this 'Huckleberry Finn' village.

Situated on the Buffeljags River and sheltered by giant oaks, Suurbraak is fast becoming a popular stop-over with travellers. Crafters are busily at work: the 'Suurbraak Skrynwerkers' fashion outstanding hand-made chairs from canary pine and woven grass seats. Visit 'Xairu Crafts' offering home-made jams, chutneys, grass brooms and painted tiles.

Suurbraak home in the Main Street

Suurbraak children

The fertile valley encourages agricultural activities, such as the cultivation of grains, deciduous and citrus fruits, dairy farming and small scale vegetable production.

Presently Suurbraak, 'The Sour Fallow Land' has a population of about 3000.

Beyond Suurbraak, the road swings sharply northwards to begin the unhurried ascent of the

Tradouw Pass, built with convict labour by Thomas Bain and opened in 1873.

Tradouw in the Khoi language means 'Woman's Pass' suggesting perhaps an easy way across the mountains. In late spring, early summer the upper hills to the east are carpeted in mauve and pink erica blossoms.

The route follows ancient San and Khoikhoi paths. The Attaqua Khoi lived in the Suurbraak area which they knew as Xairu, meaning 'Beautiful'. The earliest Dutch settlers aptly translated it as 'Paradise'.

For 17km the Tradouw Pass swings along the eastern slopes of the mountains and in the shade of the Grootvadersbosch Mountain Reserve. The river below gurgles deep below and waterfalls cascade down the steep hillsides in winter.

Don't rush through 'paradise'. Numerous view sites invite to pause and marvel at the beauty around and at one's feet. Once across the Langeberg Mountain, the world of the Cape Folded Mountains lies behind, ahead waits the world of the

LITTLE KAROO

For millennia the Little Karoo has known a permanent population. The nomad San roamed the hills and mountains, the Khoikhoi populated the fertile valleys. The first white man to penetrate into this region was ensign Schrijver in 1689.

Tradouw Pass

Karoo, a dry, hard and sparsely covered land, means 'Thirstland', a word from the Khoi language. The land is thirsty indeed. Its annual rainfall varies from 50 to 200mm, quickly absorbed by the parched land that swelters in summer temperatures which can exceed 38° Celsius. The Karoo lies about 600m above sea level.

Survival?

For centuries this land, framed by mountain to the north and south has also been known as Kannaland. The *kanna* shrub belongs to the mesembryanthemum family (figs). The *kanna* genus *sceletium* numbers 22 species. The word *sceletium* describes best, particularly to the non-botanist, the leaves which, when withered resemble a durable *skeleton*. The khoi chewed these leaves eagerly as they contain a narcotic mesembrine which has tranquilising or purgative qualities.

The Karoo plain broadens to about 100km and stretches to over 300km in length. Brilliant red-orange coloured sandstones laid down between 250 and

350 million years ago as sediments beneath water and then warped and tilted by powerful pressures as they dried in more recent times, characterise the region. Numerous rivers traverse the plain. These rivers have their source in the Great Karoo beyond the Swartberg Mountain, but claw their way through this barrier. Smaller streams join the watercourses that finally enter the Little Karoo. The most important river flowing across the plain is the Olifants (Elephant) River. The Olifants eventually unites with other rivers, such as the Gamka, or 'Lion River'. Their combined flow is called the Gourits River. The river bears the name of a Khoi clan name, the Gouriqua.

Where the Tradouw Pass (R324) meets the R62, turn right for

BARRYDALE
the western gate-way to the Little Karoo.

Barrydale

The Tradouw Pass certainly facilitated the growth of this small town, probably named after Joseph Barry & Nephews (see page 31). Strange,though, as by the time Barrydale sprung from the dry soil of the Little Karoo, the Barry commercial empire had ceased to exist.

Typically, the town grew around the first church, *Ou Kerk* (Old Church), built in 1877. Then a successful Jewish trader stepped in and filled the commercial void left by the Barry bankruptcy. This entrepreneurial businessman in the end owned the General Dealer, Hotel, Draper's Store, Shoemaker and Gunsmith shops. Further growth of Barrydale was largely dependent on the economic development of the district which concentrated on dried fruit and sheep farming and, temporarily ostrich farming.

The main fruits grown are apricot, pears, Kakamas peaches and grapes. The Barrydale Co-Op was formed in 1940, a distillery set up and a switch from dried fruit farming to canning occurred. The 25 members of today's **Barrydale Wine Cellar** produce some delectable and award-winning chardonnay, sauvignon blanc, merlot, cabernet sauvignon wines.

Climatically, Barrydale enjoys an annual rainfall of approximately 300mm Despite frequent hail storms in summer and frost in winter, Barrydale has grown into a buzzing, popular town offering refuge to many Capetonians for weekend getaways.

Rustic restaurants along the route sustain the traveller. Route 62 see-saws easterly through the arid plain, shadowed by the Langeberg to the right and the Swartberg looming to the left. Out of the lonely landscape suddenly rises **Ronnies Sex Shop.** Curious? Motorists stare in disbelief, some speed on, others lift an eyebrow, others brake hard to have a good look. To their surprise an innocent little restaurant bids welcome. Ronnie, the original owner, long ago painted his name on the dilapidated cottage on his land, planning to convert it into a farm stall. Whilst away on business, his friends played a prank on him by adding 'Sex Shop'. Ronnie's initial anger soon turned to a broad smile when he realised the potential appeal of the name in the middle of nowhere: he restored the building and turned it into a popular pub and tourist stop.

Shortly after Ronnie's Sex Shop, a gravel road turns left to

WARMWATERBERG SPRINGS
about 3.5km away. The springs are slightly radio-active and rich in iron. At source the springs have a temperature of 40°C. A small and pleasant resort has developed around the springs.

The R62 meanwhile crosses the often dry Koeniekuils River, then masters a couple of sharp bends on the approach to the Bosvlakte River, to be greeted by a very different landscape. Dry and low hills dot the valley which has opened up wide. Another gravel road branches off towards Plathuis, situated on the banks of the Touws River which, like us, rambles through this sandstone wasteland. It eventually joins the Groot River, a contributary of the Gourits River. Though seemingly a barren land where acacias are scattered on the hills, nature performs a veritable miracle in spring when vygies (mesembryanthemums) paint the dull, sandy flats and low hills in riotous colours.

The R323/Garcia's Pass to Riversdale, 83km away, (see page 85) veers off to the right, shortly afterwards a turn-off to Laingsburg, situated in the Great Karoo on the national road N1. This is not our destination, and so we traverse more dry and hilly countryside, pass a turn-off to Van Wyksdorp and finally enjoy a magnificent view of the Towerkop (2130m). This is the 'Bewitched Mountain' with its fabled cleft, rising to the skies just outside **Ladismith**. An angry witch, frustrated in her attempts to escape the loneliness of the Karoo, struck the mountain with her wand, splitting it in two...if legends can be believed?

The western half of the cleft was held to be unclimbable, until proven wrong in 1885.

One day, six daredevil youths from Ladismith set off to attempt the climb. The inexperienced young mountaineers, led by Gustav Nefdt, carried neither food nor water. Their secret and arduous climb led them, totally exhausted, to the foot of the cleft. The youths realised they were in trouble. Whilst some flashed signals to Ladismith, Gustav Nefdt disappeared. Anxiously they waited for his return or at least, for some signal from him. Nothing..dejectedly and fearing the worst, they sat down. Suddenly, out of nowhere Gustav re-appeared triumphantly claiming he had scaled the cleft. As proof, he said, he had left one of his socks under a rock! Spirits uplifted, the group made it safely downhill, back to town, to a not altogether sympathetic parental reception. But their story was believed, at first. Then doubt nagged the townfolks' mind. Curious to prove Gustav Nefdt right or wrong, a group of adults ventured out, this time well equipped. They failed to scale the cleft. Angrily they accused young Nefdt of cheating and lying, an accusation he had to refute. Once more he set off, accompanied by the townspeople and the boys of the original climb. Once at the foot of the cleft, Gustav nimbly scrambled up a 30 cm wide ledge, then disappeared from view. His invisible route took him to the top. From here he lowered a string with which he pulled up a rope to assist another climber. The hazardous climb - Nefdt swore he would never attempt it again - was only repeated 22 years later, by another party - albeit by another route.

The 'Bewitched Mountain' lies at a safe distance from the R62 and won't challenge you as you enter

LADISMITH

At the town's entrance, one passes the imposing Carl Otto Hager designed church. It was completed in 1873 in his favoured neo-gothic style.

In the early years, the Klein Karoo fell under the magistracy of Swellendam (see page 29). As the stories of farmers, hunters and adventurers unfold, so the growth of new and small settlements became known.

Carl Otto Hager

Hager, son of the legal advisor to the government in Saxony (Germany), was born in Dresden on 16 October 1813. He studied architecture and portraiture at the Royal Academy in Dresden. When he arrived in Cape Town in 1838, Hager earned his living as portrait artist and drawing master. What was to be his first breakthrough as architect, the design of the Roman Catholic Cathedral St. Mary's, in Cape Town, came to naught because of unfortunate misunderstandings with his partner, Sparrman. In his distress, Hager contemplated a return to Germany. Just before his planned departure, he visited Stellenbosch and fell in love with the town. He made it his home, married Cornelia, his German neighbour's daughter and settled down to family life and success. The couple had eleven children. He died in Stellenbosch at the age of 85.

Ladismith (spelt with an 'i' to differentiate it from the town in Natal) was established in 1851 by the Dutch Reformed Church on portion of the farm *Ylands Valley*. It bears the name of Juana Maria de los Dolores de Leon, Governor Sir Harry Smith's youthful Spanish wife. The Governor, very much her senior, had set eyes on her at the sack of Badajoz in 1812, during the Peninsular War (1808-14) caused by Napoleon's invasion of Portugal and Spain and ending with the emperor's abdication. The young beauty, she was only 14 years, totally bewitched him. They eloped and married two weeks later.

Ladismith achieved municipal status in 1903 but growth was sluggish, mainly because the town lacked an efficient transport system. Growing demands for a railway link led to the visit by the Prime Minister of the Cape, Cecil John Rhodes in 1893. The usual promises were made, but a railway line reached the town only in 1925. This railway line was completely washed away in the great floods of 1981 and never repaired.

Early real development, as with most towns and villages in the Little Karoo, coincided with the flourishing ostrich industry in the later half of the 19th century.

Spanspek melon

When you enjoy the Spanspek melon at breakfast, remember young and figure-conscious Juana Maria de los Dolores. Not wishing to join her husband's breakfast of rich fried eggs and bacon, she would routinely ask to be served a sweet melon instead. This request prompted the kitchen staff to refer to the melon as 'the Spaansche vrou se spek' – the Spanish Lady's bacon.

Sugarbush

Ladismith enjoys a healthy, invigorating climate where sunny days by far outnumber rainy days. The annual rainfall varies from 500mm in the Klein Swartberg mountains to a meagre 150mm in the outlying areas of the district.

The vegetation in the Ladismith district ranges from mountain fynbos to karoo broken veld, spekboomveld and succulent karoo in the *koppies*, the 'small hills', and plains.

A unique thatching reed flourishes in the area, *roodecoma arida*, whilst an endemic plant put Ladismith on the botanist's map: this is the *Freesia speciosa.* The vast freesia bulb export industry in the Netherlands is based on varieties developed from the *Freesia speciosa.*

Other floral wonders of Ladismith are the *Protea aristata* and the rare *Protea pruinosa,* a prostrate shrub up to 0.5m. It is found on ridges and summits from 1800 to 2100metres.. The *Protea aristata* is an erect, stocky shrub and grows to a height of about 3m. It loves the rocky kranses (ridges) and sandstone slopes.

To appreciate the area's floral abundance, visit the **Ladismith Klein Karoo Nature Reserve.** It is situated 4km outside the town and is the property of the municipality. To get there, follow along Kerk Straat(Church Street),turn left into Noord Str which bends sharply right, and then leads towards the reserve.

The reserve can be viewed by car or on foot, along the circular 12.6km Klapperbos Hiking trail. Fabulous views reward the hiker from the highest point (733m).

Snakes..

The vegetation consists mainly of Spekboom and Karooveld. Animals too may be spotted, such as the eland, duiker, Mountain zebra, steenbok and a host of smaller species.

But there is more to Ladismith than just flowers. Agriculturally, Ladismith is a major grape and deciduous fruit producing area. The district can boast of intensive wine and table grape plantings in the Southern Cape.

Apricots, plums, nectarines and peaches thrive in the Ladismith climate. In the commercial drying yards the produce is dried to delicious, high quality fruit exported to the world. It is a picturesque sight indeed, a drying yard covered with colourful trays of fruit laid out in the sun! (The early settlers used apricot pips for flooring).

Then there is the tasty cheese produced in the town which has found favour with cheese lovers countrywide.

Wine enthusiasts can indulge in the wines produced by the **Ladismith Wynkelder/Wine Cellar,** established in 1938. The approximately 750 hectare of land planted out to vine yield about 8500 tons of grapes.

A short drive around the town reveals interesting architectural styles. One of them is known as the 'Ladismith' style, a simplified Georgian design. Most buildings date from the 1830s.

The **'Ladismith' style** can be admired in Kerk Straat (Church Street) nos 23,78,82 and Konigin Straat (Queen Str) nos 31,42, 54.
The Gothic style is exposed in the Carl Otto Hager Church; the Lutheran Church with its parsonage in Kerk Straat; the former Synagogue and the Assembly of Christ Church in Becker Street.
The **Victoria style** can be seen in Koning Str 40, Suid Str.2; Albert St nos 21,27,44,65,68,76;
The **Rural style (Karoo)** is expressed in Kerk Str 41,58 and the small school situated higher up Kerk Str which forms part of the Lutheran complex.
The **Regency style** shows itself in the Old Royal Hotel, on the corner of Kerk and Noord Streets.

It's good-bye to Ladismith. Route 62 moves on eastward. About 10km away, in a lush green valley, lies the farm **Hoeko**, birthplace of C.J. Langenhoven, writer of the former South African national anthem, lawyer and passionate writer about the country. Hoeko means 'Don't know' or possibly 'Why' from the Afrikaans 'Hoe kom'. The farm is situated on the banks of the Huisrivier.

The route winds leisurely through unspoilt countryside, green fields and fruit orchards towards the quaint but poor villages of

ZOAR and AMALIENSTEIN
The 'Zoar Church' of the 'Verenigende Gereformeerde Kerk' welcomes the

visitor. Follow the bumpy village lane where children play and wave, old people sit in bowed doorways, smiling a timeless smile.

Zoar Church

Zoar was established in 1817 by Petrus Joubert of the South African Missionary Society. The mission was named after the biblical Zoar, where Lot took refuge after having been ordered to leave the wicked Sodom, about to be destroyed by God (Genesis 19, verses 15-23). The mission station encountered financial difficulties, and when Joubert left Zoar in 1833 the Berlin Society was approached to continue the vital work. The Berlin Society though sympathetic, was also convinced that in time the SA Missionary Society would return; it therefore agreed to assist but simultaneously purchased the adjoining farm Elandsfontein and renamed it after its benefactress, Amalie von Stein, **'Amalienstein'.** Here it established its own missionary station. Farming lessons were given, an impressive church and school built (1853). Amalienstein became well known for the superb quality of its dried fruit. Its first missionary, Reinhold Gregorowski also cared for Zoar from 1837 to 1842.

A long serving missionary was superintendent August Schmidt 1857 to 1894.

During the First World War, the station was taken over by the Dutch Reformed Church.

A visit to the church is inspirational. Afterwards experience farm life, riding in a donkey cart, the traditional means of transport!

A unique destination in Amalienstein is 'Aunt Carolina's Guest House'. It offers self-catering accommodation to a maximum of 6 persons. Aunt Carolina was the longest living resident of German descent on this mission station. She was born on 10 July 1870 at Amalienstein where her parents, August and Carolina Briest had settled in 1867. Her father, a schoolmaster built the only watermill at Amalienstein.

Berlin Missionary Society

The Berlin Missionary Society on 29 February 1824. Its full title was Gesellschaft zur Beförderung der Evangelischen Missionen unter den Heiden zu Berlin. (The Society for the Futherance of the Evangelical Mission amongst the Heathen).

Prospective students were very carefully selected. Some of the acceptance conditions were:

to have a thorough knowledge of the Bible, a sincere belief, appropriate Christian maturity and solemnity; acquire knowledge of modern languages such as English, do courses in the 'heathen'languages; undergo manual skills development and possess an elementary knowledge of medicine.

The course lasted 4½ years. The first five students graduated in 1833 and were sent to South Africa. These were: Gustav Krau, a clerk – August Lange, a weaver – Johannes Schmidt, a carpenter – August Gebel, a theologian and Reinhold Gregorowski, a teacher. Before departure they were sent to the Rhenish Missionary Society in Barmen to learn Dutch and finally sent out with vague instructions …'to Africa, Botswana'.

After arrival in South Africa, the five men parted company, unsure of the road ahead. Gregorowski stayed in Beaufort West, the others found their way north and worked north of the Orange River where they founded 'Bethanie' at the Riet River.

A dusty street in Zoar

Just outside Amalienstein, the **Seven Weeks Poort** Pass branches off to the north, connecting the Little Karoo to the national road N1 near Laingsberg. It snakes through rugged, magnificently colourful countryside, cutting its way through the Klein Swartberg mountains. It was completed in 1862. Motorists beware: the route crosses and re-crosses many riverbeds – vulnerable to flooding and should be avoided after heavy rains.

The origin of the peculiar name 'Seven Weeks' remains a puzzle. Some suppport the theory that it is named after the Reverend Zwerwick, a mission-ary at the Zoar Station. Others believe it took seven weeks to build the road. The most appealing definition tells us that brandy smuggling wagons on their way from Cape Town to the interior rumbled along this forlorn road to avoid the beady eyes of revenue officers.

This torturous journey took the wagons seven weeks. Even the everlasting flowers, the 'Seven Weeks Flowers', here so abundant, are likely originators of the name.

But whatever the origin, the pass is a superb route through the Swartberg. On its eastern side, the pass is dominated by the highest mountain of the Swartberg, the 2328m-high Sevenpoort . A festival of colours awaits the trav-eller: quartzite cliffs, red vertical sandstone, yellow lichened crags and blue coloured slate.

KLAPPERBOS'
Nymania capensis
(Often also incorrectly called: Chinese Lantern) is prominent in the Little Karoo.

It is an evergreen that may reach a height of up to 3m in the less arid parts of the Karoo. It grows from Namaqualand in the north to the Eastern Cape The incon-spicuous flowers grow irregularly on the branches. The 'lantern' is the decorative, papery four chambered pink fruit. When swaying in the wind, the seeds sound a tiny timbre.

Klapperbos

For you, the R62 rises and descends, the wide valley narrows, *klapperbos* jingle from the roadside in early spring. In October, November, aloes stand proud on the otherwise sparsely vegetated hills. Daily the mountains glow a warm golden-red as the sun rises or sets.

Now the road traverses a rocky mountain wonderland following the undulating **Huisrivier Pass II and I.** Far below, in narrow green belts, farming activities are overlooked by majestic, folded sandstone mountains. Traces of the adventurous original pass route, cut narrowly into the mountain slopes to the left, are visible. The modern pass climbs to a height of 662 metres.

View from Huisrivier Pass

Then the Gamka River, (Lion River), and Nels River are crossed whilst the towering mountain world yields gradually to gentler, lower hills.

Soon there is a turn-off to the Calitzdorp Spa.

CALITZDORP SPA
Around the mineral rich hot spring with a temperature of 50° Celsius at source, a pleasant resort has developed. Particularly stressed out urbanites would find that the water, rich in iron and manganese, works wonders for them. Those seeking privacy can plunge into individual hot water baths, otherwise an indoor Roman Bath and the two outdoor pools (one hot, one cold) can be enjoyed.

Travelling on, glance across to the mighty Swartberg. A remarkable and grand rock formation comes into view, an ancient red sandstone formation, glowing perfectly in the morning sun. The '**Red Hills**' red and orange coloured sand-and mudstone were laid down between 250 and 350 million years ago as sediments beneath water, then warped and tilted by powerful pressures as they dried. This gave the landscape and mountains their extraordinary shape and equally amazing colours. Locally they are known as the **Red Hills**.

A detour via **Kruis River** *will display the splendour.*

This scenic drive through the Nels River Valley branches off the R62 outside Calitzdorp and emerges after about 20 km at the foot of the Swartberg Pass, on the R328 which links in a southerly direction with Oudtshoorn. The road is narrow, some bends extremely tight and after heavy rain it should be avoided, when the many causeways by means of which the road crosses and recrosses the river are likely to be flooded.
Grain, fruit orchards, vineyards, some farms run down and neglected – yet altogether an aura of a bygone age.

Hopefully you are not neglectful of the mountain splendour to your right, where the Langeberg mountain range has changed its name to **Outeniqua**.

Thoroughly content ostriches are scouring the veld for food, prancing about, or simply gazing at the motorists with their beautiful, melancholic eyes from behind the fences.

Another cheerful country town lies ahead:

CALITZDORP

It nestles happily in a valley known by the Khoi as *Cango*. This probably means 'Valley between the Hills'. Ensign Schrijver, on his journey to the interior in 1689, refers to the *Xanga* valley on the southern slopes of the Swartberg. Geologically, the Cango Formation is the oldest in the Little Karoo, consisting of slate, conglomerate and limestone. The Cango valley is about 120km long and seldom wider than 16km. The first European settlers arrived around 1756. They had trekked across the Outeniqua Mountain via the Attaqua Kloof, from the south.

Then, buffalo roamed free and wild and it does not come as a surprise that the future town would be laid out on the *Buffelsvlei* farm which belonged to the Calitz family. The land was granted in 1821. The large family popularised the area which soon assumed the name Dorp van Calitz or 'Calitz Village'.

On this vast farm, the settlers gathered under an orange tree for church services before Calitz portioned off some of his land on which the growing farming community could build a church.

Title deed restrictions limited the sale of land to members of the Dutch Reformed Church which hindered development. Nonetheless, the original village church was enlarged magnificently in 1880. It is built of sandstone transported from the nearby Vleirivier (Lake River). The re-design was by Carl Otto Hager's son. Its first minister was Richard van Reenen Barry. Maybe he too contributed to the growth of the town in his own way: through his first marriage he had ten children to whom he added another six in his second marriage. (His first wife had died in childbirth).

Calitzdorp NG Church

Calitzdorp became a municipality in 1913 and when finally the railway reached the town in 1924, it developed as a prosperous agricultural centre.

Don't just drive through Calitzdorp. A stroll down its streets, particularly the narrow lanes with their cosy and colourful *tuishuise*, is a genuine pleasure.

This, of course can be followed by a little wine and port tasting. After all, Calitzdorp is the Port capital of South Africa, a title that may have to change as usage of the word *port* is phased out. Only Portugal can lay claim to it! The three wineries – Boplaas, Die Krans and the Calitzdorp Wynkelder produce an excellent variety of white, red and dessert wines.

The town, a mecca of fresh and dried fruit, is also known for its six different kinds of aloes. These can be admired in the Hennie Cloete Nature Garden, from where one also gains a spectacular view of Calitzdorp.

Tuishuis

Tuishuis

On the town's doorsteps lie the **Groenefontein** and **Gamkaberg Nature Reserves.**

GAMKABERG NATURE RESERVE

The Gamka Mountain (Gamka means 'lion') lies between the Swartberg and the Outeniqua Mountains. The Nature Reserve extends over an area of 9 428ha . It was established in 1974 to conserve a small, remnant herd of the endangered Cape mountain zebra.

Succulent mountain shrub, mountain fynbos and renosterveld characterise the reserve which enjoys an annual rainfall of 500mm in the summit area and 300 mm on the lower slopes.

Cape Mountain zebra, ratel, leopard, eland, grys-buck, klipspringer, duiker, steenbok, baboon and of course, a variety of birds, reptiles, insects and smaller animals have made it their home.

Deep ravines cut into the rugged landscape of the Gamkaberg. The Tierkloof Ravine can be explored on foot, a magic outdoor experience, heightened by a stay in the bush camp built of thatch, wood and reed.

Less taxing paths of varying length and exertion have been laid out.

GROENEFONTEIN

The 4 800ha farm was purchased by the World Wide Fund for Nature South Africa (WWFSA) in 1999. The purchase was made possible by the generosity of a keen succulent enthusiast, Mr Leslie Hill. The property is now managed as part of the Gamkaberg Conservation Area.

The R62 now hurries across the Kansa River and eventually comes to a turn-off for **Volmoed. If you wish to visit the Highgate and Safari Ostrich Farms, you can take this minor road. The major turn-off to the farms on the R328 still lies ahead.**

Otherwise continue the drive through flat, typical Karoo vegetation where occasionally the black-white feathered male ostriches practise their graceful courting dance.

Now the **R328 - Robinson Pass** (see page. 94) comes in from the right. The Pass connects with coastal plateau at Mossel Bay and leads to the well known **Safari** and **High Gate** ostrich farms. Both farms offer fascinating tours, including an ostrich ride for the daring.

Oudtshoorn lies straight ahead. The R62 now becomes **Voortrekker Street.** Perhaps you should count the lamp posts: have you ever seen so many street lights anywhere? Anyway, Voortrekker Street soon comes to a mag-nificent sandstone building rising to the left, on the corner with **Baron van Reede Street**. This is the former Boys School, today it houses the superb **C.P. Nel Museum**. But before exploring the town, lets trace its history.

OUDTSHOORN

Oudtshoorn, the 'Ostrich Capital' of the Little Karoo is situated in the Olifants and Grobbelaars River valley. Izak Schrijver found his way here in 1689, travelling along an elephant path. Stock-farming settlers followed in the mid-dle of the 18th century.

The town developed haphazardly around a church on the banks of the Grobbelaars River, on land donated by Cornelis Rademeyer. Here, farmers gathered for nagmaals (communion), traders and hawkers set up business and built their homes. The town was laid out officially by the surveyor J. Ford in the late 1840s. The residents of George haughtily and derogatively spoke of the fledgeling village as Veldskoendorp, (veldskoen is a type of casual home-made shoe), but the villagers named it after a descendant of the aris-tocratic van Reede van Oudtshoorn family. This descendant was Geesje Ernestina Johanna van Oudtshoorn, married to the first Civil Commissioner of George, Egbertus Bergh.

Oudtshoorn awoke from its quiet life style towards the end of the 19th cen-tury when the ostrich feather boom catapulted it into the limelight of fashion and commerce. The boom brought immense wealth to the region.

The boom resulted from the ingenuity of South African farmers who proved that the ostrich could be bred in captivity and farmed commercially. In Northern Africa, ostrich farming had been practised for hundreds of years, albeit in a primitive way. But the general belief was that the bird would not mate in captivity.

The Gilles de Binche Feathers

In 1549, Mary of Hungary gave a feast in honour of her brother, Emperor Charles I at Mariemont near Binche, in Belgium. Aztec Indians, invited to the royal banquet, wore their traditional costumes adorned by animal designs and a feather headdress, which deeply impressed the hostess and her guests. The royal court issued an order for an imitation of the costume: ostrich feathers were used for the headdress and the animal design on the Aztec costumes was replaced by the crowned lion of the Belgian Coat of Arms. The first tailor to make this garment was named Gil. This costume has become today a traditional carnival costume.

Throughout the ages, ostrich feathers were beloved by royalty. A magnificent ostrich feather fan with an ivory handle was discovered in the tomb of Tut-ankh-Amen in 1922; Roman and Greek helmets were adorned with ostrich feathers; servants attended the Assyrian kings with feather wands; Queen Nefertar, the 'Charming Companion' donned headplumes, as did the royal soldiers of the pharaohs and high priests; the Black Prince popularised the feathers in England as the symbol of the Prince of Wales after the Battle of Crecy; King Louis XIV of France, Marie-Antoinette, Chaka's Zulu warriors - all had a liking for them and so it seems that the love for the feather is as old as humanity.

The feather is unique in that its two sides are equi-distant from the central rachis.

The demand for ostrich feather was associated with the introduction of 'art nouveau' building style in Europe, America and Japan. Art nouveau, inspired by nature, emphasizes the elaborate shapes of trees, flowers and feathers in all forms of art, including architecture. This quite boisterous style is evident in numerous buildings in Oudtshoorn.

The local sandstone with its pleasing, warm colours was easy to work with and became a dominant exterior feature of the many exquisite private homes, the 'Feather Palaces', manor houses and public buildings.

A well-know architect of public and private buildings in the region was Charles Bullock. Working with sandstone, he decorated the homes with imported stained glass, wrought iron, teak panelling; attractive ceilings of paper mache, and as many 'follies', ornaments and elaborate decorations as the finances and tastes of his clients allowed .

One of his grand designs is the former Boys' High School, now the museum.

The feather boom attracted people from all over the world to Oudtshoorn which at one time, was even nick-named 'Little Jerusalem'.

The South African Jewish community grew substantially after the Russian-Turkish War of 1877 and the assassi-nation of Tsar Alexander II for which the Jews were blamed. The ensuing *pogrom* brought nearly one hundred families to the Oudtshoorn area. The majority came from Kelm and Shavel in Lithuania.

C.P.Nel Museum/formerly the school

At first they worshipped in private homes, but later met in the Feather Market Hall. Major fund raising efforts made the purchase of land in Queen Street possible and to build a *shul.*. The shul was designed by George Wallace (sr) (who also designed the first stage of the magnificent Dutch Reformed Church in High Street). It was inaugurated in 1888. For over 50 years the founder minister, the Rev. Myer Woolfson, served his congregation, until 1947.

Not everybody felt at ease with his services. The more orthodox and tradi-tion-bound Jews from the provincial town of Kelm felt that Woolfson was under the influence of German and English Jews. They also disapproved of the more cosmopolitan lifestyle of the Shavel Jews. A division within the Jewish community was inevitable: the Kelm congregation established its own congregation in 1892 and by 1896 had built its own shul in St. John Street. One outstanding feature of this shul is the 'Aron-Ha-kodesh' – the Holy Ark. It was modeled on the ark of the main shul in their home town of Kelm (destroyed by the Nazis in 1941).

The feather boom which had brought them to the region was rapidly nearing its end by late 1913. The European markets were grossly overstocked and feather sales slumped. Feather export was not Government controlled, nor did it conform to the economic principles of supply and demand. Traders simply stockpiled huge quantities in London, whilst banks and great merchants continued to advance credit: farmers continued to despatch their feathers without paying heed to market demands.

In 1914 South African ostrich farmers had a stock of more than 1,250 million birds of which more than 60% belonged to Oudtshoorn farmers and the greater Little Karoo.

There were other factors which negatively influenced the market, such as the passing of the Anti-Plumage Bill in Europe which led to the boycott of plumaged garments.

Moreover, in the capricious world of fashion, the ostrich feather was fast losing appeal, as the new dress mode called for a more casual, relaxed style. The advent of the motorcar contributed also to the demise of the boom: the motorcar called for snug-fitting motoring helmets, rather than large wind-catching hats, bedecked with plumes.

When war erupted in September 1914, farmers panicked and sold their feathers at whatever price they could realise. When the feather became cheap, it lost its appeal and was thought common by fashionable women who would hardly bother to look at it. The entire feather industry was doomed, leading to the insolvency of many farmers, businessmen and local traders.

Several Jewish families left Oudtshoorn, and both synagogues encountered a drop in attendance figures. In 1918 the Jewish community still numbered 1073. This figure dwindled to 555 in 1936. In the early 1950s, the Queen Street Synagogue closed down and services were held in the St. John Street Synagogue. In 1973

Art nouveau

When exactly the new style started cannot be said. The first impulse was given by painters who, by the end of the 19th century, tired of the overladen stucco and plush of the cities. Now theylooked in the countryside for inspiration. Book illustrations, ornamental borders for book printing followed and gradually the new style influenced the design of furniture, vases, cutlery and finally buildings.

Characteristic of art nouveau is the curve: a rising line which bends to the left, then seems to want to bend to the right, but checks this desire by bending a little further to the left, before finally changing direction.

The art nouveau trend lasted from about 1890 to 1910. In England is is often referred to as 'New Style' and in Germany as 'Jugendstil'.

though, the community returned to the Queen Street Synagogue, and the St John Street property was put up for sale.

When the **C.P. Nel Museum** moved into the old Boys' High School in 1972, Isadore Barron, a member of the Museum Board of Trustees suggested it incorporate a 'Jewish Corner', to reflect the influence and contributions of the Jewish community to life in Oudtshoorn. The idea caught on, and a Jewish Gallery was established and simultaneously opened with the inauguration of the C.P.Nel Museum. This gallery grew into a miniature synagogue in 1976 when the Holy Ark, Bima and some synagogue benches from the St. John Street Synagogue were installed.

The Synagogue in the C.P.Nel Museum is still used today for one special service during the year, and other particular occasions, such as weddings.

C.P.NEL MUSEUM –3 Baron van Reede Street
Charles Paul Nel, a succesful businessman and collector of antiques, entrusted his valuable collection to a Board of Trustees, a day before his death in 1951. This collection formed the basis of the Museum, housed in the former Boys High School.

The museum show-cases the region's life in a most appealing and lively way. The visitor steps back in time. Daily life is illustrated in a wide range of exhibitions: the chemist shop is particularly well presented, acclaimed world wide as a fine replica of an early 20th century pharmacy. But step also into the office of a feather-merchant, the Standard Bank, a typical general dealer; admire the porcelaine, transport vehicles, bedrooms, dining room; see the Pauline Smith exhibition, a well loved writer of the Little Karoo.

A well-known resident of Oudtshoorn was C.J. Langenhoven who opened his legal practice in the town in 1899.. Not only was he a successful attorney, but also a prolific writer and champion of the Afrikaans language. He died in 1932. His home **'Arbeidsgenot'**, was presented by his widow to the nation. 'Arbeidsgenot' exhibits his personal belongings, many old carvings such as the one of 'Herrie', the little elephant who features in his book 'Sonde met die Bure' ('Sins with the Neighbours') Langenhoven also wrote the words of the former national anthem which is partly incorporated in the country's new anthem.

Arbeidsgenot

Pauline Smith

Pauline Smith was born 1882 in Oudtshoorn and died 1951 in England. She was the daughter of an English doctor who had settled in South Africa for health reasons. As a child she loved to accompany her father on his rounds in the Little Karoo during which she gathered a wealth of knowledge of the people, their cultures and traditions. Pauline developed a deep love for the Little Karoo, but sadly for her, she was sent to school in Scotland at the age of 12, and shortly afterwards also lost her beloved father. To find solace, Pauline began writing sketches and poems which were published as 'Platkops Children' almost 40 years later.

Whilst holidaying in Switzerland, Pauline met the English novelist Arnold Bennett who became her friend and mentor. He urged her to develop her Karoo stories, insisting too that she keep a diary during her stay at the Cape in 1913-14. Years later, 'The Little Karoo', a collection of stories and 'The Beadle', a novel, were published.

A walk through the streets and lanes of Oudtshoorn will display much of the architectural splendour of the past. One magnificent landmark in **High Street** is the **Dutch Reformed Church**. The architects involved were Carl Otto Hager and George Wallis.

NG Church, High Street

A shaky experience will be the crossing of the **Suspension Bridge** in **Church Street**. The bridge spans the Grobelaars River. It was built in 1913, made by Rowley & Sons of London. It was imported in pieces and re-assem-

bled under the supervision of the local engineer, F. Helfritz.

The streets come to life, particularly at Easter when the annual 'Klein Karoo Kultuurfees' is celebrated. Taste the *boerewors* (farmer's sausage), dance and listen to traditional music, watch new and old plays, sing and party with the people!

Suspension Bridge

Oudtshoorn splendour

Oudtshoorn villa

The Ostrich (Struthio camelus)

The South African ostrich is related to the emu in Australia, the kiwi in New Zealand and the South American rhea and cassowar.

The bird lives on a strange diet indeed. It devours vegetation, insects, sand, bits of metal, glass, bullets, bones and stones. The stones are necessary to grind food in the gizzard. Even cans and bottles are swallowed and after being ground in the gizzard, digested effortlessly.

The adult bird can survive for long periods without water, the chicks go without it for the first 8 to 10 months of their life. Though flightless, the ostrich is versatile enough to swim.

It has two-toed feet and very muscular legs which enable the bird to attain enormous speeds of about 60 km per hour though it cannot sustain this speed for a long time.

Normally the bird is docile. During the mating season, however, the male can turn vicious. During courting the skin on his beak and feet turns bright pink and he perform a graceful dance, displaying his feathers of which he has 35 white ones in each wing, yielding 1 kg. Swaying with open wings from side to side before the lady of his choice, he waits patiently for an answer. The hen, if willing, will 'kneel' before him.

The hen lays her first egg about 14 days after mating and thereafter every second day, until a clutch of 12 to 15 eggs is in her nest which is a simple, scraped out hollow in the ground. Each egg weighs about 1kg and provides an excellent scrambled egg! Quantatively it equals 24 chicken eggs. Both, male and female sit on the eggs: the female during the day - hence her brown feathers, and the male at night when his black feathers provide the perfect camouflage. The incubation period is 47 days.

The female is smaller than the male who grows to an average height of 2 metres and has a mass of about 100kg.

The average lifespan is approx. 40 years.

The bird is almost voiceless, other than the lion-like roar that the male can produce. The female is 'dumb', perhaps thus endearing herself to the male? Reputedly stupid - not surprising with a brain weighing a mere 40gram - the birds however, do not bury their heads in the sand as told by the Roman author, Pliny. What they do however, is to lower their head and lay the long neck along the ground to avoid discovery, and to protect their eyes.

Ostrich jockeys

Of course, Oudtshoorn is not only about ostriches, feathers and boerewors (and apparently the town with the highest divorce rate in the country) – Oudtshoorn is also the town of thrilling caves. Let's head for the awesome world of stalactites and stalagmites, the

CANGO CAVES

Leave town in a northerly direction along the Baron van Reede Street. It becomes the R328 and winds gradually uphill, with fine views of the Grobelaars River valley to the left. The total distance to the caves is 26 km.

Immediately outside town, it passes the **Cango Wildlife Ranch**. Huge 'crocodile jaws' welcome the visitor.

The Ranch cares for a variety of animals. An informative tour leads past the crocodile enclosure where close to 300 crocodiles lurk in the water or laze in the sun.

Crocodiles

Crocodiles are cold blooded, social reptiles. They can die in cold water below 8° C and cannot digest food when it is very cold but can go without food for about one year.

Slaughter age (for leather):	between 3 - 5 years
Teeth:	regrow, every 2 years.
Tongue:	yellow (the alligator has a red tongue)
Speed on land:	about 8 km/h
in water:	about 45 km/h
Prey:	is dragged by the ankle or neck and left to become putrid before consumption
Sexes:	No external differences are visible. Sex is determined by temperature: all eggs hatched above 34ºC are males 50 - 80 eggs are laid between October and November.

The snake park houses a fascinating collection of slippery reptiles, and from the safety of an elevated boardwalk one can leisurely observe the big cats of the wild: cheetah, white Bengal tigers, lions, jaguars and puma. A pack of wild dogs, pygmy hippos, emus, wallabies, flamingos, peacocks, bat eared foxes and the world's largest rodent, the capybara add thrill, noise and colour to the visit.

Just beyond the Wildlife Ranch, the **'Oudtshoorn Ostrich Show Farm'** offers 45-minute tours which include an ostrich race and the chance of riding the giant bird.

The road traverses the verdant Schoemanshoek valley, passes rickety drying sheds, labourers' cottages, and then reaches another popular ostrich farm

'Cango Ostrich Farm', a last opportunity to make acquaintances with the world's biggest flightless bird before coming to the caves.

A very different attraction awaits the traveller at the **'Angore Rabbit Farm'** and just beyond, at about 22km outside Oudtshoorn, a sign points to the **Koos Raubenheimer Dam** and **Rus en Vrede Resort.**

If you venture along this road, do not drive much further than the dam. Beyond that point, this country road, though idyllic, should only be explored on a fine, dry day. On a wet day it can turn the trip into a slippery and muddy affair. The valley it traverses is dotted with colourful farm cottages. Citrus trees splash the valley golden, ostriches and sheep browse in the green fields and small vineyards are planted out along this narrow and twisting road which emerges near **De Rust**, *about 30km away (see page..).*

The valley close to the caves narrows, and the road passes one more tourist attraction **'Wilgewandel Camel Rides'**. Apart from the thrill of precariously balancing high up on the camel's back, you learn interesting facts, such as that camels have a fifth foot and can consume up to 100 litres of water at one time!

Then, after a last glance into a lush, peaceful valley to the right, you arrive at the caves.

No cardigans, woollies or torches are necessary for a visit: the temperature inside averages 18 °C and the humidity level is high. The passageways are well-lit during the duration of the visit to negotiate the steps and passages, but lights are switched off once a visitor has passed through to avoid damage to the formation. The light is strong enough for photography. Wear sensible shoes.

If time allows, visit the museum, watch a video explaining the history of the caves, browse around the shops, relax in the restaurant, bar or coffee shops.

Tours of different lengths and difficulty are offered, from the 'Standard Tour' to the 'Adventure Tour'. For the latter one needs to be fit and slim as one is

literally 'posted' through some very narrow slots!
In 1780, a Khoi herdsboy, searching for missing cattle, nearly stumbled into a massive hole. Excitedly he alerted his employer, farmer van Zyl. Curious, van Zyl set out to explore further. Secured to a rope and equipped with just one candle, he was lowered down into a dark, cavernous hole, today's 'Van Zyl Cave'. Engulfed by almost total darkness, van Zyl's account of the cavern's dimension were understandably vastly exaggerated.

One of the first accurate accounts of the caves came from the pen of the Swedish naturalist Victorin. He remarked in 1855 that 'the cavern entrance is spacious, but as one goes on, the rock walls close in so that in places it is no more than 1,5 m wide and 3m high and only one can pass'.

A survey of 1897 established a network of passages totalling some 4,5km though the cave penetrated into the foothills of the Swartberg for only about 800 metres.

The first accurate survey of 1956 determined the correct length of the known caves in one line to be 775m and that the caves never rose or fell more than 16m and always returned to the same level. The survey also found that the side passages were not as extensive as previously thought and that there were definite bottlenecks. It suggested that, if these could be opened up, the flow of traffic could be eased.

This survey also showed that when the atmospheric pressure outside dropped, there was a flow of air out of the caves, and when the barometric pressure mounted outside, there was a reverse flow of air into the caves. This proved the existence of a continuation of the cave sequence. In the last recognised sequence, the Devil's Workshop, speleologists tracked the source of a draught to a small crevice. After months of working on this crevice, they finally broke through into a wonderland. This 270m-long extension is called the 'Wonder Cave' or 'Cango Two'. Continued exploration led to the discovery of a perennial stream flowing back towards the entrance and disappearing into a course about 20m below the level of the caves. In 1975 a pump was brought in and this reduced the water level sufficiently to allow workers to clear obstructions which prevented further exploration of the stream. The team ultimately entered what is known as Kango Three, a sequence of chambers measuring about 1600m, with a further extension known as Cango Four. These sequences are closed to the public - the dripstone formations will thus be saved from destruction: body warmth heats the air in the cave, limited supplies of oxygen are replaced by carbondioxyde and artificial light stimulates the growth of algae. Another problem can be caused by foodstuffs thrown on to the cave floor. in so humid and sheltered an atmosphere, this leads to serious invasions of bacteria and cockroaches.

Green algae on a formation

The first sequence of caves, today known as **Cango One**, is the only one open to visitors. The entrance to the caves is at a height of 560m above sea level.

What one sees in the Caves (Standard Tour):

VAN ZYL HALL
Burst into song as you descend into the cave: the acoustics are excellent. The van Zyl Hall is approx. 95m long x 46 m wide and about 16m high.

Look up to the ceiling: the stalactites are known as the 'Oudtshoorn tobacco leaves'. Towards the left, the magnificent flowstone 'organ'. It is about 700 000 years old. Not far from it, a 10m-high and 150 000 years old stalagmite rises towards the ceiling, referred to as 'Cleopatra's Needle'.

Following the passageway to the right, you enter the **BOTHA HALL** which was discovered 1792; the entrance to it was then to the left of the 'Organ' in the previous chamber; a rock wall was subsequently broken through to create today's passage.

The unusual 'Tower of Pisa' greets the visitor. Here stalagmite and stalactite have joined to form this massive pillar. It is 16 m high and about 270 000 years old.

In the ceiling a massive crack is visible, caused by an earthquake, 4000 - 6000 years ago. Still to the left of the hall, the incredible 'Weeping willow', a flowstone formation, shows itself. It is about 1,5 million years old. Then, to the right, one sees the aptly named ' Victoria Falls' and five 'temple curtains'.

A surprise awaits the visitor when the lights are switched on to illuminate the entire hall, the beauty is breathtaking.

Botha's Hall

Victoria Falls

In the **RAINBOW CHAMBER** , or **CHAMBER OF GOOD AND EVIL**, ' Nick the Cave Devil' makes his appearance, together with the 'Family Bible', the 'Cross', ' Angel's Wing' and the ' Baptism Font'.

Look at the holes in the ground: they are up to 30m deep. One can just make out the original visitor's route by looking at the blackened ceiling; candles were used until 1928 for cave visits.

Walking on to the **BRIDAL CHAMBER,** the 'Cango Babies' hang down from

the ceiling; stalactites grow 5-7 cubic mm in 100 years, so these babies are are about 500 - 700 years old.

The **DRUM CHAMBER** is the last cave on the standard tour. Here the collapsed ceiling causes pressure on the crystal stone which are not hollow. These stunning formations are transparent and resonant.

From here, steep and narrow steps lead towards the 'Adventure Route'.

It is also time to wave good-bye to Oudtshoorn.

The Cango Caves and Little Karoo: geology in brief

About 600 to 800 million years ago, the land was under the sea and algae float-ed on top, known as stromalotites. Over time, the shell and skeletons of tiny sea creatures dropped to the bottom of the sea and formed ultimately a limestone belt which is approx. 140km long and 1000m thick. This formation became known as the Kango Group. Where the limestone belt remained on the surface it weathered to the blue-grey rock "Elephant Stone".

Further sediments were deposited over and around the limestone belt forming the Cape Supergroup. These layers were warped and folded when either the land rose or the sea receded. But once more the sea flooded in and submerged the basin of the Little Karoo. This occurred nearly 250 million years ago. Wave action now erodes the mountains which resulted in soil and pebbles being deposited as richly red conglomerates at the foothills of the parent mountain. These conglomerates, known as the Enon conglomerates, were finally exposed when the sea withdrew again.

Up to now, the original limestone belt had been left fairly undisturbed. But things changed when about 20 million years ago, earth movements forced this belt into the weathering zone close to the surface. The earth movements also caused fis-sures and cracks through which acidic rainwater begins to soak, eating away at the limestone.

Nearly one million years ago, a general uplift occurred and the water gathered in the chambers seeped away, leaving empty spaces. Cave air has a lower rel-ative pressure of carbon dioxide than air in the soil, since the caves are venti-lated. So a drop of water will pick up calcium carbonate on its way through the cave roof and deposit the calcium carbonate when it reaches the cave and loses carbon dioxide. It is this simple process which has produced the stalactite and stalagmite formation. Stalactites hang from the roof and stalagmites grow from the floor. A third formation in the caves is the flowstone which forms curtains and drapes.

Gradually stalagtites were formed, fashioned by rainwater. As it dripped down, it picked up carbon dioxide from the humus in the soild, formed bicarbonate by dissolving the limestone and then deposited this on the ceilings, walls and floors.

OUDTSHOORN via SWARTBERG PASS TO PRINCE ALBERT

After the miracle of the Cango Caves, the journey continues northwards for about 4km along the R328 towards the stunning **Swartberg Pass.** This pass traverses the Swartberg and leads to **Prince Albert. It is untarred, extremely narrow in places and cannot be taken by cars with trailers or buses. It should also be avoided in wet weather conditions.**

THE SWARTBERG PASS (1881 – 1888)

Thomas Bain was not far off the truth when he stated that the pass would be steep. The awe inspiring route took four years to complete. Bain, with hundreds of convict labourers, followed the folds created by the crumpling of the earth's crust. Supported by massive retaining walls, the pass snakes relentlessly uphill, with seemingly endless curves but out-of-this-world views, before it reaches the summit at 1 585 metres above sea level.

In 1988, in its centenary year, the Swartberg Pass was declared a National Monument

The torturous 20km-long descent towards **Prince Albert** is equally thrilling and scenic.

Remnants of stone buildings which housed the convicts are still visible just below the summit on the northern slopes of the Pass.

When you have explored Prince Albert, return to the Little Karoo and Oudtshoorn via the magnificent **Meiringspoort** (see page.145)

Half way up the Swartberg Pass, on the Oudtshoorn side of the mountains, a turn-off leads to

DIE HEL and GAMKASKLOOF NATURE RESERVE

Where exactly does one find 'Hell', this fertile, green valley? There, where the Gamka River, the Lion River, chisels through the Swartberg Mountain by means of the huge Gamkaskloof Gorge. Better known as 'Die Hel', the valley is about 20km long and 600m wide; it runs in an east-west direction. A fair access road of 37km leads to Gamkaskloof itself. Sharp bends over the last 4km call for caution. **The road is unsuitable for trailers, towed caravans and buses.**

From the top, the road snakes downhill and drops nearly 1000 metres to the valley floor.

Die Hell and Gamkakloof tell a fascinating story that reaches into the distant past of the Stone Age people - numerous San rock paintings bear testimony to their lives here.

The first Europeans to settle in this remote part of the world were Afrikaners (Boers) when they sought to evade British authority at the time of the 'Great Trek' in the 1830s. They lived in total seclusion. Decades later a Boer commando stumbled upon this community. The commando, ironically, also sought an escape escape route out of the Little Karoo which was teeming with British soldiers. A vivid description of the first encounter speaks of 'a shaggy giant in goatskins speaking an outlandish Dutch, a man named Cordier and his brood of half-wild children..' Unbeknown to the commando, Cordier, 'that shaggy giant', was fully aware of his arrival as one of his children had long tracked him down in the mountains. He was finally led out by some of the children.

But why does this little earthly paradise bear the name hell? If stories can be believed it was the stock inspector Piet Botha who dubbed it thus in 1940. On one occasion he was forced to climb down 'The Ladder' on his inspection tours, at which point he exclaimed:it's 'Hell'.

The name stuck, whether liked or not by the people of the valley. In his book 'People of the Valley', P.B. du Toit writes: *A letter at the Post Office in Prince Albert was addressed to a 'Mr H.Mostert, The Hell, P.O. Prince Albert'. This happened to be an income tax return. Mr Mostert read the address a number of times and then slowly scrawled across the envelope: 'First find out whether people in the Hell also pay income tax', and returned it to the mailbox.*

The first farmers living in this hidden mountain paradise were the Swanepoel, Cordier, Mostert, Nel, Marais, Snyman and Joubert families.

Ouplaas, the first farm to be surveyed, was registered in 1841.

Despite its isolation, the valley provided a satisfactory standard of living. Its climate suited the cultivation of fruit, vegetables, wheat and rye. Goats and cattle provided milk and meat, whilst donkeys pulled the ploughs, threshed the wheat and hauled loads up the steep mountain tracks.

The farmhouses were built from local materials. On stone foundations rose walls built of unbaked bricks. Indigenous olive trees were used for rafters, whilst the roofs were thatched with rye straw. Ceilings consisted of local reeds, tied together with strips of bark from thorn trees. Often mud was laid on top of the reed ceiling which served then either as fire protection or attic floor. The attic provided additional storage.

Compacted earth and cattle dung, mixed with resin from the sweet-thorn trees made up the flooring.

Children attended school on 'Boplaas Farm', later on in the second school-house built in 1928 on the farm 'Middelplaas'. The school only closed 1980. Both the school and the teacher's dwelling, built in 1938, have been restored.

Spiritually the people of the valley were cared for by ministers of the Dutch Reformed Church in Prince Albert.

Lenie Marais, a much loved local midwife with vast knowledge of herbs and traditional remedies, acted as the local doctor. For an emergency, a Doctor Luttig from Prince Albert was called to 'The Hell'. He would ride on horseback along the Gamka River.

There was also the 'Flying Doctor' of Prince Albert. Dr Manie Coetzee. A landing strip was built for this purpose. He flew a Tiger Moth. One of his patients was bitten by a donkey and the 'Flying Doctor' wanted to transport him on his plane to Prince Albert, which the patient refused being too frightened. The doctor produced his biggest syringe which persuaded the patient to board the plane.. he survived both, plane ride and donkey bite.

Such then was the old life in 'Die Hell' which was to change drastically as from 1959 when the then administrator of the Cape, Otto du Plessis, rode into Gamkaskloof . He promised the people a proper road. This road was designed by the engineer O'Reilly in just over two years completed. With the road, an era ended, signalling the death of 'The Hell' as its early, hardy people had known it. They began to drift out of the valley – but new arrivals, tourists drifted in, tourists.

Gamkaskloof was declared a national heritage site in 1997, and is managed today as part of the **Swartberg Nature Reserve.** Life in the valley today is very different. The modern traveller is spoilt by comfort. Seven of the original valley cottages have been restored. Everything is provided, other than toiletries, food and drinks.

The vegetation within the vast reserve is amazingly varied. It features mountain fynbos, Karoo-veld, spekboom veld, numerous bulb species, renoster-veld.

The **Swartberg Trail** *offers two very basic overnight huts at Bothashoek and Gouekrans. The latter has four rooms and a cooking/dining area built into the rocks. Fires are not allowed at these huts. All the hiker will find are bunk beds, mattresses, cold showers and toilets. The trail is limited to 18 people.*

Campers can overnight at the top end of the valley. The campsite has 10 sites, with ablution and braai facilities. At the bottom end of the valley there is a basic dormitory sleeping 12.

The 4x4 Route
The route stretches over just 72 kilometres, cutting more or less straight across the top of the Swartberg. Vehicles, drivers and passengers will be tested on parts of the route. A minimum of two and a maximum of twenty vehicles are allowed. Gate keys must be fetched from and returned to the nature conservation offices in Oudtshoorn, or tourism information centre in Prince Albert. To complete the route put aside a whole day! Overnighting is possible at the 36km mark. Rain can lead to closure of the route.

Mountain Biking
In his book 'A guide to Mountain Bike Trails' the author Paul Leger states that 'no visit to the Karoo is complete unless the road to Hell and back and the Swartberg Pass have been tackled'. He favours also a back up vehicle.

Tips:
Petrol is not available in Gamkaskloof
Permits are required for the hike and 4x4 routes in the valley
There is no cell phone reception in the valley.

The choices for the nature and outdoor enthusiast are wide. Hiking, cycling, driving – all is possible.

OUDTSHOORN – DE RUST - MEIRINGSPOORT – PRINCE ALBERT.

The total distance is about 110km, without deviations.

To escape from the Little Karoo, take the R29/N12 from the town centre, in an easterly direction. The picturesque town of De Rust is reached after 37km. It is named after the eponymous farm once owned by the man who proved that there was indeed a way through the massive mountain massif – and had this magic mountain pass with its incredible passageway through lofty, lichen coloured sandstone cliffs named after him – Meiringspoort.

De Rust, with its delightful Victorian buildings, sundrenched vineyards and fruit orchards spreads happily over low hills. Snow capped mountains may look down on it during the cold, but sunny winter months when temperatures drop to uncomfortable 3 to 5°C. The summer heat reaches the high 30s.

De Rust home

Shopping in De Rust

Casablanca Cafe

Beyond De Rust, ignore the turn-off for Uniondale/R341 and continue northwards on the N12. After another 4.5km you enter the amazingly beautiful

Meiringspoort
which also falls within the Swartberg Nature Reserve.

In 1854, Petrus Johannes Meiring, from the 'De Rust Farm', followed a narrow river gorge in the Swartberg, carved out by the Groot River. Towering rock walls closed in on him, serrated mountain peaks and the rush of the river guided him through the Swartberg. He eventually emerged on the other side, at the edge of the Great Karoo. For years his path was the only link between Prince Albert and the Little Karoo.

In due time, a road was constructed and formally opened in 1858. It clung perilously close to the river and, not surprisingly, was washed away by a series of floods in 1885. It was rebuilt the following year. Meiringspoort still keeps the river company today and the danger of flooding persists. Over the 17km that it snakes in between the massive sandstone cliffs, the road crosses the river 32 times.

The writer C.J. Langenhoven (see page 132) loved Meiringspoort. He created the much-adored circus elephant *Herrie* which in his book *Sonde met die Bure (Sins with the neighbour)* hauled an old tramcar from Oudtshoorn through this mountain passage. He carved the elephant's name into a rock, now a National Monument, which lies to the left of the road, as you enter the passageway from De Rust.

Lichen coloured rocks in Meiringspoort   *Herrie Stone*

After emerging from Meiringspoort, the N12 passes the hamlet of Klaarstroom, and reaches the R407. This veers off to **Prince Albert.** Though situated in the Groot Karoo and not part of our travel explorations, a few words about this cheerful little Karoo town.

PRINCE ALBERT

situated in an arid region, is blessed however, with ample water from the Swartberg Mountains. Its superb climate, spectacular night skies and bright, crystal clear sunny days for most of the year has enticed many a star gazer to settle here.

Water furrows zig-zag through the town with its beautifully preserved Cape Dutch, Karoo and Victorian buildings, many of them National Monuments. The restored Alberts Mill, (1850) grinds its corn again!

The local **'Fransie Pienaar Museum'** tells the town's story and that of its people.

Meiringspoort

The town developed from the loan farm 'Kweekvallei', 1762, run by Zacharias de Beer in 1762. The Dutch Reformed Church was established in 1845. A 'gold rush' erupted in 1891 when a shepherd discovered a gold nugget on the farm 'Klein Waterval' (Little Waterfall) – but only 1 504 ounces of gold were ever mined. Clearly not enough to sustain a mining industry!

A British garrison was established at Prince Albert, named after Queen Victoria's husband, during the Anglo-Boer War (1899-1902). The Boer rebel Commandant, Gideon Scheepers, played a prominent role in the district during this war.

The town is a visual and culinary delight – try the locally made cheese, wines, home-grown olives and figs.

Gideon Scheepers

was born in the Transvaal and joined the Republic's Staats Artillerie in 1895. During the Anglo-Boer War, he was seconded to the Orange Free State Artillery and promoted to commandant. He and his men blazed a trail of destruction for those who were unsympathetic to the Boer cause. For a while they eluded their British pursuers, but Scheepers was eventually captured on the farm 'Kopfeskraal' near Prince Albert, tried by a military court on more than 30 charges, and executed by a British firing squad outside Graff-Reinet beside an open grave in January 1902. His execution caused an outcry as it was felt that a British military court was not competent to sentence a non-British prisoner of war to death during the war.

ROUTE SIX

GEORGE TO KNYSNA VIA THE SEVEN PASSES ROUTE (OLD ROAD)

Allow about 2.5 hours for the drive, excluding stops. The road is part gravel, part asphalt, but safe to travel in wet conditions. The total distance is about 81km, without deviations.

How to get to the start:
At the top end of **York Road (where one finds the George Museum)** bear right at the traffic circle and follow **Courtenay Road** which becomes known as the **Knysna Road.** This is a busy commercial part of George, numerous traffic lights tend to slow the traffic flow. Once across the railway bridge watch out for the **Saasveld Road turn-off to the left, about 6km from the town centre**.

The road winds through thick forests, gently climbing and falling before one is directed to Saasveld, home to the Forestry College until the late 1980s**.**

The name Saasveld originates in Holland where the castle *Saterslo* (1250) changed its name in the mid-1550s first to *Saatselo* and finally to Saasveld. The castle was home to the Lords of Saterslo, powerful vassals of the Bishop of Utrecht. In 1360, the last daughter and heir, Aliken van Saterslo, married the knight Bernt van Reede, whose descendants became known as the Reedes van Saasveld. Descendants of this family settled in the province of Utrecht, near the village of Oudtshoorn and became known as the **Reedes van Oudtshoorn**. One of them, Pieter, reached the Cape in 1741 as a naval officer and became a highly ranked Company official. He eventually went back to Holland. When Governor Rijk van Tulbagh died in 1772, Pieter van Oudtshoorn was appointed his successor. He could never take up this post as he died on the return voyage to the Cape. Van Oudtshoorn was buried in the Groote Kerk, Cape Town, where his tombstone can be seen in the north wall of the church. His second son became a succesful merchant in Cape Town where he built his home 'Saasveld' between 1791 and 1804. This house was pulled down during the 1950s, though parts were saved and incorporated in the Huguenot Museum in Franschhoek.

The College grounds, established in 1932, were purchased by Baroness Gesina van Reede van Oudtshoorn, wife of E.J. Bergh, a retired magistrate and Civil Commissioner. She named that land Saasveld.

History lessons are over, and the Old Passes adventure continues.

The Old Road to Knysna, a National Monument, was built by Thomas Bain and completed in 1882. It is the original main route between George and Knysna and took 15 years to build.

The Old Road was cut through difficult terrain, across rivers which forged steep ravines into the mountains. The road winds through these gorges, crosses the rivers and streams by way of narrow bridges. Forever climbing and descending, it is a lifeline to the small villages and forestry stations.

Today, the road is often called **Seven Passes Road,** after the Swart River, Kaaimans, Touw River, Hoogekraal, Karatara, Homtini and Phantom passes.

A worth while turn-off is reached soon after crossing the narrow bridge which spans the Silver River: the **Wilderness Hoogte Road/Wilderness Heights Road** joins in from the right.

Bridge across the Silver River

Travelling down this tarred road, the Bundu Shop and Methodist School are reached. Here a gravel road turns off to the **Map of Africa/Kaart van Afrika.** The road ends near a bench, duly marked 'Map of Africa':below, an amazing view of a' map' of the African continent, carved out of the wooded hills far below by the powerful forces of the Kaaiman and Silver Rivers can be seen.

Bundu shop

After this short detour, return to the Old Knysna Road.
Now the comfort of tar also yields to the occasional discomfort of a corrugated gravel road. Open fields dominate for a while, farms lie scattered about. Soon the turn-off for **Woodville** is reached.

Stop for a rest in the shade of the **Big Tree,** or take a short circular walk through the forest. The Big Tree reaches a height of about 33m and its crown spreads over 29m. It's age? About 800 years.

Numerous connecting roads for the **Lakes Area near Wilderness/N2** *are encountered.. Amongst these are the turn-offs to* **Hoekwil (tarred),** *from near* **Woodville** *towards* **Rondevlei/Sedgefield (gravel),** *then from near* **Karatara** *to* **Ruigtevlei/Sedgefield,** *and from* **Barrington via Homtini** *to* **Ruigtevlei/Sedgefield.** *The last two are tarred link roads. One interesting church building can be discovered on the Karatara link road, nearer the lakes: 'Evangelische-Lutherische Kirche, Rondevlei'. This small Lutheran church dates back to 1931, beautifully situated on a hill with commanding views over the vlei. In its grounds also stands a miniature model of the 'Voortrekker Church' in Pietermaritzburg/Natal.*

Lutheran Church near Wilderness

After the turn-off to Ruigtevlei (Thicket Vlei), the route takes on the name Hoogekraal Pass. It descends quite steeply in sharp bends, reaches a river of the same name which is spanned by an age-worn bridge. Then, at **Karatara,** the road dips steeply towards the river. Karatara probably means zebra; the village was established in the 1930s to resettle displaced foresters,

Past another turn-off for Sedgefield, and you arrive at **Barrington.**

The small village developed on farmland, the property of the Honourable Henry Barrington, son of the 5th Viscount Barrington. He had settled at the Cape in 1842 and purchased from Captain Duthie (see p.186) the Portland Estate. Though a lawyer by profession, Barrington's first love seemed to be farming. He showed a particularly keen interest in silk worm cultivation, honey production and growing apples for cider. He was a prominent figure in public life and elected Member of Parliament for George, 1869. This was also the year when the Great fire broke out, from near his farm, which destroyed vast tracts of land right up to Humansdorp in the Eastern Cape.

Beyond Barrington, the road soon swings southward for the start of the Homtini Pass. It climbs, meanders for a while, then drops through forested land, with wonderful views of valleys far below. 13km away from Barrington lies **Rheenendal,** named after the van Rheenen family. The village is also a starting point for a number of exciting forest walks, such as the Millwood Mine walk, in pursuit of gold. (see page 170)

The main excursion continues past **Portland Manor House,** the former stately home of the Barrington family.
Southwards one traverses a fertile plateau, then the **Phantom Pass** branches off to the left. The Seven Passes road carries on to Keytersnek where it joins the N2, about 2km outside the town of Knysna. The Phantom Pass also

Portland Manor House

emerges on the N2, but closer to the Knysna Lagoon.

The **Phantom Pass** (named after the Phantom Moth) descends into the verdant Knysna valley, where the Knysna River leisurely finds its way towards the lagoon. At the bottom of the valley, the road clings for 5km to the river bank and then joins the N2.

Knysna River valley

ROUTE SEVEN

GEORGE TO KNYSNA VIA WILDERNESS/N2

The total distance is 56km, without deviations.

At the traffic circle where York and Courtenay Streets meet, turn right into Courtenay Street which becomes known as the Knysna Road.

George suffers one draw-back, it lacks its own beach. Sunseekers, surfers and bathers have to travel eastward towards Knysna for about 8km, and then turn-off to

VICTORIA BAY

The country road traverses the coastal plateau with fine ocean and mountain views before its gradual descent towards the bay. Parking is access controlled. A board walk just above the road makes for relaxed walking towards the beach.

The whistle of the Choo-Tjoe steaming past above the bay and disappearing into a tunnel, adds to the colourful atmosphere of Victoria Bay.

Choo-Tjoe above Victoria Bay

As you frolick in the sheltered waters, spare a thought for **Baron Josef Wilhelm von Mollendorf,** son of a Prussian field-marshal. He arrived in the Cape in 1788 where he boarded the vessel 'Maria', intending to settle on the south coast. Though he had deposited most of his money in a German bank before leaving Europe, a large iron box, filled with gold coins and other treasures, accompanied him on his ship voyage. Disaster struck the vessel near Ballots Bay, close to Victoria Bay. The 'Maria' was wrecked, but incredibly, the baron succeeded in building a raft and to salvage his treasured box. Then, unexpectedly, a huge wave knocked off the box and badly injured the stricken man. He lost one arm, and the box went under and settled, tightly wedged, between two rocks. The baron was saved and after his recovery, regularly went down to the sea to spot the place where his box had disappeared. But he failed to salvage his lost treasure.

Return to the national road which sweeps across the Swart River in the first curved bridge of its kind built in the country. For another 2km it weaves in generous bends along the eastern river bank with stunning views of the coast: watch for the signpost **'Dolphin Point Lookout'**, so named because

Dolphin Point

the hill on the far side of the river resembles a dolphin's head. The tunnel through which the Choo-Tjoe steams is the dolphin's eye. Parking is to the left of the road; steps immediately above the parking area give a wonderful view, but walk also the boardwalk underneath the bridge.

The mists rising from the sea, the Choo-Tjoe puffing across the Kaaimans River railway bridge, a vast, sandy beach and breaking rollers welcome us to **WILDERNESS.**

Wilderness

The **Kaaimans River** was originally called 'Keerom', not surprisingly as the treacherous mountain crossings would have forced many to *turn around.*

Kaaimans River Bridge

Sadly, the national road bi-sects this very popular resort with its unusual name. Legend has it that a love-stricken young bride quoted Mendelsohn's 'O for the Wings of a Dove' to her sweetheart when he disclosed his intentions to take her away to the southern Cape; she replied, then in 'the wilderness build me a nest, and there let me forever be at rest'.

Urban encroachment on the hills and dunes has impacted on the tranquility of Wilderness. But its charm and appeal remain in tact. Do not rush by! It is after all the only village in the country that can boast of its own National Park, and thus a good starting point for a number of interesting day excursions and activities.

Exploring the Lakes

Touw River Estuary and Serpentine
For the exploration of the lakes, leave the national route behind and travel the 'Lakes Route'. From the 'Protea Hotel Wilderness Resort' in the centre near the estuary, turn first left, then right into **Waterside Road**. This is the start of the **Lakes Road** from which numerous roads branch off to the north, connecting with the **Seven Passes Road** (see Route Six), as well as to the south re-connecting with the N2.

*For a short enjoyable walk, cross the grassy area in front of the hotel and look for the sign "**Kingfisher Trail'**. The trail itself is about 10km long and easy to* *follow, but at the start, a short, 800m-long* boardwalk *under the canopy of mostly milkwood trees has been built. It follows the river bank, a wonderful opportunity to exercise the legs.*

The motorist finds himself on a gravel road which follows the lakes as close as is possible. At times bumpy, it is by far the most scenic way to experience the splendour of these wetlands. The Choo-Tjoe line runs the same course.

Rail and Road meet..

Watersport enthusiasts will enjoy the Touw River estuary and the river which snakes its way through marsh and reed country, aptly called the Serpentine. The Serpentine allows the waters of the three linked lakes to the east of it to flow by way of the Touw River estuary to the sea at Wilderness.

The **Ebb and Flow Nature Reserve** with its picnic sites, campsites and rondavels is an ideal holiday destination.

Soon **Island Lake** with its 'Dromedaris' hump is reached. Here sailing and windsurfing are permitted as well as powerboating and canoeing. But landing on the 'Dromedaris' Island itself is prohibited. Island Lake is connected to the estuary by the Serpentine.

The Serpentine

Shortly the start of the 'Brownhooded Kingfisher Trail' is reached as the road hugs the northern shore of Langvlei. A narrow channel connects Island Lake to **Langvlei and Rondevlei**

Langvlei is an inundated low-lying area, caught between dunes which are estimated to have been formed some 2000 to 15000 years ago. This is truly the birdwatcher's paradise as these two lakes have been set aside for conservation. In the surrounding reed beds and on the water rare bird species gather. Motorists beware.....

Owls on foot...

Swartvlei
This is the largest and deepest of the lakes. It averages about 6m in depth. The lagoon is open to the sea and is therefore tidal to an extent. It is thought to have been formed as a drowned river valley. Popular with holiday makers who are keen on watersports, jogging, mountain biking and hiking. Birdwatchers again are spoiled by the presence of rare species in the vast expanses of reed beds around the lake. The larger part of the lake, north of the railway bridge, has been set aside for recreational purposes and the eastern section for conservation. Here, no sporting activities are allowed.

WILDERNESS NATIONAL PARK

extends to about 2500ha, knows five rivers and lakes, two estuaries. It controls nearly 28km of coastline. An extra 8100ha of privately owned land is also under the control of the SA National Parks. The Wilderness area offers therefore a vast variety of habitats. Wetlands, forests, rivers, lakes, floodplains and the sea wait to be explored. Birdlife too abounds. About 160 species of birds have been recorded which can be observed from hides on the edge of the lakes.

How were the lakes formed?
Geologically, the lakes are fairly young, dating back some 7 000 years. They were formed by recurrent cycles of rising and falling sea levels , which in turn were caused by the formation and thaw of polar ice caps. About one million years ago the sea level was about eight metres higher than now. With the gradual recesssion of the shoreline, south-westerly gales led to the formation of consecutive lines of dunes in an easterly direction. Island Lake, for example, was formed as a result of a dune ridge being created south of the Serpentine channel, and isolating an expanse of water. The hump in the centre, is actually the remains of a fossil dune.

Brownhooded Kingfisher Trail

It is an easy 3 hours walk, there and back. The total distance is 6km.. No permit is required.

Take the 'Lakes Road' from Wilderness until it meets the tarred Hoekwil Road. Turn left here and after about 800m, turn right into a minor road at the Langvlei sign. The parking area is another 3km further down this gravel road.

This lovely trail follows first the Duiwe River (Dove) - which feeds the Island Lake - along a grassy track. Riverine shrubs such as Black-eyed Susan and Wild grape line the river banks.

A wooden bridge spans the stream which is re-crossed shortly afterwards. Then it follows the river giving the walker a lovely view of the other side of the riverbed with its aloes and many bulbuous plants. Then the path bends to the left and the trail crosses the stream onto an island. Another crossing follows to the opposite bank where you clamber up an often damp and slippery bank. Shortly afterwards, the trail bends to the right and once more follows the Duiwe River. As the river swings right, you cross it on a bridge of concreted rock. Not far from there four paths converge.

Take the path heading for the 'Pool' which continues along the stream. The stream is crossed several times before it suddenly reaches a magnificent pool, surrounded by rock walls. While away a moment here, breathe in the beauty as the pool marks the turning point of the walk – retrace the path to the 'start'

Pied Kingfisher

KINGFISHERS – family *HALCYONIDAE*

Five kingfisher species are resident in the southern Cape, mainly in and around the wetlands. They are distinguished by their long, strong and straight bills, short-tailed and compact bodies, shortish legs and colourful, sometimes striking plumage. They nest in holes which they usually excavate themselves in earthbanks along rivers and streams, occasionally even in tree trunks. Not all of them actually hunt for fish or other aquatic animals, despite their name. Some are birds of the bush and woods and feed on insects, lizards and other smaller creatures. They share one habit: perching on telephone or power lines, or convenient branches from where they plunge-dive for their prey.

The **brownhooded kingfisher** (Halcyon albiventris)prefers the woodlands and bushy vegetation, hunting mainly for insects, but it is not averse to eating lizards, small rodents, scorpions, small snakes and birds. The powerful red bill is black-tipped which contrasts strongly with his overall brownish appearance.

The **pied kingfisher** (ceryle rudis) is mainly black and white and can be spotted near pools on the seashore, dams, canals or inland waters and estuaries. Frequently they perch on wires along the national road near the Swartvlei, a give-away is their raising and lowering of the tail when perched. They hunt for fish, insects, crustaceans and tend to hover over the water as they hunt, their bodies almost vertical and bill pointed downwards. It has a high-pitched twittering call.

The **giant kingfisher** (Ceryle maxima) is the largest at 45cm long. He is also the truest to his name as his prey is mostly fish, although he does dot sneer at the occasional frog or insect meal. He holds the prey in his heavy beak, pounding it, before he takes it to its nest or eats it. The male bird has a mainly black back and brownish breast, the female reverses this colour scheme.

The **halfcollared kingfisher** (Alcedo semitorquata) is seldom spotted, despite its brilliant plumage. Its bright blue back is his outstanding feature. This kingfisher prefers also the faster flowing rivers and heavily wooded banks of rivers and lakes for his fishing ground.

The **malachite kingfisher** (Corythornis cristata) is the most beautiful of all. Its bright red bill, turquoise back and reddish-brown breast make this small bird(14cm long) a true jewel amongst the kingfishers. It is a common resident in the reed beds of the lagoons, and on thickly wooded river banks. A thrilling sight

Riverbanks

indeed to watch this flash of colour fly low over the water.

Its good bye to Wilderness. The national road occasionally overlooks the tranquil lakes below, but traffic is mostly too fast to savour the splendour. Shortly you cross a low bridge spanning the Swartvlei and arrive in

SEDGEFIELD

Sedgefield Station

Reduce speed – the traffic wardens are keen to collect money! The town developed around the construction of the railway line from George to Knysna in 1928.

Commercial outlets line the main road. Choo-Tjoe enthusiast can board the train at Sedgefield's quaint railway station.

Don't rush through the town. Explore the lovely lagoon and sandy beaches at the Swartvlei's outlet to the ocean., such as Cola Beach with its high cliffs and white sands.

Swartvlei mouth and Gericke Point/Sedgefield

Four kilometres outside Sedgefield, **Groenvlei** (Green Lake) comes into view. It forms part of the Wilderness Lake area. Groenvlei developed during the last glacial period, some 20 000 years ago. It became landlocked because of changing sea levels about 5000 years ago. Groenvlei is a fresh-water vlei although no permanent river flows into it. Seepage and run-off water from the surrounding dunes supply it with its water. Reeds and indigenous dune forests, dominated by milkwood trees, characterise the southern part. Birdwatchers and walkers alike are spoilt by the abundance of walking and watching opportunities in the area. The angler too will not be disappointed as apparently the vlei is so well stocked with bass (an angling permit is needed) that they die of old age. A fisherman's tale?

The road to **Karatara/Ruigtevlei** (see page151) branches off to the left, perhaps the Choo-Tjoe is panting past. The railway bridge across the Goukamma River and coastal road is a favourite for train spotters. The coastal road leads to **Buffels Bay**, a popular holiday resort and **Goukamma Nature Reserve.** The Reserve stretches from the western side of Groenvlei across to the western bank of the Goukamma River.

Goukamma Nature Reserve

Goukamma derives from the Khoi 'Ghaukum', the name of the sour fig plant Carpobrotus deliciosus; a popular plant as the ripe fruit is a genuine thirst quencher. They also form a natural barrier against sand erosion on the dunes and can be seen along many coastal stretches. The sour fig flowers between August and October.

The Goukama Nature Reserve stretches over 2230ha and includes the Groenvlei freshwater lake. Its dune forest dominated by milkwood trees, riverine forest along the Goukamma River, patches of dune fynbos and the 14km-long sandy and rocky seashore characterise the Reserve. It offers the nature lover a wealth of different habitats from wetlands to forests.

About 210 bird species have been recorded , many of them associated to the Groenvlei habitat. Bushbuck, blue duiker, grysbuck hide in the woodlands, maybe one even sees the re-introduced eland and bontebok.

Various walks explore the Goukamma Reserve. The longest day hike is to Groenvlei, up over fossil dunes and down through milkwood forest (16km; 4-5 hours).

The circular route from Goukamma (8km) leads through a milkwood forest.

One could add a beach walk to this.

Carpobrotus edulis

Dune Rat

Beyond the turn-off for Buffelsbaai/Buffels Bay the national road N2 climbs and rises, passes the turn-offs for Rheenendal/Portland Manor House (see Route Six) and descends in a grand swoop towards the Knysna Lagoon. The Phantom Pass joins at the bridge, known locally as 'White Bridge'. Take note of the turn-off to **Belvidere** which will be explored later.

For 6km the road glides past the lagoon shore and then enters the bustling town of

KNYSNA

The name is probably derived from the Khoi language and means 'Place of Wood' or *Xthuys Xba*.

Knysna

A romantic story is spun about the town.

A few settlements existed around the Knysna Lagoon as early as 1798. But raids by indigenous tribes in the early years turned life at times into a nightmare. Amongst the first European families in the area were the Meading, Read and van Huysteens who all selected sizeable tracts of farming land. Best known was 'Melkhout Kraal', (Milkwood) granted in 1770 to one Stephanus Terblans. His initial loan period of one year extended in the end to over twenty years. His land contained the entire lagoon basin. after his death, his widow managed 'Melkhout' until 1798 when she sold it to Johann von Lindenbaum, whom she shortly afterwards married and equally quickly divorced. 'Melkhout' changed hands again, was raided, plundered and destroyed in 1802, before it finally became the property of George Rex, rumoured to be the son of the English monarch,King George III in 1804. The story is told how the young prince George who was to become King George III, fell in love with Hannah Lighfoot, a commoner. Authorities got wind of the blossoming romance and the royal court swung into action. The prince's grandfather and his mother decided that Hannah Lightfoot be married off to a grocer named Isaac Axford. This plot, however, did not take the cunning of young lovers into account. The prince, barely 16 years, arranged with Hannah that she should consent to go through with the marriage, but that she should not show any opposition to a kidnap attempt at the chapel's door. Thus the young bride, as she arrived at the church, was snatched away from her groom, the grocer, and driven off in a travelling coach. Many versions of the kidnap exist, but all agree that Hannah was whisked away, and she vanished for ever, never to be seen again by family or friends.

Six years later, George and Hannah are said to have been legally married at Kew Chapel, by a Dr. Wilmot. The couple apparently had three children: George jun.(Rex), John and Sarah.

In 1760 George II, the prince's grandfather, died, and George ascended the throne as George III. A year later he married Charlotte of Mecklenburg-Strelitz who, it is rumoured, was aware of the Hannah affair..

But as the years went by, the stage was set for another legend: George III was to discover that his daughter, Princess Amalia, unaware of the relationship between them, had secretly married her half-brother George Rex. It is out of this last legend that one can understand the banishment of George Rex to the Cape.

In 1797 George Rex was appointed 'Marshall and Serjeant at Mace of the Vice-Admiralty at the Settlement of the Cape of God Hope' where he lived in a house called Schoonder Zigt (Beautiful View). He married the widow Johanna Rosina (Ungerer) with whom he had four children: Edward (1801), John (1802), Elizabeth (1804) and Jacob (1805). Johanna lived with George Rex for about eight years. Then she seems to fade into the mists of time.

When Britain was forced to return the Cape to the Netherlands in 1802, George Rex lost his various posts and, like many of his compatriots was

interned briefly in Stellenbosch. In 1804, he was granted permission to settle at Knysna where he purchased Melkhout Kraal.

George Rex rebuilt the ruined Melkhout farm which became known as the
'Old Place'. As time went on, he became the biggest landowner in the area.
His properties included present day Eastford, Westford, Brenton, Belvidere,
Hunter's Home, Woodbourne, Rexford, Jakkals Kraal in the Pisang Valley
near Plettenberg Bay and part of Leeuwenbosch on which later, the
Honourable Henry Barrington established his Portland Manor.

After Johanna Rosina's death, George Rex married her daughter Carolina
Margaretta (born Ungerer). He was about thirty years her senior.

George Rex died in 1839.

His large family, six sons and seven daughters, were all well educated. His
daughter Caroline married Lt. Thomas Duthie who settled after their marriage at 'Belvidere'.

Another enterprising businessman lived at the time in Knysna. This was the
master shipwright James Callander.

In 1798, Callander was appointed 'Inspector of all the Government
Woodlands to the eastward of Mossel Bay'. Apart from his thorough knowledge of woods and woodlands, Callander also had a passion and knowledge
for all things nautical. Meticulously he examined the coast between
Plettenberg Bay and Mossel Bay, and the woods along the banks of the
Knysna River, particularly near the lagoon. From his observation he con-
cluded that the lagoon could be entered by ships at low tide.

James Callander lived in fair comfort near the Heads, at the entrance to the
lagoon, literally a neighbour of George Rex.

George Rex teamed up with James Callander to develop Knysna as a port.
The Naval Commissioner at Simon's Town, Sir Jahleel Brenton, had keenly
supported Rex's scheme to establish farming families on the northern shores
of the lagoon. Timber was to be had in abundance 'within ten or twelve miles
of the river's bank, where there is a sufficient quantity of fine timer to build a
whole navy' thus wrote Sir Jahleel.

Accordingly, the Royal Navy sent the transport brig 'Emu' on an experimental visit. Unfortunately, she struck a rock at the entrance to the lagoon, but

with no loss of life. 'Podargus', commanded by Capt. Wallis, was sent to assist the 'Emu'.

The captain commented favourably on Knysna and shipbuilding started. To this end, George Rex donated 16ha of land which he named **Melville**, after Viscount Melville, First Sea Lord at the time of the British occupation. The first project was abandoned when a fire destroyed the hull. Some of the brig's salvaged wood was used to build the triangular table in the Council Chambers of the town.

In 1831, George Rex launched his own vessel, 'Knysna', sailed by his son, John, to explore the coastline. She was the first ship to enter Buffalo Bay near East London. Almost fifty years later, the 'Knysna' was still in service in England, transporting coal.

The story of shipbuilding in Knysna is, however, synonymous with the **Thesen** family.

Thesen House

The Thesens, of Norwegian origin, arrived in 1869. The family was actually on its way to New Zealand, but a storm off Agulhas drove their schooner, the 'Albatross' back towards Cape Town. One son sailed to Knysna on contract, liked what he saw and persuaded his family to settle here. 'Thesen Island' , today a luxury estate, became their property and serious boat- and furniture building began. Business flourished in the town. Its lifeline was the jetty at the very end of Long Street.

Thesen House

The first jetty was built of untreated timber in 1882, but replaced by a concrete jetty in 1913. From here the creosoted yellowwood railway sleepers from the saw-mills in the forests and in town were shipped.

Shipping traffic intensified towards the end of the 19th century despite the hazardous lagoon harbour entry: A total of 92 steamers and 3 sailing ships tied up at the jetty in 1892. But when the SAS Pietermaritzberg steered into the lagoon in 1953, it signalled the end of an era: Knysna port was finally closed to shipping. The arrival of the railway line had been the death knell; when the harbour was de-proclaimed, the last harbour pilot, John Benn, 4th generation of Benn's in that post, was transferred to Port Elizabeth.

The Benn Family

The year 1855 marked the beginning of a remarkable era in Knysna.

When the 27-ton ketch 'Musquash' piled up on the rocks at Coney Glen, the young shipwright, John Benn, who came from a long line of seafarer, was sent for. Hastily he bundled his young family and their worldly belongings and, by oxwagon, rode from Mossel Bay to Knysna. By the time they reached Knysna, the ketch had broken up. John Benn now launched his own ship-building venture. His vessel was the 'Annie Benn', a 50-ton schooner. She was later wrecked in a gale off Mossel Bay. In between he volunteered his services as pilot, a role which four generations of Benns were to fulfil with distinction.

Guiding vessels across the bar and through the Heads was demanding work, requiring skill and courage. The first pilot was dismissed in 1820, because of absenteeism; the second pilot drowned in the lagoon, and after two further unsatisfactory appointments, the post was closed down: the safety of ships for the next 30 years was left to volunteers, particularly members of the Rex family. Tirelessly they would climb the eastern Head, watching for ships, signalling ships when passage was safe. It was not unusual for vessels to lie waiting for days.

In 1841 the schooner 'Sovereign' was totally wrecked; another shipping disaster in 1855 made it abundantly clear that the increasing shipping traffic through the Heads would inevitably lead to more damage, loss of life and ships unless an official port control was established. The Colonial Secretary was urged to appoint a pilot. John Rex who had done this job, unpaid, for long years, was recommended for the post. The recommendation was accepted, but sadly, John Rex died shortly afterwards leaving a void which John Benn was to fill.

Intrigued by his father's activities, his young son, also John, often joined him at his look-out post. The younger Benn shared his father's love for the sea. Until 1865, when his ship the 'Galatea' was wrecked, Benn junior worked in the boats. Now he teamed up with his father as assistant pilot, and eventually took over as chief pilot when his father died in 1877. He was to serve for an amazing 44 years.

Another brother, young Donald, assisted him and between them many lives were saved from the furious seas. Their loyal service certainly was recognised by the community which insisted that a pilot's house be built for them on the Look-Out Hill.

Lagoon entry

One day in 1882, sitting on his bench at the foot of the hill, he noticed a fishing boat in serious trouble near the entrance. Desperately the fishermen tried to manoeuvre their boat safely into the lagoon. It was not to be. The boat capsized. John and Donald Benn rowed out and managed to save the fishermen

Today's signal at the Heads

from certain drowning. A similar incident occurred in 1899 when a boat attempted to cross the bar against the pilot's signal. Again, the Benns saved the sailors' lives.

It was not the first time that ships had disobeyed the signals. The barque 'Friedheim', laden with creosote, had been lying outside the Heads for several days, waiting for the pilot's signal to enter. Growing impatient, and with total disregard for safety, the captain made for the Heads on an outgoing springtide and gale force winds. The 'Danger Flag' on the hill went up – too late. The ship was thrown onto the rocks at

Coney Glen and disintegrated within minutes. John Benn saved three sailors, half blind from creosote. Ropes were fired across to sailors clinging desperately to wreckage, and brought in. The entire crew was saved except the sailmaker who refused to jump across and to take off his boots. His body was found nine days later.

GOLD PROSPECTING

Knysna, since 1882 a municipality, grew out of the two hamlets 'Newhaven-on-Knysna' and 'Melville-on-Knysna'. They combined as a result of the steady population growth due mainly to the flourishing timber and shipping industry, and the discovery of gold.

Long before the town came into existence, people had drifted into the forests following elephant trails. Once roads were constructed, timber became the main activity in the Knysna area. Water wheels powered the many sawmills that sprung up. One of these mills belonged to the Thesen family and became known as the 'Mill in the Wood' – today's **Millwood**. It operated from 1870 and was managed by a Mr Franzsen.

In 1875, James Hooper found a particularly heavy pebble in the Karatara River and believed it to be a gold nugget. He took it to the local pharmacist, Mr Groom. He, in turn, consulted Charles Osborne, a civil and mining engineer with experience of the Californian goldfields. Osborne shared Hooper's belief, approached the Cape government and was given a grant for further investigation of the area. The two men sank a shaft and searched the Karatara River, nearby creeks and gullies, but without any further finds. Their search area was about 15 kilometres from Millwood.

Mining tunnel in the Millwood area

Despite the failure, rumours of alluvial gold persisted. In 1886 the government proclaimed the land 'above and below the Main Road drift on the Karatara River' a public diggings. John Barrington was appointed Gold Commissioner.

John Osborne, after a brief stay in Port Nolloth, returned to Knysna in

1886 and continued prospecting on a full time basis. Still, the Karatara River yielded nothing. Osborne then turned his attention to the Homtini River up towards Thesen Hill and to a gully which became known as the Millwood Gully. Here his probing proved more successful. Together with Thomas Bain, the district Inspector of Roads, he submitted a report to the government in which recommended that the area should be opened to the general public and allow them sluicing.

Many inexperienced prospectors were lured to the 'gold fields' in the forests, their health badly affected by the extremely wet and cold winter conditions of 1886. That same year, they formed a Diggers Committee and put rules into place. For the administration of the fields, 1 shilling per month was exacted per claim. Gold prospecting now began in earnest. The Government Surveyor, Mr Newdigate, laid out a village of 135 stands and soon 75 wood and iron cottages, 6 hotels, 4 boarding houses, a hospital, Methodist Church, a number of general dealers, bakers. butchers, banks, a music hall and 3 newspapers could be found at Millwood Village. In time the alluvial gold find attracted over 1000 men.

Pitt Street cottage at Millwood

Millwood's growth ensured years of fair material comfort for the Knysna area. Even the social calendar filled with dates, as people flocked to the town.

The diggers meanwhile had contact with Knysna through a post cart service. Despite the torturous journey, it operated three times a week. A red flag with a white cross signalled its arrival at the post office.

By 1888 over 1400 claims were staked out and about 40 companies and syndicates involved in gold extraction, both alluvial and reef. The government scored best, its revenue coffers bulged with taxes collected.

But the good fortune was about to end. Gold had been discovered in the north of the country. The slump started in 1890 and caused the collapse of the Millwood gold mines. Almost all companies went bankrupt, and most diggers moved on to Barberton for greater fortunes. Some stayed behind, hoping, but recovery never came. By 1890 only 3 shops remained and 5 government officials. Mr Charles Osborne was the only one still digging!

The population at Millwood dwindled to 162 in 1892, to 7 in 1893. Equipment, some of which was retrieved and brought back to Knysna, lay scattered and abandoned in the woods. In 1924 the area was officially deproclaimed and prospecting became illegal.

Most of the machinery on display at the Bendigo Mine was found deep in the forest, in gullies and ravines. The Department of Forestry was responsible for much of the recovery of machinery, whilst the **Millwood Goldfield Society**, keeps the memory of gold alive. The Society, established in 1988, organises regular excursions to the former gold fields.

The Millwood Mining Walk

Allow about 2 hours for this 6km-long, easy walk.
Directions: take the Rheenendal turn-off on the national road N2. At Rheenendal itself watch for signposts 'Bibby's Hoek, Millwood, Goldfields'. Turn off for Bibbys Hoek towards the parking area. Here you find an information board, including distances to Krisjan se Nek, Jubilee Creek and Millwood walks. Take out a self-issue permit, then drive towards the starting point, pass the boom signposted 'Millwood Goldfields 8km' and continue driving for another 1.5km. Then bear right for Krisjan se Nek picnic site, a fabulous spot in the shade of an ancient Outeniqua yellowwood tree. Maybe you are fortunate enough to hear the raucous cry of the beautiful Knysna lourie. a rough 'kraa, kraa' betrays its presence as the shimmering scarlet and green plumage is only seen in flight.
Beyond the picnic site, another fork in the road is reached, here bear left. A lovely cool drive past trees and ferns for about 4km when yet another fork is reached: let to Jubilee Creek, right to Materolli/Bendigo/Millwood Hut. Bear rigth and head for the mines. Don't be deterred by the numerous forks in the road, the route is clearly marked. At last, a signboard welcomes you to the 'Millwood Mining Walk'. The walk passes the 'Matterolli Tea Room - Mother Hollie'. Step inside: apart from refreshments, it houses the small, but fascinating Mining Museum. The building itself is a survivor of the gold digging days.
Start with a circular walk via the old village site. Solitary street sign bring to mind the busier times: there was a Main Street, even a Victoria Street. Memories of the past linger on, particularly also at the mining sites where some of the adits have been restored.
The near-by toolshed allows an insight into the workings of the mine. All around, railway tracks, broken equipment lie lost in the grass. From here, the path finds its way back past the cemetery towards the tea room and museum.

Millwood Museum

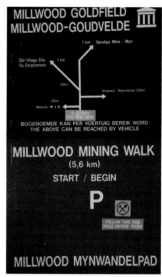

Direction finder

Abandoned Machinery

Victoria Street

Machinery at Bendigo Mine

The Knysna Lourie

The Jubilee Creek Walk

It is an easy walk of under 4km along a path that gold miners used. It also is part of the Outeniqua Hiking Trail. You need to put aside 1-1.5 hours.

Tree ferns

Retrace the drive from Millwood and bear right (signposted) for **Jubilee Creek.** *Another 3km along this downhill route leads directly to the picinic site on the banks of a gently flowing stream, known as 'Forest Creek'. Today, a delightful place to picnic, but in days gone by, the riverbanks teemed with life of quite another kind when gold diggers were at work. A most refreshing walk leads past a number of miners' diggings to the* **Waterfall,** *a total distance of 3.2 km there and back.*

Tree ferns (Cyathea capensis) shade the path, forest birds chirp as

Cyrtanthus purpureus/Knysna Lily

one follows the stream. The small pool and waterfall mark the turning point. A second waterfall (unmarked) directly above the lower falls is reached by stepping along the edge of the pool to the other side and clambering up the hill.

Jubilee Creek yielded mostly alluvial gold. A couple of hundred metres upstream there is a pit, to the left of the path, testifying to the old alluvial gold diggings.

Things to do in Knysna

A walk through town:
In the centre of town, on the square behind the War Memorial, stands the

Knysna Library
built in 1893 and officially opened by S.W. Thesen. Until then a Reading Room on the corner of Long and Main Streets had quenched the literary thirst of the residents. The opening ceremony was a colourful affair with flags and bunting bedecking the town, young and old marching to the spirited tunes of the local brass band, the Knysna Rangers.

Use was made of local timber, such as stinkwood and witels for the entrance door, panelled jamb linings and ceilings.

The library has been extended twice, the last time in 1987 when the north wing in more modern style was added.

The Square and War Memorial
The War Memorial honours the Fallen of both World Wars and the Liberation struggle.

The Memorial was designed by C.P. Walgate and crafted by John Donald. The carving of the wreath and sword is the work of Mrs Marion Walgate. The stone used was quarried on the Brenton Hills and ferried across the lagoon by boat.

During the unveiling ceremony in 1922, it was draped with the same Union Jack that the Rev. Captain A.G. Duthie had used at burials at which he offici-ated in Flanders while on active service as Chaplain in the Union forces.

From the Memorial, turn left (east) and walk down Main Street. Just before the traffic lights stands the double-storeyed

Melville Centre
with its large gables, heavy plaster mouldings and rusticated corners - one of the finest buildings in Knysna.

The original building, erected by the carpenter and undertaker William Patterson Milne, was let out to the Standard Bank and served both as bank and manager's residence.

The Thesen Company purchased it in 1912 and gave it its name. The popular General Dealer's store 'Melvilles Limited' closed in 1976, when Thesens were taken over by Barlows Ltd.

Melville House

Further down Main Street stand the

St. George's Churches
One enters the tranquil grounds through the lych gate made of solid teak. The roofed gate was traditionally the place where the coffin awaited the clergyman's arrival. The gate was donated by the Thesen family in memory of Bessie Thesen, born Harison. She was the daughter of Captain Christopher Harison, first Conservator of Forests for the District. The red ironstone was quarried locally, as was the stone for the wall surrounding the church yard.

'Old' St. George's
Soon after Bishop Robert Gray's arrival in the Cape (1847), a deputation from Knysna requested the services of a clergyman. The petition fell on receptive ears and the Bishop visited Knysna a year later. A service was held in the school which, until the building of a church, would serve as the licensed place of worship.

'Old Rex Church'

Funds were raised, and the foundation stone laid in April 1849 by John Rex.

In November 1850, Robert Gray once again visited Knysna but was deeply disappointed at the lack of building progress due to lack of money. With a little talking, six townsmen were persuaded to find the necessary funds to complete the building. At last, in October 1855, the church was consecrated by Bishop Gray, just two days before he was to consecrate the 'Duthie' church at Belvidere.

Wide yellowwood floorboards, whitewashed walls and timber ceiling, stone window traceries with slightly different design at the top combine to create a feeling of warmth and welcome.

The first clergyman was Dr William Andrews, a physician from London who had been ordained Deacon in 1849.

The New St. George's Church
The foundation stone was laid in September 1926 by the Right Reverend Henry Sidwell, the first Bishop of George – as the 'Old Church' could no longer accommodate its growing congregation.

The first builder went insolvent when the church was only half built and other masons and carpenters had to be engaged. Finally, the new St. George's stood proud and ready to receive the parishioners in 1928. But only in April 1937 were all debts cleared and the church finally consecrated by the new Bishop of George, the Right Rev.Herbert Gwyer.

Inside, ones eyes are drawn towards the magnificent stinkwood chancel screen with its theme on interlinked thorns, the reredos, the stinkwood pews and carved choir stall. The choir stalls were a gift, in memory of their mother, by the children of Johanna Metelerkamp, a granddaughter of George Rex.

The Knysna Trades School created the pulpit, and Mrs Wynne Cloete designed and made the cross on the reredos. Pew ends from the old St. George's were used for the panelling in the sanctuary.

The four sanctuary windows are in memory of Bishop Robert Gray.

Now walk across to the

Cemetery
where to the north of the Old Church the graves of various members of the Rex family rest in the shade of ancient oaks, including Jacob, John and Caroline Rex.

To the right of the New Church lies the grave of John Benn, the first of the Benn family of Pilots at the Heads.

Next to the church one finds

The Royal Hotel the oldest hotel in town. It was originally a small thatched building, known as St. George's Tavern, built for Master Mariner Captain Thomas Horn.

The hotel achieved fame in 1867 when Queen Victoria's son, Prince Alfred, spent his first night here en route to the forests for an elephant shoot. Prince Alfred was accompanied by the Governor of the Cape, Sir Philip Wodehouse, Maj. General Bisset and Sir Walter Currie. After the successful elephant hunt, the prince returned to Simon's Town with his trophies of two elephant heads and the skin of one. He granted his host the privilege to name his tavern the 'The Royal Hotel'.

The hotel has known different owners since then and was re-designed in 1939.

Turning into Queen Street, you meet the town's first public building, the

Old Gaol
It was built by some convicts assigned to Thomas Bain, the road engineer, who was to build the road linking Knysna to the Longkloof valley. This pass became known as the **Prince Alfred Pass** (see page 221). The four erven on which the gaol was built were purchased from John Sutherland in 1858.

In a festive atmosphere, the magistrate, John Fichat, laid the foundation stone in 1859. Dignitaries and townsfolk alike marched through town to the building site.

The Gaol Bell also sounded the fire alarm and, curiously, to keep the public off the Post Office verandah; a double peal was rung 15 minutes before postal deliveries began.

In 1965 planning for a new jail commenced and in 1991, the Old Gaol was declared a National Monument.

Presently it houses the Angling Museum, Maritime Museum, Knysna Art Gallery, Gift Shop and a Café.

When the Old Gaol still operated as a prison, the crossroads formed by Queen and Main Streets where one finds the Royal Hotel, Police Station, Gaol and St. George's Church, was called by the locals '**Temptation, Condemnation, Damnation and Salvation**'.

Further down Queen Street, on the left,

Millwood House – The Knysna Museum Complex

bids welcome. This quaint wood and iron house with its equally quaint out-buildings is typical of the homes built in the 1880s in the mining village of Millwood in the forest.

Millwood House

The Millwood House was transported in sections and re-erected in Queen Street. At Millwood village it had been the Scott's family home, in Knysna that of the shoemaker Cook and his family who rented it from the new owner, Mr W.D.McFarlane. Mr Cook paid a monthly rental of £2, on top of which he was required to keep the house in 'fair wear and tear'. He was repaid £1 on the 1st December every year, if he had kept it satisfactorily.

Museum buildings, Knysna

To the left of Millwood House, a National Monument, stands

Parkes Cottage
also from the Millwood village and brought down in pieces. It was first re-built in the Main Road, then moved yet again in 1905 to a site in Rawson Street, (named after Rawson W. Rawson, Colonial Secretary) before finding its final place in 1992.

If the story of George Rex seems unbelievable, study the documentation and genealogy exhibited in this building – there may, after all, be some truth in it.

Step also into the corrugated iron Company shop behind Parkes Cottage. This was once owned by the timber company Geo. Parkes & Sons and a neighbour to Parkes Cottage in Rawson Street. The workers and staff of the sawmill used the shop which today houses a timber display.

The third cottage, also corrugated iron, was built in 1904 by George Parkes as accommodation for one of his employees. In 1998 it was moved to its present site and displays Anglo Boer War memorabilia and photographs.

Now walk down Queen Street, past the municipal building and turn right into Union Street. Here, at the corner with Long Street, stands

Thesen House
The double storeyed house was built in 1916/17 and designed to house the offices of the Thesen Steamship Company downstairs, and a wholesale store upstairs.

Thesen House

It once sported round turrets on its north and south west corners. Turrets were a popular feature at the time. Unfortunately, the Thesen House turrets were destroyed by a devastating fire in the 1920s which burnt down the entire upper storey. The turrets were subsequently replaced by the pointed gables one sees today. A little of the Thesen family story is told by the plaster work on the gables: the Viking ship on the north rounded gable points to the Thesen's Norwegian origin; the white star on a red background is the logo of their Shipping Line which was depicted on their ships' funnels and on their house flag. In the west gable one sees the house flag in a shield and the two construction dates. The south-west pointed gable is decorated with an anchor on a deep blue background; the south rounded gable displays the house flag with its white star on the red background.

Step inside and climb the striking yellowwood staircase to the upper floor and browse through the gallery of photographs, telling the Thesen story.

From Thesen House it is only a short distance to relax in Knysna's

Waterfront, the Knysna Quays.
Colourful boats lie at anchor, shops compete for visitors' attention as do the many restaurants.

Knysna Quays

Hopefully the Choo-Tjoe steams across the lagoon and into the railway station whilst at the quays.

Choo-Tjoe at Knysna Station

A leisurely boat excursion towards The Heads or across to Featherbed help unwind before an unusual site is visited, the

Knysna Fort
It is situated above the Knysna Provincial Hospital in Main Street. At the traffic lights in Main Street turn into the hospital grounds for parking at the back.

The Knysna Fort locally known as 'Thompson's Folly', never saw action. Climb the concrete steps and follow a fairly rough and also neglected footpath to the left. Immediately after the fenced-in Reservoir turn left again and the path takes you to **Verdompskop Hill**. Here you find the remnants of the most southerly fort built during the Anglo-Boer War.

Knysna Fort

It comprised two loop-holed circular towers with vertical slits in the wall at the north-east and south-west corners. These were connected by a dry-stone perimeter wall. In the centre of the enclosed area was a circular stone base on which the flagpole and two small guns stood. It is said that the two small guns came from the first ship to ever have entered The Heads in February 1817, the 'Emu'. (These guns can be seen in Knysna's Main Street at the entrance to the Old Gaol).

South of this stood a two-roomed rectangular garrison office with crenellated battlements. Today one can still see walls of the north-east tower and the garrison office, the south-west tower and parts of the south and east perimeter wall. But why a fort at all in Knysna?

The Anglo-Boer War erupted in 1899. A year later, when General Kritizinger's commando of 2 000 Boers invaded the Cape, many towns began to look seriously to their defenses.

News of Boer attacks on Willowmore and Avontuur in January 1901 led to the declaration of martial law in Knysna. Even a Town Guard was formed as suspicious men had been spotted near the Knysna Bridge who, as it turned out, were harmless mule drivers from Pacaltsdorp. A curfew was imposed and, as a precaution, the books and assets of the Standard Bank sent by sea to Mossel Bay for safe keeping.

In August 1901, a Boer commando led by Gideon Scheepers (see page 181) clashed with a British force, based at Uniondale, in the Longkloof (see page 224). This battle was the nearest the Anglo-Boer War ever came to Knsyna.

Enjoy the superlative views across the town and lagoon from the fort, named after the Town Guards commanding officer.

One inescapable drive is to the famous

Knysna Heads
the two magnificent sandstone cliffs that guard the treacherous lagoon entrance.

Heading eastward out of town, turn right onto the concreted, busy and bumpy **George Rex Drive.** It is also the access road to the industrial area which explains the frantic traffic. It passes picnic grounds, the municipal golf course and a turn-off to fashionable **Leisure Isle**. Once truly an island known as 'Steenbok Isle', George Cairn bought it in 1929 from the Duthie family and subsequently built the causeway.

Speed bumps slow down the drive near the steep turn-off to the left to **Cony Glen Driv**e and the **View Point** on the eastern Head. The road then narrows and passes luxurious homes to end at an access controlled parking area.

To the left of the parking area and restaurant, a paved path ambles towards the Heads, accompanied by the sound of pounding waves and screeching gulls. A little cave-like opening is reached, continue on the lower track which traverses a rocky slope – watch out for waves at high tide – and then leads across a short wooden bridge to the viewpoint at the foot of the eastern 'Head'.

Allow thoughts to travel back in time. Imagine the year 1903 and the ship 'Paquita' in the lagoon. The 460-ton schooner had plied its trade between Goteborg and Guam over the past two years. This time, she had called at the Cape to discharge her creosote cargo at the Knysna harbour. Once completed, she took on sand as ballast in Featherbed Bay, the western shore of the lagoon. John Benn, the pilot, became suspicious. The size of the ship would need at least 15 sailors to operate her – now he could only spot 5, the rest had disappeared. Benn kept a sharp eye on the 'Paquita' who looked as if she were waiting for a favourable wind to sail out. When night approached, John Benn left. That same night, the 'Paquita' fouled her anchor and drifted across to Steenbok Island.

The master of the vessel was forced to discharge his cargo of sand during a spring tide which occurred about twelve days later. Crowds flocked to the scene, always eager for a bit of diversion. Questions, never answered, were asked: how did the 'Paquita' get to the island in the first place. Was it an accident, was it intent? Rumours floated about a possible insurance scam...Eventually the vessel was auctioned, but few bidders came. The 'Paquita' looked as if she would soon sink. A second time she fouled her anchors, drifted away from the island and sank just in front of today's green harbour light where she still manages to intrigue divers her wreck, apparently, is visible in clear water. Later inspections revealed that no damage was ever done to her anchor.

caves near 'Featherbed'

Just as the Benns used to sit at the same spot, gazing out to sea, ready to sound the alarm or give the green light for vessels to enter the lagoon, you too have now a chance to study the

The Knysna Lagoon
Is it a lagoon or an estuary? An estuary generally remains open to the sea, whereas lagoons are characterised by sand bars which may build up and prevent fresh water flowing out into the ocean during certain seasons.

In Knysna, no sandbar blocks the river's outflow to the sea; the lagoon is therefore theoretically an 'estuary'. But practically, to the people of Knysna, it is their beloved lagoon.

The Knysna River has its source in the Outeniqua Mountains, 64km away. Its waters are swelled by its contributaries, the Swartkops, Steenbras, Gouna, Rooiels, Lelievlei, Witels, Dwars, Palmiet, Kruis, Oubos and Lawnwood Rivers.

A deep shipping channel allows ships to sail upstream for some distance. Then, only small and shallow draft vessels can continue as the channel decreases in depth. At its widest point, the lagoon measures 3km.

The river mouth is about 230m wide with a depth of about 3.9m in the navigable channel. It is known as **The Heads,** flanked on either side by impressive rock formations. The river mouth is notoriously dangerous because of currents, submerged rocks and unpredictable winds.

At low tide, salt marshes and sandbanks are exposed in the lagoon. Salt marshes are a favourite hunting ground for sea birds and waders. For the birder, the best place to observe is at the Woodbourne Marsh, along George Rex Drive, opposite the causeway to Leisure Island.

Mesmerised by the boisterous sea, the warm glow of the sandstone rocks, the preying gulls gliding through the air, one tends to forget the smaller creatures that live in the lagoon. One of them is the

The Knysna Seahorse - *Hippocampus capensis*
This tiny 7cm-long creature is is the only known estuarine seahorse species in the world. It is present in the Swartvlei, Knysna and Keurbooms estuaries. The seahorse, a protected species, lives off estuarine vegetation which is increasingly destroyed by human encroachment along the shores.

Seahorses belong to the genus *Hippocampus*. Because it can move its eyes independently and change its colour, it is also known as the 'chameleon of the sea'. It is a poor swimmer. Its strong tail grasps submerged vegetation, once comfortably secured to the plant, the seahorse uses its toothless mouth to suck in minute crustaceans. If absolutely necessary, it will swim free from its anchorage and pursue its prey.

The Knysna Sea Horse reaches sexual maturity between 6–9 months, depending on the water temperature and availability of food.

An interesting feature is that the male has the brood pouch into which the female deposits the eggs for fertilisation. A lengthy courting ritual has preceded this. As soon as the eggs are deposited, the pouch closes, the male sways cautiously for a moment to settle the eggs, and the female is free from any further duties. The young are born, after about 100 days.

Another smaller creature of the lagoon attracts almost world-wide culinary attention, this is the cultivated **Knysna Oyster.**

The oyster is a mollusc of the class *Bivalvia,* with two shells or valves. As a filter feeder it processes up to 15 litres of water per hour, extracting single cell micro-organisms for food.

Common oysters indigenous to the Southern Cape

Red Oyster (Ostrea atherstoni)

Weed Oyster (Ostrea algoensis)

Pearl Oyster (Pinctada capensis) has flakey amber-grey shell valves and is fixed to rocks by threads. Its shells are thrown up on the beach showing the shiney 'mother-of-oearl' interior. It produces real pearls. They are found along the coast between Algoa Bay and False Bay.

The Common Rock Oyster/Coastal Oyster (crassostrea margaritacea) is the most common edible oyster and found along the coast from the Transkei to False Bay.

The crassostrea genus releases its eggs and sperm into the sea; fertilisation therefore takes place externally, a process known as spawning.

The female oyster can produce more than 150 million eggs per season which, once fertilised, begin swimming within 24 hours by using an organ known as velum. The velum is covered with fine hairs that propel the organism. Depending on temperatures and other factors, remain free-swimming for about 21 days.

After 48 hours it begins feeding on plankton which, together with bacteria and decaying organ matter will be its diet for the rest of its life.

At a later stage of larval growth an 'eyespot' forms. This is sensitive to light and gravity and used to select a suitable place to settle.

Then a 'foot' is developed which is used to crawl and excrete the glue needed to attach it to the selected surface. It is also used to control its vertical movement whilst swimming – when retracted the larvae will drop. Once they are attached, the larvae become known as 'spats' and begin to manufacture their shells. This they do by binding calcium and carbonate collected from the sea water.

Natural oysters live in the intertidal zone between the mean sea level and low water neap tide. As one of the shell valves is secured to rock, the oyster has no power of locomotion. They normally live in solidly packed colonies on rocks. They open their shells at high tide and feed by filtering water through their gills. The shells close as the tide recedes, but trap enough water to prevent dehydration.

The Knysna Oyster Company was established in 1948 as a joint undertaking by the Fisheries Development Company and Thesen & Co. The first oyster beds were built with asbestos roofing tiles in Featherbed Bay, with oysters imported from Britain, Portugal and Australia. This venture failed and other sites in the lagoon were looked at, different rack designs and oyster species investigated. Eventually, in the 1970s the Pacific Oyster, *Crassostrea gigas,* was found to be the ideal species for production purposes in the Knysna lagoon, and oyster farming could start in earnest.

Today, the Knysna aqua farm is using the intertidal rack system. The oysters are imported as spats from hatcheries in France and Chile when they are about three months old. At this stage they measure a mere 3 to 4mm in size. On arrival in South Africa they are placed first in the 'nursery' waters of Algoa Bay and finally taken to Knysna. Here they are placed in fine mesh bags and lashed onto racks in the intertidal zone. As they grow they are turned regularly, sorted, sized and moved to bigger bags to facilitate water flow and feeding. In the lagoon water they develop strong shells which close tightly when they are removed from the water.

Once taken from the Knysna lagoon, the oyster is returned for another three months to Algoa Bay.

When the oysters are ready for harvesting, they are cleaned with high pressure hoses, before being sorted and packed.

The Knysna Oyster Company is one of the largest single producers of oysters in the world. It has grown from producing 1,4 million oysters in 1999 to 2,4 million in 2002.

Knysna Oyster Festival

is celebrated annually in July. Since its inception in the 1980s, the festival has gained in popularity. The first festival saw the South African Navy sailing through the dangerous portal at the Heads, an exciting and spectacular event for the town. The Navy received the Freedom of Knysna on 21 September 1985. The most recent attendance figures (2004) have soared to over 35 000 visitors – book accommodation early!

Oysters dominate the celebrations: oyster cooking and eating competitions are organised, where opposing teams establish who can open and eat the most oysters in 60 seconds. Waitrons race against each other whilst golf, bowls tournaments, and angling competitions, flea markets, beer and braai tents, camel rides, dog shows, variety shows and live music all compete for the visitor's attention.

Another festival highlight is the Forest Marathon. The 42,2km run through breathtaking forest landscapes leaves many a runner literally breathless!

A visit to Belvidere

Head out of town in a westerly direction towards George. On White Bridge, spanning the lagoon, move into the right lane, as you turn off right. The road swings towards the lagoon past an amazing cycad garden, then goes underneath the bridge to emerge on the Brenton route, gently winding uphill. Below, the green roofs of Belvidere Estate line the lagoon shore. Follow the directional signposts to

Belvidere House

which rests beneath shady oaks on the western shore of the Knysna Lagoon. Its story begins with a young and love smitten army officer, garrisoned at the Castle in Cape Town. His name? Thomas Henry Duthie. Born 1805 in Stirling, Scotland,, he joined in 1828 the 72nd Highland Regiment at the Cape and visited Knysna on a hunting trip in 1830. Here he met and fell in love with Caroline, daughter of George Rex. By 1833 he had hung up his military boots, married Caroline and become a gentleman farmer. After a year in England, Duthie returned to Belvidere Estate which he had bought from his father-in-law. He was its owner from 1833 to 1857.

The homestead became known as 'Belvidere House', built in traditional Georgian colonial style from mainly local materials. Later additions changed its appearance somewhat, such as the verandah and the flat roofed section at the rear, one room of which served as the Belvidere Post Office for a number of years.

Ancient oaks, planted by young Duthie, lend some cooling shade. The acorns were a gift from his father-in-law.

Holy Trinity Church – the 'Duthie Church'

This charming church, a beautiful example in miniature of the Norman style of the 11th and 12th centuries, was built by Thomas Henry Duthie as a place of worship for his family, friends and their servants.

Sophia Gray, wife of the Bishop of Cape Town, provided the architectural plans. The Hon. Henry Barrington of Portland generously supplied much of the stinkwood and yellowwood for the timberwork, and the captain's brother, Rev. A.H. Duthie, collected funds in England. The sandstone was quarried nearby and shaped by three Scottish masons. Ox-drawn sledges transported the stone to the building site. The slate roof tiles arrived from England in 1849 on the brig 'Apame'.

Bishop Robert Gray consecrated the 'Duthie' Church in October 1855. The last direct descendent to hold the estate in the Duthie name was Miss A.V. Duthie, a well-known botanist who died in 1963. She is commemorated by the stained glass window in the north wall of the nave. Her grave, like that of many other family members and friends, lies under the oaks in the peaceful churchyard.

The bell above the main door was cast in England. On its journey to the Cape, it was dropped overboard and retrieved from the lagoon silt months later.

The pulpit, except for the parapet, was carved out of a single block, the 'Monster Block'.

The Royal Arms and those of the Diocese of Cape Town are shown in the central window in the west front, flanked by windows depicting the Arms of the Duthie and Barrington families.

The Rose Window above is the work of the stained glass expert C.Groves from England. It is dedicated to Miss Annie Armstrong who was a much loved governess and companion to the Duthie family.

After this step back into the past, re-join the road towards **Brenton,** home to the **Brenton Blue Butterfly,** a rare species for which a small sanctuary has been established in the village. The road rises, passes a turn-off to Brenton-on-Lake, crosses the Choo-Tjoe railway line, and offers tremendous views of the lagoon. Stop at a parking area to the left to savour the spectacular surroundings. Speed humps slow the journey, just as well, as traffic is fast, everybody rushing to Brenton-on-Sea. The descent weaves past holiday homes and ends at the beach.

From here, steps lead to the most magnificent beach imaginable. Kick off your shoes, feel the sand between the toes as black oyster catchers nervously watch, sea gulls screech overhead, anglers cast their rods and you finally reach Buffels Bay at the other end of the beach, a few kilometres away. If not walking, dip the toes into the mostly pleasant water near the impressive rocky outcrop, 'Castle Rocks'. Be careful though, swimming is dangerous. 'Castle Rocks' is also a favourite spot for anglers who may hook galjoen and kob or, east of the rocks, white steenbras, white musselcracker and garrick.

Brenton Beach

Invigorated from the walk, return to Knysna.

What the forests offer
Search for timber had brought the white man to the Outeniqua region in 1728, leading to inevitable large scale destruction of the forests. Early control measures made unauthorised felling illegal in 1788. Governor van Plettenberg went even further: he closed down the Outeniqua timber post and channelled all timber traffic through the new Plettenberg settlement, east of Knysna.

The first forest policy allocated all forests west of the Kaaimans River to free use by the public; the eastern side to use by the government, whilst the southern part was closed to allow regeneration.

A licence system had been introduced by the time the town of George was established. But the tasks that faced the overseers were enormous: they had to inspect the woods daily to see that the woodcutters obeyed the regulations and to report any wrongdoing to the landdrost.

Despite its good intentions, the government's interest in forest control soon declined. Had it not been for the foresight of men such as Thomas Duthie of Belvidere and the Rex brothers, the forests might not have survived. Felling was finally declared illegal in 1847.

But with what effect on the woodcutters to whom the forests had been home and a source of livelihood for well over a century? Not surprisingly, they resented the appointment of Captain Harison to the post of full-time Conservator of Forests in the area.

Harison explored the vast forests on foot and was appalled by the wasteful felling over the years. For 15 years he stayed in his post and then took up work in Cape Town. Captain Harison returned to Knysna eventually where he died in 1897.

The Comte de Vasselot de Regne, a graduate of the School of Forestry at Nancy (France) succeeded Captain Harison. He arrived in Cape Town in March 1881, accompanied by his wife and eight children.

Where Captain Christopher Harison had introduced the 'section system' for felling in an effort to control over-exploitation of the forests, De Vasselot wanted to preserve the forests in a more balanced way: timber was to be exploited on a sustainable basis, allowing it to be removed at a rate which matched the growth of the indigenous forests.

In 1882 the Cape Parliament passed the first Forest Act, which made demarcated forest inalienable, and established a Forestry Department with de Vasselot in control. Professional forest research led to the first scientific plan for forest management.

Unfortunately de Vasselot also insisted on the planting of exotic trees around the indigenous forest, particularly on the summits of mountain ranges. This way, pine trees, blue gums and the Australian blackwood found their way into the indigenous forests.

When de Vasselot's contract expired after 12 years, he had established a solid foundation for forest management.

The woodcutters' fate was finally investigated by the government which realised that some drastic action was needed to ease their life.

A first step was the introduction of a lottery system in 1913. Only registered woodcutters could participate in the lottery and only certain marked trees could be felled. A nominal fee for each tree was payable. The lottery system survived for a quarter of a century, but neither woodcutter nor government benefitted from it.

The woodcutter's population gradually declined. By 1932, about 500 registered and 200 unregistered woodcutters, making up a population of nearly 4000 people, lived scattered in the forests.

Just before the outbreak of the Second World War, a mere 258 woodcutters were still registered. In 1939 the lottery system was abolished and the Woodcutters Annuities Bill passed. Through this bill the woodcutters became pensioners at 25 pounds a year, except those who were eligible for old age pensions.

Today South Africa has a total of about 255 000ha of indigenous forest and nearly 972 000ha of exotic plantations. Only 1% of the land surface in the country is forest.

In the southern Cape and Tsitsikamma region, 35 765ha of indigenous forest and 5339ha of fynbos is managed by the Directorate Indigenous Forest Management (DIFM) of the National Department of Water Affairs and Forestry (DWAF). The land is scattered on the narrow coastal strip to the south of the Outeniqua and Tsitsikamma Mountain ranges, between George in the west and Kareedouw in the east, a 177km long and 16 km wide belt.

The area is divided into three forest estates:
Farleigh Forest Estate: areas between George and the Knysna River

Diepwalle Forest Estate: between the Knysna River and Plettenberg Bay

Tsitsikamma Forest Estate: to the east of Plettenberg Bay
The indigenous forests stretch from sea level to altitudes of 1000 metres and above. A total of 465 plant species is known to occur in these forests.

Of the large number of exotic plants that have invaded the indigenous forests, the Australian Blackwood (*Acacia melanoxylon*) is the most important invader plant. It was introduced to the southern Cape in 1856. It has become an important timber tree in the region.

Though an invader, the tree is less harmful than previously thought. Research has shown that it regenerates poorly .

Timber from the indigenous forest is used mainly for the manufacture of high quality furniture and ornaments, an important industry in the local economy. Harvesting is limited to forest types and sites that are the least ecologically sensitive and takes place on a 10-year cycle. Harvesting is carried out on about 600 to 650ha annually.

The harvested timber is usually sold on public auction.

Forests and elephants

The Knysna forests once teemed with buffalo and elephant which had adapted to life in the forests. The poisonous arrows and cunning hunting skills of indigenous people were the elephant's only enemy until the arrival of the European. He brought his gun from which there was often no escape. The worst enemy was the ivory hunter. Elephant hunting was totally uncontrolled until 1885 by which time it was already too late for the buffalo whose herds had been extinguished. A few hundred elephants still roamed free.

Though shooting of elephants now required a permit, the permit was issued free up to 1908. Only when the elephant population had dwindled to about twenty animals did the government intervene by proclaiming elephants royal game.

Elephants cooling down at a waterhole

By 1925 the herd had shrunk to about twelve, including two calves. For some time the population figures remained stable at this level. But any hope for increasing the numbers was dashed by the high mortality rate amongst the calves.

An inspection tour of the forests in 1951 revealed that the relic herd contained no more than four elephants, one rogue bull, one old cow and two others whose spoor only had been seen.

Experiments, not entirely successful, were carried out to re-introduce elephants to the Knysna forests. Today, maybe four of the gentle giants survive.

The Knysna elephants were lovingly and respectfully known, particularly by the woodcutters, as *Big Foot*.

(For a warm insight into the woodcutters' life read Dalene Matthee's books, such as 'Fila's Child', 'The Mulberry Forest', 'Circles in a Forest'.)

Now it is time to explore the forests on foot or on bicycle, the opportunities are endless. Obtain maps or other reading material from the local informa-tion office, easily spotted in the Main Street as a huge elephant skeleton fills the window. In central Knysna explore the **Pledge Nature Reserve,** about one block away from the Main Street. To reach it, follow Grey Street and turn into Bond Street.

The reserves stretches over 10 ha and pleasant footpaths allow you to enjoy rich birdlife. Walking is very easy.

Elephants

The gregarious elephant normally roams the veld in groups of 10 to 20. The group size can increase substantially because of outside pressures felt, or towards the end of the dry season.

The family, led by its matriarch, follows a highly developed social structure. Bulls of different ages are part of the family until they attain puberty at between 10 to 12 years. They then seek to establish their own units.

Breeding occurs throughout the year. A cow produces a single calf every five years or so after a gestation of 22 months. The calf weighs in at about 120kg, and stands about 90cm high. During the first year of its life, the young is able to walk under its mother's belly. Between the forelegs it will find two mammae and it will suckle until the age of two. The adult elephant will ultimately attain a mass of up to 7000kg. This staggering weight is reached by spending 16 to 18 hours daily eating. The diet is simple, nonetheless between 180 to 270kg are con-sumed by the bull and large distances covered in the search for food.

Nearly 80% of their diet consists of grass, but elephants are not averse to leaves, branches, roots, wild fruit and seed pods of the acacia species. Thorns present no problem. Whilst foraging they strip many trees of their bark – but to make up for this destructive behaviour, they frequently rock seed-bearing trees. In doing this the elephants open up the soil and allow seeds to enter the ground. Whilst feeding, they move continuously.

They use their forelegs to dig up roots and shallow water holes. Up to 100 litres can be consumed during a visit to a water hole.Elephants are able to survive long periods without water, but do depend on it.

The trunk is used for smelling, food gathering, drinking and as a weapon.

Though the eye sight is poor, nature compensates by giving elephants acute hearing.

Wounded elephants are particularly dangerous, or when they are continually pursued or females separated from their young. A danger sign is a rocking motion and the swinging of one foot. A storming or charging elephant can reach a speed of up to 40km/h, an enormous increase from the usual 9 – 12km/h.

ROUTE EIGHT

KNYSNA TO STORMS RIVER ALONG THE NATIONAL ROAD N2

The national road N2 continues easterly out of Knysna. Exercise special caution for the first few kilometres as pedestrian traffic is intense and visibility often poor.

Seven kilometres outside Knysna the massive Khayelethu township marks the first turn-off. Here the the R339 veers left to **Uniondale** (see page…) and also provides access to the three **Elephant Walks** of various lengths near the Diepwalle Forest Station, the **King Edward VII Big Tree** and the stunning **Prince Alfred Pass** (see page 220).

Opposite this turn-off, a visit to

NOETZIE
beckons. The minor road descends to a cliff-top parking area, about 5,5km away. Do not leave any valuables in the vehicle.

Noetzie means 'Black' after the dark colour of the river feeding the lagoon. The colouring is caused by humic acids leaching into the water from the indigenous forest floor.

Over 100 concrete steps must be negotiated before the lovely little beach and lagoon can be enjoyed. Swimming in the lagoon is safe, but the sea is dangerous because of a steep slope. The beach is dominated by the 'castles', which are private residences.

Return to the N2 and drive for a few kilometres to visit the

BRACKENHILL FALLS
which overlook rough terrain covered by old natural fynbos and indigenous forests. They start as a series of minor cascades and end in a sheer drop of great height into the gorge of the Noetzie River.

Back onto the national road, eucalyptus and pine plantations momentarily line the route. then the coastal road re-enters indigenous forest and passes the aptly named

GARDEN OF EDEN
which offers a short (1.5km), beautiful and easy walk under the dense canopy

of trees. It is a typical wet high forest with many examples of tall stinkwood, kalander (*Podocarpus falcatus),* witels (*Platylophus trifoliatus)* and many other species of the moister forest types. An 800-metre long trail has been established for wheelchairs.

An entrance fee is payable.

Note: Out of season, mountain bike enthusiasts must obtain permits for 'Harkerville Biking' at the Garden of Eden.

Harkerville Biking
Four routes have been developed through the indigenous forest, plantations and coastal fynbos. They are colour coded: yellow, blue, green and red. Each route is of a different distance but all four start and finish at the Garden of Eden, on the N2. Alternative access roads are available from the Kranshoek Road Gate, or the Kranshoek Picnic Site. During the season permits are available at the Kranshoek Road Gate.

The Harkerville Forest Reserve lies barely 2km further along the coastal road. To get there, turn onto the gravel road to the right and drive for about 11km; the road then ends at a clearing from where a path leads to the lovely **Kranshoek viewpoint** over the rocky coastline.

Kranshoek Coastal walks
A short route of 3.5km or a longer, circular route of 9.5km can be walked.

Kranshoek coast

The longer route is fairly tough. It demands a descent and ascent of 200 metres.

The route traverses interesting ecological systems which are explained on interpretation boards. You walk through high forest, cross sections of coastal fynbos and are rewarded with some breathtaking scenery of the cliff-coast. Swimming in natural rock pools or at the pebble beach near the mouth of the Crook River adds to the pleasure.

The serious hiker may be tempted by the challenging Harkerville Trail.

> ### Harkerville Coast Hiking Trail
> *The trail of 24 kilometres starts and ends at the Harkerville Forest Station. Booking for the Harkerville and Sinclair Huts (limited to 12 hikers) is essential.*
>
> *The trail is dangerous for the inexperienced. Risk is involved at certain places despite safeguards such as stepladders and chains. Persons suffering from fear of heights may experience problems at some of the steep rock faces.*
>
> *A part of the route traverses the Sinclair Nature Reserve, some 1282 ha in extent, which is not normally open to the public.*

Back to the N2, the national road weaves through forested countryside and meets with a minor gravel road to **Plettenberg Airport,** branching off to the right. Shortly afterwards, a very genuine encounter with elephants adds a thrill to the journey at the Knysna Elephant Park.

The park offers daily scheduled tours on the half hour from 0830 to 1630. Guests are transported to the elephants in open game viewing vehicles. Visitors have the opportunity to touch and help feed these magnificent animals. There are no fences or barriers to spoil your adventure.

Back from this encounter with the wild, the landscape assumes a different mantle. Forests momentarily give way to wide open meadows and fields.

Within a few kilometres, a sign points to **Wittedrif**, a little hamlet situated on the Bietou River. The road to Wittedrif, 8km away, is initially gravel but changes to a comfortable tarred surface. It joins the **R340** which carries on to the **Prince Alfred Pass** via **Uplands** on tar, then on gravel to **Avontuur** (see page 226).

Incidentally, the butchery at Wittedrif sells tasty boerewors (farmer's sausage) and excellent biltong (dried meat).

Just outside Plettenberg Bay the Kwanokuthula Informal Settlement spills

Sheep grazing

over the low hills almost onto the national road. Near the **New Horizons** suburb follow a route through the **Piesang Valley** (Banana) to **Plettenberg Bay**, instead of taking the later main turn-off into town.

The Piesang River

The picturesque Piesang Valley Road winds downhill in harmony with the eponymous stream towards the sea, past smallholdings, humble and luxurious homes, but sadly, also past increasing commercialisation. At the bottom of the valley, it joins the **Robberg Road**, which leads to the spectacular Robberg Nature Reserve and connects to the airport road.

For the moment continue towards the Beacon Isle Hotel which enjoys compelling views over the ocean, a gorgeous beach, the mountains and hills. In the grounds of the hotel stands a replica of the **beacon** erected by Governor Joachim van Plettenberg. The Governor's party came here on 6 November 1788 and recorded that '..arrived at a bay where the Keurbooms and Piesangs Rivers flow into the sea'.

Plettenberg Beacon

Return now to the traffic isle and continue along the Piesang Valley Road towards town. Bearing right it crosses the Piesang River, past **Central Beach** and curves uphill in a broad but quite steep bend towards the town centre. Look for **Meeding Street and turn right into it**. Follow it until you reach the

TIMBERSHED (1787)

which is a good point to introduce the history of Plettenberg Bay.

The town's recorded history stretches back to the 15th century when Portuguese explorers reached its shores and named it the 'Bay of Lagoons'.

Bartholomeu Dias and Vasco da Gama no doubt were the first to have set eyes on the bay. Plettenberg Bay, shielded by the enormous rocky promontory of Robberg, also known as Cape Seal, offered sailors shelter from storms, and rest before the onward journey.

Tsitsikamma mountains

The majestic Outeniqua/Tsitsikamma Mountain ranges as backdrop led later Portuguese seafarers to name the bay 'Formosa'. This name is still attached to one of the mountain peaks in the Tsitsikamma Mountains and the Anglican parish in town. Musical chairs were played with the name: it became known as 'Bay of Content', 'Piesang's River Bay', and 'Keurboom', before Governor van Plettenberg named it after himself. He erected a stone beacon on Beacon Isle (see above) as a mark of possession by the Dutch East India Company.

In 1630 the '**Sao Gonzales**', a Portuguese East-Indiaman, commanded by Fernao Lobo de Meneses, put into Formosa Bay to repair some leakages. The ship dropped anchor near the Piesang River mouth where, however, she was wrecked. The disaster claimed 133 lives. The survivors camped on the beach for several months while they built two small boats. One headed eastwards and eventually reached Mozambique and safety, the other set sail for Portugal. The boat reached Table Bay where the 'Sao Ignacio de Loyalo' picked up her sailors and headed home for Portugal. Tragically she was wrecked near Lisbon and all aboard perished.

Before they headed off, the sailors inscribed a simple message on a sandstone, 'Here was lost the Sao Gonzales, year 1630. They made two boats'. Apparently this stone was found buried in the sand in 1860 by somebody looking for relics of the ill-fated ship.

The Dutch appeared in the area towards the end of the 17th century. These were the cattle-traders, sent out by Governor Simon van der Stel to barter among the Attaqua and Outeniqua Khoi. Hunters followed, then the first farmers. Yet genuine growth only commenced with the exploitation of the forests as the demand for timber steadily grew.

Following van Plettenberg's visit, the VOC directors ordered the authorities at the Cape to investigate the possibility of developing the bay as a harbour. The investigative team set off in 1786. Their favourable impressions resulted in the establishment of a woodcutter's post to which Johann Friedrich Meeding was appointed as its first overseer.

Meeding hailed from Prussia in Germany and settled at the Cape in 1751. He was a well educated, reliable and honest man, devoted to his work. Within a short while, eight other officials, a wagonmaker and seven wood-cutters ,worked under him at the timber post. To store the loads of timber, Johann Jacob Jerling was tasked with the building of a store. Jerling, at the time, was the only free burgher living east of the Plettenberg Beacon.

Plettenberg Bay Timber Shed

The first shipment of timber left from Plettenberg in 1788 on the 'Meermin' commanded by François Duminy.

Meeding continued with his work until his death in 1813.

Plettenberg Bay remained an important port of call for the timber trade until 1817, by then the forests were nearly denuded from ruthless exploitation.

A building close to the timber shed ruins is the **Old Rectory** in Van Plettenberg Park, also once known as the 'Barracks'. Since at least 1777, it served different purposes, changing from barracks to a military store, to a home of a whalerman and until 1939, the home of Anglican clergy.

Many settlers left indelible marks on the region. One of these was William Newdigate, married to Caroline Duthie of Belvidere, the eldest daughter of Captain Thomas Henry and Caroline Duthie, and granddaughter of George Rex of Melkhout Kraal (see Route Seven).

William Newdigate had settled in the Cape in 1848 where he purchased three farms, Redbourne, Buccleugh and Forest Hall which lies beyond the Keurbooms River. On his Redbourne farm in the upper Piesang Valley (the turn off to this church on the Piesang Valley Road is marked) he built a small yellowwood church, **St. Andrew.** It was meant as a *temporary* place of worship for his family and to serve as a school. The church was consecrated by Bishop Robert Gray in 1855.

Meanwhile, Newdigate's father, unaware of the Bishop's visit, continued to raise funds in England for the building of a permanent church. The money collected provided the source with which the Anglican Church on the hill above Plettenberg Bay was built in 1880.

When Bishop Gray re-visited the region in 1869, (on horseback he had ridden from Uniondale over the newly built Prince Alfred's Pass to Plettenberg Bay) the district had been devastated by the Great Fire of the same year. Through an auction sale, he acquired a house with eighteen acres of land which was to accommodate the missionary J.C. Samuels and a small school.

St. Peter's Anglican Church – Parish of Formosa
The robust stone church of St. Peter stands on the site of a small schoolroom-cum-chapel that devoted Coloured parishioners of Plettenberg Bay had built. They toiled day and night to complete the humble building in time for the arrival of Bishop Robert Gray in 1856. It served the small community for 19 years before it was destroyed by a gale in 1875.

The building of a new church was entrusted to the contractor William Jones who also donated several items of furniture, including the lectern, prayer desk, reredos, altar railing and kneeling benches. In May 1881, the Rev. Edwin Gibbs, a member of the Building Committee and first incumbent for 21 years, was able to write to Cape Town, that 'the church here is so far completed that we used if for Divine Worship on Easter Sunday..'.

St. Peter's Anglican Church

The church was consecrated by the then Anglican Bishop (later Archbishop) William West Jones, on 14 August 1881.

A vast area, stretching from Harkerville in the west to Storm's River in the east is covered by the Chapelry of Formosa – a hundred years ago taxing travel indeed for the clergy.

In 1912, a Norwegian company leased Beacon Isle from its owners, the Anglican Church, to establish a whaling station. The small village had vigour and life breathed into it as for eight years whaling fleets came and went. When the company left, its buildings served for a number of years as a hotel for fishermen, until the striking modern hotel made its appearance.

Today's industry is tourism. Ten kilometres of grand beaches, between Beacon Isle and Robberg and Lookout Beach, provide ample opportunity for leisurely strolls and fairly safe swimming.

Beacon Isle Hotel

A walk through the town

To explore the town, follow an easy to walk circular town and coastal trail. The starting point is at the municipal nursery, but can be picked up anywhere along the marked route. It straddles at first the Piesang River bank, reaches the Central Beach from where it goes on to Hobie Beach and to the Lookout Rocks. From here it leads to the Lookout Viewpoint, then leaves the beach area and swings back towards the town. You reach Church Street (St. Peter's

Anglican Church), from where it continues towards Meeding Street (timber shed) and then winds its way back towards the starting point.

Once the historical sites have been visited, spend some time exploring the magnificent

ROBBERG NATURE RESERVE

Situated a mere 8km south-east of the town, the Nature Reserve extends over 175 hectare. Signposting to it is not brilliant. From the centre of town take the Piesang Valley Road towards the traffic circle near the Beacon Isle Hotel. Bear left and follow the airport road. **Watch out for a sudden left turn**.

Robberg

The Robberg Nature Reserve is open daily from 07:00 to 17:00 and until 20:00 in December/January. An entrance fee is payable. It welcomes hikers, sunworshippers, archeologists, birders and fishermen. Fishing (with permit, available from post offices) is restricted to rock and surf angling inside the Marine Protected Area which extends one nautical mile (1,852km) seawards around the entire Reserve. Its name means 'Seal Mountain'.

Robberg's vegetation is characterised by coastal fynbos and thicket, beloved by the over 100 species of birds that have been recorded.

The promontory's rocks go back to the early Cretaceous period, (130 to 110 million years ago), and the break-up of Gondwanaland, that prehistoric supercontinent which split up about 120 million years ago into today's South America, Africa, India, Australia and Antarctica. The underlying rock is hard Table Mountain sandstone on to which more recent layers have been deposited, including conglomerate rock of rounded pebbles held in a sandstone mould which has become quartzitic through the deposition of silica.

Imagine a time when this rocky peninsula was home to Middle and Later Stone Age people, a good 120 000 years ago, when the sea level had dropped. Several caves on the peninsula bear testimony to their presence.

At **Nelson Bay Cave** an interpretation board tells their story.
Wind has played its part in shaping the 4km-long Robberg: the southern

slope is gradual, the northern shore boasts almost sheer cliffs.

View across Robberg towards Plettenberg Bay

Walking Robberg

There is a choice of three circular routes from very easy to difficult. The round trip via The Point takes four hours (11km) and should not be attempted by hikers suffering from serious fear of heights. It is dangerous at high tide. It is also not recommended for young children. Take water, sun protection and good walking shoes.

The two shorter walks lead via comfortable and safe paths to either The Gap (2.1km) or down a massive snow white drift sand dune towards the beach at Die Eiland/The Island (5.5km).

From the car park (Braai facilities, toilets) and after having studied the informative museum kiosk, follow the path marked 'The Gap'. and 'The Point', to the left of the field museum.

The stony path drops gently through coastal fynbos and then continues almost level through the thicket above the cliffs on the northern side of Robberg. Interesting stone and rock formations can be observed , whilst across the vast bay, Plettenberg Bay stretches along the endless beach. At The Gap, a safe boardwalk leads to a cosy little beach on the southern side of the promontory. You can now retrace the walk to the starting point, or continue towards Die Eiland and The Point.

Die Eiland/Island at Robberg

Then the path climbs the steep, rocky slope. It is not difficult as the rocks provide a good hold and cement steps have ben built, but exercise care.

Way below, hundreds of Cape Fur seals frolick in the water, bellowing and barking. They flock to the rocks between Kanonkoeëlgat and Grasnek. Further out to sea, keep your eyes open for dolphins and whales, particular-

---

The Cape Fur Seal(Arctocephalus pusillus)

 seal is a member of the family Otariidae or 'eared' seals.It is endemic to the south western shore of southern Africa. 25 breeding and 9 non-breeding colonies are known along the 3000km of shoreline. 19 breeding colonies are situated on small, rocky near-shore islands and 6 on the mainland. Close to 75% of the pups are born in the mainland colonies.

Dutch sealers began to hunt the seals from the early 17th century, later joined by French, British and American hunters who killed for the skins, meat and oil. In all likelihood, 23 island colonies became extinct as a result of uncontrolled hunting. Since 1973, the seals are protected by the Seals and Seabirds Protection Act.

This playful, intelligent animal possesses exceptional hearing under, as well as above water. They close their nostrils and eyes when diving which forces them regularly to the surface in order to breathe. Older animals can stay under water for about 30 minutes.

The average life expectancy is 20 years. The female, which matures faster than the male, bears the first young at the age of four. The male reaches sexual maturity only between the ages of 8 and 12 years. During the mating season, the male abstains from food and relies solely on fat reserves. The pups are born late November, early December. At six weeks, the pup makes its first attempt at swimming, but ventures out alone only at the age of about 5 or 6 months.

ly the humpback and bottlenose dolphins which make frequent appearances. The Bryde's whale is attracted to Plettenberg Bay waters all year round. Plettenberg Bay was one of the 16 shore-based whaling stations in the country. All whaling was outlawed in 1980.

On top of the ridge (about 89m high), the path leads past montane fynbos which has adapted to the extremely harsh coastal conditions. Then it emerges on an enormous sandbelt that cuts the peninsula in half. The Witsand sand dune is one of seven climbing-falling dunes on the Cape coast. The Island traps the sand driven ashore from the southwest wind and by currents. Dry sand is blown upwards to a height of about 80 metres before it slides into Plettenberg Bay. To the north (towards Plettenberg Bay), the sand is unstable and walking on to it is extremely dangerous. Please keep clear, as is indicated by a wind-battered signboard. Turning downhill through the soft, sandy gully you reach **Die Eiland/The Island**.

The sanddunes at The Gap

Submerged rocks surround The Island, offering food and shelter to reef fish. A badly neglected boardwalk clambers up and across, – take care.

The beach looks enticing but the rip currents make swimming dangerous.

If you decided to descend to the Island, return via the marked path along the southern slopes of Robberg to the starting point.

Beyond the drift sand, the path continues to **The Point**. You encounter occasional sheer drops and care should be exercised, particularly on a windy day. The path descends to the rocks at The Point where huts, belonging to the

Angling Club, surprise the unsuspecting walker. At The Point, terns, gannets and cormorants thrive on the riches of the Agulhas Bank, feeding mainly on pilchards and anchovy.

Higher on the hill stands **The Cape Seal Lighthouse,** 146m above sea level. This is the highest navigational light on the South African coast. Its rotating solar-powered beam has a range of about 27km. It was built in 1950.

Beyond the hut, the walk turns into a magic experience. Depending on the tides, it meanders across massive rock platforms, past lichen coloured boulders and dark rock pools – whilst all the time the sea is pounding the coast, sending plumes of white foam to the shore.

Rock pools

Then the route leaves this rocky paradise and ascends to the edge of a sandstone cliff. Shortly beyond this point, the path reaches an intimidating spot: unless it is low tide when you simply continue walking at the foot of a large rock, you have to negotiate a narrow ledge on a vertical rock face above the sea. A chain will help you get across. Recently a path has been established above the rocks that avoids the chains.

Once beyond this spot, the walk gets easy on the nerves and feet. Meandering along the shoreline, rock pools invite you for a swim and soon you reach the Island. As mentioned earlier, swimming is dangerous because of rip tides, (which is a strong seaward moving current caused when waves are parallel to the shore) but linger long enough to explore the Island. Take care with the rickety steps leading to it.

Take off your shoes and let soft sand trickle between the toes as you walk westwards. Perhaps plough snails digging into beached jellyfish entertain you for a while, or you are fortunate to find a fragile nautilus or pansy shell.

At the end of the beach, the path leads across the rocky outcrop. It leads

below Guanogat, a large overhang cave, and is clearly marked. But if you think it is all plain level walking, Robberg holds a little surprise in store: the last short section from The Gap leads steeply uphill onto the south-facing cliffs. A well placed bench allows a short rest on the plateau, from where you enjoy a leisurely stroll back to the car park.

Plough shells

The Paper Nautilus (Argonauta argo)

This beautiful shell is found between April and August, at the end of the spawning season. Unfortunately it rarely survives the hammering of the sea to be washed up undamaged.

The female nautilus has eight arms, two of which are flattened. These she uses to build and hold the shell in which she seems to spend her entire life. The protective shell helps with flotation and serves as a brood chamber. The male has no shell and is only one-twentieth of her size. It is believed that the female dies after spawning, and the male after mating when his sperm sac has broken to fertilize the eggs.

Nautilus Shell

Just beyond the parking area, a signboard points to the site where the Portuguese ship, 'Sao Gonzales' went down. From here it is back to town.

No visit to Plettenberg Bay is complete without knocking on the doors of **Father Bannert's** home. His house, situated above the Main Street, on the corner of Church and High Streets hides a most unusual treasure:
FLOWER PICTURES
Father Bannert, a retired priest of the town's Roman Catholic Church , glad-

ly welcomes visitors to admire his amazing wildflower collages. He collected thousands upon thousands of flowers in the area, dried and painstakingly assembled them with pins into powerful religious 'paintings'.

The Last Supper

'Ave Maria'

The Risen Christ

From Plettenberg Bay town join the N2 either via Marine Drive, or follow Beacon Way which is the continuation of Main Street till you meet the coastal road. The signposts direct you either to Knysna (left) or Humansdorp (right). The coastal road N2 continues north-easterly.

The Tsitsikamma Mountains loom on the horizon, hills roll towards the Bitou

River. The lush, natural surroundings contrast sharply with the nearby polo field. Here too, the signpost **R340/ 'Uniondale/Wittedrif'** steers drivers westerly, off the national road. The first few kilometres via Wittedrif are tarred until Uplands, then it becomes gravel and joins the Prince Alfred Pass (see page 220) near Kruisvallei.

Carry on straight. After bridging the Bitou, the N2 reaches the magnificent Keurbooms River, named after a tree species, *Virgilia divaricata*. This pretty, fast growing, evergreen tree bathes the countryside in pale pink when in bloom (October to December). Its pea-like flowers have a very sweet scent.

Slow down to savour the magnificence of the countryside. Look up-river, into the dreamy, mysterious river gorge which can be explored by canoe.

The Aventura Campsite is an ideal starting point for exploring the river and its stunning estuary, perfect for all watersports. Once across the the bridge, a tarred road leads to

Keurbooms River

KEURBOOMSSTRAND
where rocky outcrops interrupt the lovely sandy beach, popular with surfers, whilst anglers cast their lines from the rocks.

From here return to the national road which now finds its way through the splendid **Tsitsikamma Forests.**

In the language of the Khoi people, Tsitsikamma means 'very wet'. Dense natural forest and deeply cut gorges characterise the narrow coastal plateau, which seemed impenetrable, even to early European travellers.

In the west, the Tsitsikamma Mountains are bordered by the Salt River near Knysna, and in the east they stretch as far as the Kareedouw turn-off, covering a distance of about 80km. The mountains climb to over 1700 metres. The coastal plateau at their feet ranges between 200 and 300 metres in height and drops abruptly to the sea. Natural forest, patches of fynbos and exotic plantations live side by side. The annual rainfall of 1 100 and 1 250mm ensures lush surroundings. Generally the climate is mild, where the soft, soaking rain tends to fall at night.

Tsitsikamma stillness

The botanist Thunberg describes the area in 1772 as'..a land abounding in grass, wood and buffaloes. Beyond the river lay the dense forest of what is now called the Tsitzikama'. Three years later, the Swedish scientist Sparrman almost echoes the impressions. He 'saw mountain sides ..covered with a pink mist of sweetsmelling Keurboomsblossom..the lion no longer liver there permanently..'

Although vast tracts of vegetation were destroyed by the horrendous fire in 1869, the same fire laid bare a possible route from Plettenberg Bay towards Humansdorp, some 160km away. Thomas Bain's report favoured the construction of this coastal road which was completed in 1884.

Not far from Keurboomsriver, one passes **Whiskey Creek.** Then, 17km later, **The Crags.** Slow down, to visit

Monkeyland
a primate sanctuary, where guests are taken on safaris to meet many different species of monkeys as well as a large variety of forest birds.
To reach it, take the **Kurland Village/Safari** turn-off and follow the

Monkeyland signs for about 2km. The sanctuary is open daily from 0800 to 1800.

Vervet Monkeys

Return from this noisy encounter to the national road and prepare to decide between travelling along the modern highway, or taking a relaxed journey through attractive forest and wild-flower land, along the R102.

The R102 here is known as the Groot River's Pass. It snakes in sharp bends through the de Vasselot Nature Reserve and descends into a delightful world of indigenous forest which escaped the great fire unscathed, particularly in the deep gorges of the Groot, Bloukrans and Storms Rivers.

Ferns

The Seven Weeks fern (Rumohra adiantiformis) is found in forests throughout the country.

It has been harvested from the forests of the Southern Cape and Tsitsikamma since 1982. Their fronds are used in flower arrangements because of their long cut-life and many are exported to European flower markets.

Declining yields in recent years, coupled to other market factors such as oversupply of cultivated ferns, led to diminishing interest in harvesting ferns on State Forest land. At present no ferns are being harvested.

Giant yellowwood tree..

Giant yellowwood trees amidst ferns, and even wild bananas line the route which finally ends in the popular resort of

NATURE'S VALLEY
once a small, isolated holiday village, today bursting at its seams with houses big and small. The village is on the floodplain to the west of the magnificent Groot River Lagoon.

Nature's Valley/Groot River mouth

A vast tract of land (2 561ha) around Nature's Valley, was incorporated in 1987 into the Tsitsikamma Coastal National Park. The land includes the forested valleys of the Groot River, the forests of the Salt River to the west, a large part of the coastal plateau and coastline.

The magnificent beach is the leisure seeker's heaven, the wide river mouth a wonderful playground for young and old, and the valley a walker's paradise.

Permits for a number of walks are obtainable at the De Vasselot Campsite. This you find to the right of R102/Groot River Pass just past the main turn-off to Nature's Valley.

The well known Tsitsikamma Trail starts from the de Vasselot Campsite. A trail of several days which reveals the splendour of the forests, the challenge of steep hills and, sometimes, the power of the rivers.

The Otter Trail, (see page 215) probably the most popular coastal trail in the area, ends at Nature's Valley.

The Groot River Pass winds its way out of Nature's Valley first across a low bridge spanning the chocolate-coloured river water, a wonderful picnic place. Then, in sharp bends it twists through the Bloukrans Forest and to the top of the plateau from where, about six kilometres later, it descends into the Bloukrans Pass route, (past Cold Stream) before it ultimately joins the high-way near the Elandsbos River. Both passes drop by about 185m in altitudes over short distances – it gives you some idea of the steepness of these stunning routes. No lorries or large buses are permitted which adds to the quiet enjoyment of the journey. The top of the Bloukrans Pass is about 50km away from Plettenberg Bay.

If travelling time is short, continue on the Tsitsikamma Toll Road/N2 which bridges the deep gorges cut by the Bobbejans, Bloukrans and Storms Rivers.

The Salt River is first crossed, followed soon afterwards by the Bobbejaans River, about 25km outside Plettenberg Bay. The coastal plain opens up and gentle mountain slopes to the north roll towards the coast. The Groot River bridge now spans the river coursing, 172 metres below, towards the sea. The coastal road has now entered the 'Blaukrans Forest' area and reaches the turn-off for **Nature's Valley/Bloukrans**. This is also the point where the free enjoyment of nature's treasure chest comes to an abrupt stop: the toll gates lie ahead: presently the fee is R9.50 per small car, up to R82 for buses and trucks. Initially the toll was introduced to fund the construction of the striking bridges spanning the Bobbejaans, Groot and Bloukrans Rivers.

Bloukrans Bridge

The massive bridges, visible from the old R102, were constructed between 1980 and 1984 by Murray & Roberts and Concor Construction. The length of the toll road is 27km – it shortens the old scenic route of the Bloukrans and Groot Rivier Passes by only 9km – but of course, leaves out the ups and downs, the twists and bends!

The national road speeds towards the Bloukrans Bridge (Blue Ridge). A stop is an absolute must. At the turn-off to view the bridge, the San Village welcomes the traveller for a little shopping and browsing about. At the viewpoint itself, an interesting display explains the construction of the bridges, true engineering masterpieces. A few adrenaline seekers make their way to a walkway along the side of the bridge: bridge walking has become popular and, unbelievable, bungy jumping from Africa's highest bridge.

Bloukrans Bungy Jumping – *216 metres*
The world's highest Bungy jump. Age restriction: 14 years

Bobbejaans Bridge:
length: *286m - arch span:165m - above river: 170m*

Groot River Bridge:
length: *301m - arch span:189m - above river:172m*

Bloukrans Bridge
length: *451m - arch span:272m - above river:216m*

The Bloukrans Bridge is the largest concrete bridge in Africa, the 4th largest in world.
Building of the bridges started with simultaneous construction from either side of the gorges that they span.
The single arches of all three bridges were constructed in stages by means of the cantilever system using temporary suspension and tie-back cables.

With the crossing of the Bloukrans Bridge, the **Eastern Cape** welcomes us.

Nature's splendour continues to spoil the eye on the coastal terrace. The road leads through huge plantations, travels across two more rivers, the Lottering and Elandsbos, and passes a turn-off to **Coldstream.** Once past the **Boskor Sawmills,** the Kleinbos (Little Bush) River cuts its way through the mountains towards the sea. Forestry activities remain evident until a few kilometres further east, beyond the Witteklip River (White Stone), a sign points to **Storms River Village/Blackwater Tubing.**

Now look for the sudden turn-off south to the TSISTSIKAMMA NATIONAL COASTAL PARK, controlled by SA National Parks.

Drive the approximate 6km past forests and plantations to the entrance gate – a fee is payable - and then continue downhill towards the spectacular, rocky **Storm's River Mouth,** one of the country's most popular holiday resorts.

The Storm's River Mouth is roughly the middle of the Tsitsikamma National Park, a narrow strip of land and sea stretching from the Groot River in the west at Nature's Valley, and another Groot River at Oubos Rand, in the east.

The river has cut a dark, narrow gorge through the high cliffs before it joins the turbulent sea. Huge waves wash incessantly over enormous rocks, scattering seagull and sending plumes of spray into the sky.

Find your way past the holiday cottages towards the restaurant which stands on the site of one of the many strandloper middens of the coast.

From the restaurant, a boardwalk, first across the small beach at the river mouth, straggles through lush indigenous forest, past a cove once used by strandlopers, towards the **suspension bridge** spanning the river. The walk across is a little shaky but safe.

The magical sea and forest area can be explored underwater on the **snorkel route, tubing** down the river, and on foot. Numerous walks of varying length and grades of difficulty have been laid out, such as the 'Blue Duiker' and 'Lourie' trails. The SA National Parks office and Museum will supply you with brochures and information.

Amongst all the walks in the park, the most popular is the **Otter Trail**. The first part is known as the 'Waterfall Route' which may be walked without a permit by all visitors to the park. Beyond that point, only hikers with a permit, which must be booked at least one year in advance, with South African National Parks, can proceed.

The trail of about 45km with four overnight stops, demands of its participants experience, a clear head for heights and loads of energy. As it ends at Nature's Valley (see above), make sure you have a second vehicle waiting for the return journey.

At each overnight stop there are two hiking huts, equipped with three mattressed bunk beds sleeping six, and a rustic table on which the daily meals can be prepared. Fireplaces and wood are mostly available, watertanks and loos, some even with a 'view' provide the basic comfort for the hiker.

Walking the Otter Trail

Otters...

Day One leads to Ngubu Hut, 2.5 hours walking away. Follow the yellow markers through coastal forest and over massive boulders. Within an hour, a waterfall tumbles powerfully down the cliffs into a dark, cold pool on the edge of the sea.

The waterfall

From here, the path continues in through coastal forest to the huts.

From Ngubu Hut, on **Day Two,** the trail finds the next overnight huts after about 4hours walking. The distance between the huts is 7.9km. Take your time to enjoy the scenery!

Within an hour, 'Skilderkrans', the 'Painter's Rock' is reached. Just beyond, the path emerges near a romantic lily pond. then the rocky Kleinbos River rushes by. This picturesque river can be hazardous to cross.

The next stopover en route could be nearby Bloubaai. The path to it branches off from the main trail. It is a beautiful but dangerous beach because of the backwash. Beware, its a steep way there and back..

After Bloubaai, another hill needs to be conquered before Scott Hut is reached. Here two nearby rivers are ideal for that quiet evening on the river bank, washing (with bio-degradable soap) or filling the water flasks. With luck, otters may frolic about..

the lily pond...

Day Three leads to Oakhurst Hut about 7.2km away.

The trail leads across the Geelhoutbos River. Today, the path clings mainly to the sea. Dolphins may be spotted skipping happily through the waves.

Otter Trail coastline

Soon you cross the Elandsbos River, a lovely resting spot. Beyond the river, the one and only steep hill surprises towards the end of the trail. A toothlike rock juts out from the mountain top to where you are heading. But once there, the path turns into a pleasant traverse through coastal fynbos, followed by a steep descent towards the majestic Lottering River.

While away some time on the sandy river banks-do not rush it, as Oakhurst Hut lies on top of the hill. Swimming at the hut is not possible, other than plung-ing in some of the natural small rock pools. You are unlikely to want to walk downhill to the riverbanks again!

Day Four to Andre Hut covers a distance of 13.2km. Allow about 7 hours. On this day the Bloukrans River is crossed. Safe crossing is at low tide – do not risk it at high tide. Consult the tide timetable as it might involve a midnight departure or very early departure with torches!

After Oakhurst, the path rises sharply and then turns into a relatively easy walk to the Witels River. The easy walking ends when you leave the forest area and trail along a rocky part of the coast. Occasional rock clambering is involved. Just before you enter the last stretch of forest look out for a magic pool to the left of the path. Look carefully for it, as the pool is not visible from the main trail which then follows a good hour through the forest towards the Bloukrans River. Below, the ocean murmurs or bellows, fluorescent colours beam up as you walk towards the riverbed.

on the way to Bloukrans River

Bloukrans River mouth

Hopefully you reach the river mouth at low tide - you may be lucky and only have ankle deep water – but follow the safest route across. The rocks on the other side are razor sharp. Once the boots are on again, walk another two hours to Andre Hut on the aptly named Klip River (Stone River). On the way, one crosses three quite stony beaches, conquers one more steep hill and traverses staggeringly beautiful fynbos.

Day Five, the last day, is a walk of about 2.5 hours to Nature's Valley.
The steep path out of the riverbed does eventually level out. Easy and pleasant walking follows, except near the halfway mark where another descent and ascent have to be negotiated.

Linger a while on the hill overlooking beautiful Nature's Valley and take care with the descent on to the sandy beach to the Groot River mouth and car.

If the Otter Trail sound too demanding, try the **DOLPHIN TRAIL,** a hike in luxury along the Tsitsikamma coast, led by trained field guides, and where your rucksacks are transported for you.

Some perhaps would like to swing Tarzan-like through the forest canopy with the Tsitsikamma Canopy Tours?

Reluctantly one leaves the stunning coast behind to continue the journey east. Return to the national road. A wonder of the forest world hides a mere kilometre away, the

BIG TREE
Park the vehicle, pay the entrance fee and follow a comfortable boardwalk (approx. 1km) through an indigenous moist forest where giant tree ferns also clamour for some attention.

Giant tree ferns

Many trees are marked for identification whilst information boards tell the story of the yellow- and stinkwood trees. The return walk is along the gravel road and not the boardwalk.

Of the 30 or more species of indigenous trees in this forest, the Outeniqua Yellowwood is probably the best known. It can grow to a height in excess of 50m and live for hundreds of years. This giant, the object of the walk, is 36.6m high, spreads its crown over 32.9m and is definitely over 800 years old.

The boardwalk continues to a tree of similar dimensions which was felled, almost like a match, a few years ago in a major storm. From an observation platform one can study the changing forest canopy and the huge opening created when this massive tree crashed to the ground.

the fallen giant...

Near the platform, the **Ratel Walk** begins, a pleasant easy meander through the forest.

Return to the car and head easterly. The national road narrows considerably which, however does not slow the traffic. Civilisation lies ahead: the Petroport Garage. But its not only filling up, shopping and eating time, but also time to walk the

STORMS RIVER BRIDGE

The Storm's River cuts its way deep below through sandstone cliffs. The bridge is 191m long and its single span rises 130m above the riverbed. It was designed by Ricardo Morandi of Rome and built like two giant drawbridges made of concrete. At first a platform was constructed on either side of the gorge. The two halves of the bridge, in vertical form, were then erected on hinges and, on completion, lowered, to connect. Anxious moments for the engineers indeed. But they need not have worried, the halves met perfectly in the centre. The bridge was opened to traffic in 1956 after 2.5 years of construction.

The walking can be daunting, but there are **Viewpoints** near the restaurant.

Storm's River Bridge

The onward journey towards Port Elizabeth is briefly described in Route Ten.

ROUTE NINE

KNYSNA – UNIONDALE - LONGKLOOF/N2
via Prince Alfred Pass
and
KNYSNA – TO OUDTSHOORN
via Prince Alfred Pass

Leave Knysna in an easterly direction, (towards Port Elizabeth). Just outside the town, a signpost points, left, to '**Uniondale'/R339**.

The lively drive through Khayelethu township spilling over the hills on to the national road is an experience in itself. In sharp contrast to the luxury homes, estates, golf courses and elegant shopping centres so far seen in Knysna, these sprawling suburbs confront us with realities not mentioned in tourist brochures. Brave attempts to live an orderly life in extreme poverty, barefoot children splashing with abandon in some muddy pools, cows, dogs and goats roaming along the path, washing hanging on doors, fruit drying on rooftops, broken carparts abandoned in ditches, men and women hanging around doing nothing – this too is the Garden Route.

The phenomenal mountain pass that transports you towards the Langkloof is known as the

Prince Alfred Pass
It is a single lane pass, unsuitable for large vehicle or cars towing caravans. It should be avoided in wet conditions.

Again, it was Thomas Bain who built this daunting mountain His father,

Prince Alfred Pass

Andrew, had carried out preparatory survey work in 1856. He was convinced that a 70km long road through the dense forest to a height of over 900 metres over the mountains to Avontuur was feasible. The daring scheme was only approved five years later, and his son started construction. Four torturous years of cutting through seemingly impenetrable forests followed. Rock had to be blasted, streams crossed and dry-stone retaining walls had to be built on steep slopes. At last, the sensational pass had conquered all its obstacles. Soon after its completion, Prince Alfred, Queen Victoria's second son, the Duke of Edinburgh, visited Knysna and was accompanied by Bain on an elephant hunt led by members of the Rex family. The pass was named in honour of the prince.

The first few kilometres towards **Diepwalle Forest Station** are tarred. The total distance to the Forest Station turn-off is just over 16km. Ignore any roads veering off to the left.

On the way another big tree stands proud in the forest, the **King Edward VII Tree** one of Knysna's well-loved yellowwood forest giants, named after the British monarch who succeeded Queen Victoria. The tree grows to a height of 39 metres, its crown spreads over 24 metres. It is over 600 years old.

'Kom se Pad' lures cyclists and walkers on the **Elephant Trails** which lead through beautiful natural woodland – indeed this is the home of the elusive Knysna elephant. Who knows, you may have your path blocked by a looming grey shadow, or stumble over some dropping as you continue north?

The pass winds relentlessly uphill – a glance back reveals occasionally the coastal plateau, whilst the hills are covered with protea.

Protea scoly mocephala

Protea lepidocarpodendron

Protea nitida

Protea nerifolia

View from Spitskop

Sharp twists over the next seven to eight kilometres demand the driver's concentration. Then a turn-off to the **Spitskop Viewpoint,** a short,pot-holed track to the summit at 933m. Maybe you should leave your car behind and walk?

Return to the R339 and visit the near-by **Valley of Ferns/Dal van Varings.** where giant ferns tower over the visitor who walks in the shade of the *Cyathea capensis* ferns, a protected species. It favours the banks of forest streams and grows happily under the canopy of moist forests. The ferns in this valley have grown to heights of 3 – 6 metres.

A wide valley looks up to the pass which swings past forestry houses at 'Sonderskuit'. Seven kilometres beyond the Valley of Ferns, a fork is reached at Kruisvallei: here the **R340,** which goes to Plettenberg Bay/N2 (see page…), joins the Prince Alfred Pass.

Memorial Plaque to T.C. Bain

Continue northwards and reach after about 6km the **Diep River Picnic** site, where a memorial plaque on the 150th anniversary of Thomas Bain was laid by the Outeniquea Naturalist and Historical Society.

A strange signpost comes up to the left: **N9 to George.** This gravel road is unmarked on the maps, but does exist. At the nearby **De Vlug** take a break in the tea garden, or visit the **Outeniqua Trout Lodge**, situated in the lush valley below.

Along the next few kilometres, rustic houses, seemingly forgotten by time, peep up from underneath the trees, a narrow bridge and drift are crossed.

The road narrows but continues its northerly direction in sharp bends and turns. About 14.5km after De Vlug, the top of the pass is reached at **Avontuur on the R62.** You have travelled about 85 km since leaving Knysna and have arrived at crossroads in your journey!

Alfred Pass bridge

If you wish to visit **Oudtshoorn,** you can follow the clearly signposted route along the **R62** in a westerly direction for 12km when it will join the **N9.** Here **turn left onto the N9.** After about 85km it meets the **N12.** Take this road in a northerly direction to Oudtshoorn. (distance approx. 135km)

However, the journey described will take you from Avontuur via Uniondale, Barandas, Diepkloof and De Rust to Oudtshoorn.

For continuation to the Langkloof turn to page 226.

Having emerged from the Prince Alfred Pass at Avontuur, a new world opens up. To the south lie the mighty Outeniqua and Tsitsikamma Mountains, to the north appear the Kammanassie Mountains. In between lies comfortably enclosed the western edge of the Langkloof valley.

Your travels continue north to **Uniondale,** 13km away, along the R339. The Kammanassie River, meaning 'Washing Water' is crossed. Then the road narrows as it snakes downhill through mountain fynbos and the rocky, extraordinary 'Uniondale Poort,' characterised by bright lichen coloured rock formations. When in season, the Poort (Gate) is ablaze with aloes. Occasionally one glances into small green valleys, and after about 6km, look out for an old pass route straddling a hill. Uniondale welcomes the traveller who might feel lost with huge white letters sprawled out on the hills.

Uniondale landscape

A quarrel erupted between two farmers in the 1850s who both owned portions of the farm Rietvallei. The two townships they laid out adjoined each other which led to the disagreement which was settled by the Dutch Reformed Church. To separate the townships a church was built in the centre of the disputed area and the townships, now united, were named *Uniondale* which achieved municipal status in 1884. The impressive rock church watches over the tranquil town of modest homes, many in the attractive Victorian style.

The dispute settled, Uniondale lived a quiet life until the ostrich feather boom propelled it into action and prosperity. Cattle, sheep and goat farming added to the wealth, as did furniture manufacture and wagon building.

The quiet town is set amidst dry surrounding, but enjoys the benefit of a perennial stream. A restored water-mill, built in 1852 by James Stewart, recalls the past, as does a small fort built by the British during the Anglo Boer War.

Outside Uniondale, the road winds uphill. Travel first the N9 in the direction of **Willowmore**, but then branch off onto the R339 to **De Rust**. To the east stretch the Kouga, to the west the Kammanassie mountains.

Traversing a high plateau, the Swartberg Mountain looms darkly to the north. Low growing shrubland spreads to either side of the road, dotted here and there by green fields. Twenty kilometres away from Uniondale, a T-junction marks a turn-off to the right for Willowmore – continue to **De Rust/R341/Barandas/Oudtshoorn.**

Heading due west now, the road passes through attractive countryside, marked by aloes, acacia thorn trees, colourful pink klapperbos and low hills. One wonders what a train journey through this spectacular mountain world would have been like – here and there the railway line appears. Road signs point to various stations, such as Snyberg in the foothills of the Swartberg. On the way to the next small settlement, **Rooiriver**, the road undulates through clay-rich, low hillside country. Flat topped hills greet the traveller, and a remarkable red glowing sandstone formation near the Diepkloof hamlet, as the road begins to quietly descend towards De Rust, 18km away. Shortly you cross the Olifants River, embellished by more red sandstone formations, and the railway line. A minor track leads to Vlakteplaas, whilst the R341 weaves its way through the foothills of the Swartberg towards De Rust. What a charming picture the small town makes, sitting prettily on the hills above a small valley. For the story of De Rust, turn to page 146.

From De Rust, the main tarmac road N12 continues to Oudtshoorn, 35km away.The road follows the valley of the Olifants River, past stunning red hills, ostrich farms and verdant fields.

An alternative, marked on the official maps, branches off the N12 just outside De Rust, marked 'Oude Muragie'. This 35km stretch leads to the Raubenheimer Dam and emerges on the main road to the Cango Caves. **Though beautiful, it should definitely not be undertaken in wet, rainy conditions.**

Longkloof valley

The journey on the R62 from Avontuur through the Langkloof

The distance from Avontuur to the N2 is 172km.

The fertile Langkloof, (Long Kloof), wedged between the Kouga and towering Baviaanskloof Mountains to the north, and the Tsitsikamma Mountain to the south, is a major fruit producing area in Southern Africa. The climate favours in particular the cultivation of apples, pears, peaches and apricots.

The valley's original inhabitants were the nomadic hunter-gatherers, the San, and the pastoralist Khoikhoi. Various 'bushman' paintings in rock shelters have been discovered.

You guessed correctly: Izak Schrijver was the first European to penetrate into this valley in 1689. Though hunters followed him, the Long Kloof waited until the 1740s before white settler farmers arrived. By 1773 a handful of homesteads dotted the valley. One of these pioneers, Coenraad de Buys, was a particularly colourful character, declared an outlaw by the authorities because of his wild and polygamous lifestyle. He had owned the De Opkomst farm near Kareedouw. He found his way to the far away North where he founded a tribe of his own, the 'Buys people', on the southern slopes of the Soutpansberg.

In the late 18th, early 19th century, during the early frontier wars in the Eastern Cape, Xhosas invaded the isolated valley, leaving behind a trail of fear and fighting.

The entire valley is traversed by a narrow-gauge railway line, from Avontuur to Port Elizabeth. This is the popular 'Apple Express', frantically busy in the fruit-picking season. It is essentially a goods train, but railway enthusiasts can enjoy a thrilling ride from Port Elizabeth to Loerie.

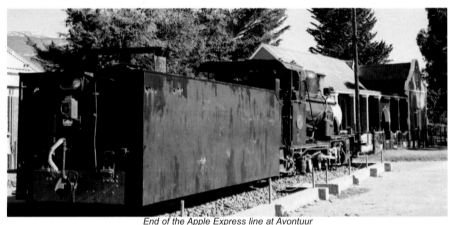

End of the Apple Express line at Avontuur

Avontuur itself is a collection of modest homes, framed on either side by the lower slopes of the Kouga and Tsitsikamma ranges. Not far away the Siesta railway siding is passed, the Driehocks and Klein Rivers crossed, and then the hamlet of **Haarlem** is reached. Quite quaintly, the village stretches out on low hills, surrounded by fruit orchards and dominated by a tall church.

Beyond Haarlem, fruit orchards give way for a short distance to drier Karoo-type vegetation. The road crosses the railway line near **Ongelegen**, and a stream of the same name, finds a turn-off to **Bo-Kouga,** crosses the railway line again and arrives at the picturesque village of **Misgund**. The name means 'Envied'.

From here the road see-saws a little, past the 'Infruitec Experimental farm'. The railway now runs to the north of the road and meets up with you again at

Louterwater (Clear Water), marked by light industrial activities. Packing sheds line the twisting route which has come to an intensely farmed stretch of the Longkloof. The next village, perched on a hill is, **Krakeel**. Houses dot the fertile valley below, overlooked by the magnificent Tsitsikamma Mountain. The Onder-Kouga turn-off is passed and shortly afterwards, you have arrived in **Joubertina,** the principal town of the Long Kloof.

Joubertina, which gives the impression of a hill-billy town, is named after the Rev. W. Joubert, a pastor from Uniondale. In 1907, the Dutch Reformed Church purchased

Road meets railway

land from the Kritzinger family to establish a church centre. Conditional to the land transfer was a prohibition on the sale of liquor, as Kritzinger was a teetotaller. Despite the restriction the village, set in beautiful mountainous surroundings, developed rapidly and became a municipality by 1971.

Joubertina NG Church

Longkloof valley

Shopping in Joubertina

Apple Express station...

For more than 40km, the railway accompanies the road towards the next major town, which is **Kareedouw** (Pass of the Karee tree). Even the Kouga River, though invisible, runs the same course as it streams downhill from its source in the Kouga Mountains. Slowly also, the Tsitsikamma Mountains show their floral wealth: leucadendron, a protea species, shine brightly on the slopes. At Kareedouw either take the R402 to link up with the N2 or continue an the R62 towards Jeffreys Bay on the coast and from there regain the national road.

ROUTE TEN

STORM'S RIVER /N2 TO PORT ELIZABETH

The total distance is about 150km without deviations.

This route falls outside the purposes of this book which explores the Overberg, Little Karoo and Garden Route. But as so many travellers continue their journey east, the route to Port Elizabeth is briefly described.

Beyond Storm's River Bridge, the national road, for some distance, resembles a minor country road. A very narrow bridge spans another mountain stream, about 69km from Plettenberg Bay, and ahead rises the formidable silhouette of Formosa Peak. Between the Tsitsikamma Mountains to the north and the ocean to the south, the road traverses a garden of trees, shrubs and flowering plants. Soon the Blue Lillies Bush Forest is reached, about 4km from the bridge. Increasingly the road swings away from the coast and farming activities become more evident.

At **Witelsbos, signposted 'Koomansbos/Witelsbos', the R102 is an alternative route to Port Elizabeth.** The R102 offers more rural charm and tranquility than the N2. The distance is more or less the same.

The N2 meanwhile rushes through cattle land. To the north, the Tsitsikamma Mountains have flowed over into the **Kouga** ('Butter') **Mountain range**..

About 32km from the bridge, ignore the turn-off to **Kareedouw** in the Longkloof (see Route 9). Travel on to pass **Clarkson**, a former mission station established in 1839 by the Moravian missionaries. The village bears the name of a co-worker of Sir William Wilberforce, one of the great campaigners for the abolition of slavery which came about in 1834 in the Cape.

Not only the mountains diminish in height, the rainfall too decreases the further north-easterly one travels. Rolling hills and wide valleys have replaced the rugged peaks in an altogether drier countryside. The next major place en route is

HUMANSDORP
once known as the 'Parish of Alexander', after the Rev. Alexander Smith, a minister of the Dutch Reformed Church from Uitenhage near Port Elizabeth. He occasionally preached here to the small resident community who, as from the 1840s, clamoured for their own church. This became a reality in 1849

when Mattys Human of the farm 'Zeekoe' donated 606ha land for the establishment of a township. This marked the birth of Humansdorp.

A detour to ST. FRANCIS BAY

which was first named by the Portuguese sailor Manuel Perestrello in 1575. The 2 750 000-candlepower lighthouse on Seal Point was built in 1876. It is 28 metres high.

In more recent times, the 1961 film 'Endless Summer', produced by Bruce Brown, propelled the town to fame and increasing popularity as a holiday resort. Swimming and surfing are ideal, as is also fishing, especially the chokka (calamari) industry.

JEFFREYS BAY

is about 4km off the N2. The modern houses belie the humble roots of the town which grew out of a trading store, established in 1849. Then, the beach served as the trading area, today keen swimmers, particularly surfers in search of the super tube, monopolise the white sand. It was named after the senior partner of the store enterprise, Messrs. J.*Jeffrey* and Glendinning.

It was declared a municipality in 1968.

From Jeffreys Bay the national road descends towards the **Kabeljous River**, named after a species of fish. Soon afterwards one traverses open sandveld countryside and the **Gamtoos River** is crossed. The Gamtoos, which takes its name from a Khoi tribe, is of major economic importance, as its broad alluvial valley lends itself to irrigation. Approximately 1% of agricultural land in South Africa is under irrigation). A popular holiday resort has developed at the river mouth.

The road now climbs quite steadily and then comes to the **Van Stadens Gorge**, named after the pioneer farmer, Martinus van Staden.

The first road to cross the gorge was completed in 1867 but was repeatedly destroyed by floods. Crossings remained hazardous even after its reconstruction because of the precipitous descent into the gorge on both sides of the river. Patience and driving skills were needed until 1971 when construction of the new bridge started. It was opened to traffic in 1975.

The four-lane bridge is one of the biggest concrete arch bridges in the world. Its main span is 198m long and it rises to 125m above the riverbed. The overall length reaches 366m and its overall width 26 metres.

The bridge was constructed by Impresa Ing. A & P. di Penta.

East of the bridge, 1km away, one finds the **Van Stadens Wild Flower Reserve.** It extends over 375ha covered with exquisite wild flowers.

The national road now traverses flat, acacia covered countryside, with numerous turn-offs inland and to the coast. After about 40km it comes to

PORT ELIZABETH
Port Elizabeth is the 5th largest city in the country and its 3rd largest port.

Before the arrival of European settlers, a Khoi tribe grazed its livestock in the area and fetched its water from the Kragga Kama River, the Stony Water. This is today's Baakens River, (Beacon). The river mouth used to be an immense lagoon, and the wide beach provided an ideal landing place in the huge bay, known as Algoa.

Portuguese seafarers knew the bay as Bahia de Lagoa, the Bay of Lagoons, stretching from Cape Recife in the west, to Cape Padrone in the east. Bartholomeu Dias, on his epic journey in 1488, sailed as far as today's Kwaaihoek (The Angry Corner), about 14,5km east of Cape Padrone. The Portuguese knew the Angry Corner as 'Penedo das Fontes' - Rock of the Fountains. Here, Dias erected a padrao in honour of St. Gregory.

As the Khoi had little to trade and barter, and the bay offered no shelter, neither the Portuguese nor later Dutch sailors made much use of it. In 1690 a Dutch vessel had sailed into the windswept bay intending to take possession of it, but the inclement weather dissuaded the white man from settling there.

In 1752, ensign August Beutler reached the shores of the bay on an overland journey, and erected a beacon at the river-mouth which since then is known as *Baaken's River.*

The Cape meanwhile was expanding its borders to the east and clashes with the Xhosa people increased.

In 1799, during the first English occupation, a stone redoubt of 24 square metres was built, overlooking the Baakens River. It was named 'Fort Frederick' to honour the Duke of York. A garrison was stationed there and a town was born: the fort was the first stone building built in the Eastern Cape.

Port Elizabeth saw its true development in 1820, with the landing of the

British Settlers. The acting governor, Sir Rufane Donkin, named the place after his late wife Elizabeth who had died of a fever at the age of 28 in India, 1818. Sir Rufane built a stone pyramid in her memory on the hill above the settlers' landing place.

In 1825 Port Elizabeth became a seat of magistracy, but construction of a secure harbour only commenced in 1928. The worst shipping disaster recorded in the bay wrecked 19 out of 28 ships at anchor. Not without reason, Port Elizabeth is also known as 'the windy city'.

Industry took root in 1811 when a tannery and smithy were opened by Fredrick Korsten. In the 1880s, Port Elizabeth played a major role in the auction sales of ostrich feathers, wool, hides, skins and fruit – today, the city is a principle centre of the automobile industry.

The city has developed into a popular holiday destination as well. Not surprisingly, as the sea temperatures are a pleasant 21 - 25°Celsius.

Some historical city landmarks

The Donkin Reserve, Pyramid and Lighthouse
The pyramid in honour of Elizabeth Donkin, after whom the city was named, stands on a hill overlooking the city. It bears two plaques. One to the memory of *'One of the most perfect human beings who has given her name to the town below'*; the other to *'The husband whose heart is still wrung by undiminished grief'*. Elizabeth Donkin never saw the city bearing her name.

The Public Library

The nearby lighthouse dates back to 1861. A time ball used to drop daily at 13:00 from the top of the signal mast to the lower rail. Today, the lighthouse is no longer functional.

The Library
is situated in the north-western corner of Market Square. The land was granted by Governor Sir Benjamin d'Urban in 1835. In 1861, Prince Alfred presented the library with a set of books. From 1854 the old building served as a courthouse. The present building, in the Victorian Gothic style, opened in 1902.

The Queen Victoria Statue
sculpted of Sicilian marble, stands directly in front of the Library. It was erected and unveiled in 1903. The sculptor was R.Roscoe Mullins, London.

The City Hall
also on Market Square, was built between 1858 and 1862 from the designs of R. Archibald. The clock tower was added in 1883. The City Hall served as a Council Chamber, concert hall, a lecture hall and offices. A fire gutted the City Hall in 1977. Numerous valuable paintings were destroyed, amongst them a portrait of Elizabeth Donkin and paintings of early Port Elizabeth. The restored City Hall was re-opened in 1981.

Monument to Prester John and Portuguese Explorers
This unique monument – it is possibly the only one in the world depicting Prester John - stands behind the City Hall, in Fleming Square. It was the quest to find the mythical king-priest, Prester John, that led to the expeditions by sailing around Africa.

The monument is a large Coptic cross. In the central circle are the figures of Prester John and a Portuguese navigator. The Portuguese royal coat-of-arms, a caravel, navigational instruments are depicted on the arms of the cross, the Coptic cross-motif, the Lion of Judah, the elephant and rhinoceros representing the fabulous kingdom of Prester John.

The monument is the work of a local sculptor, Phil Kolbe. It was unveiled in 1986 by the Portuguese Ambassador, Dr. de Villas-Boas.

Campanile
The Campanile honours the approximately four thousand 1820 settlers who were very diverse in class and creed, comprising various religious backgrounds and both, labourers and gentry. The British government at the time offered settlement schemes in its attempt to populate the Eastern Frontier: the settlers were given free passage, 100 acres of land grants and temporary supplies of government rations, as well as money deposits for each settler family. The campanile stands on the original landing site. It is 52m high, has a carillon of 23 bells and a spiral staircase of 204 steps to the viewing platform. It was completed in 1923.

The Old Post Office
opened in 1900 and was designed by the Public Works Department. It is situated at the top of Fleming Street. Its architectural style is typical of public buildings of the late Victorian era. In later years it housed the Magistrate's

Court   Police Station and Barracks.

Post Office building

Feather Market

On Military Road, not far from the old Post Office, one finds the Feather Market Centre. This produce market was originally built to house the auction sales of ostrich feathers, wool, hides, skins and fruit and was, without doubt, the city's commercial heart towards the end of the 19th century. Today it is home to a a conference centre and concert hall.

No 7 Castle Hill

In Castle Hill Road stand typical Settler houses. A fine example is No 7, the first Colonial Chaplain's home, the Rev. McMleland. It is one of the oldest buildings in the city. The lower storey was built of stone, the upper one of brick. Deep in the foundations one finds the larder, and the kitchen in the basement. Today, it is an Historical Museum, furnished in the style of the mid-Victorian period.

The Horse Memorial (on R102)

A very different monument, possibly unique in the world, is the **Horse Memorial** by Joseph Whitehead. It was erected by public subscription to honour the horses who perished in the South African War (1899-1902).

The Horse Memoiral

"The greatness of a nation consists, not so much in the number of its people or the extent of its territory as in the extent and justice of its compassion."

Are there any better words to conclude a book that has taken you on a magically diverse part of South Africa?

Enjoy the onward travels.

Slaves and Slavery

The slaves came from the Malay peninsula, India, Indonesia, Madagascar, Mauritius, Angola and East and West African countries. In time, though forbidden, indigenous San (Bushman) women and children were enslaved. A similar fate befell many Khoikhoi. Three slave owning classes existed in the Cape: the VOC, the free burgher and even the emancipated slave.

Male slaves laboured as masons, carpenters, bricklayers and lime burners. Some were fishermen, porters or vegetable hawkers, whilst a few even became grooms, coachmen, valets, cooper's assistants, pump makers, bookbinders, miller's assistants, tailors, butlers and musicians. Most, however, did menial tasks.

Slave women were mostly domestic workers. They were the cooks, cleaners, nurses, washerwomen and wet-nurses. At the Cape, slaves were the backbone of the labour force.

Many faced physical hardships, most suffered deep emotional scars and the additional loss of identity when their owners gave them new names. Old Testament names and places of origin were popular, though many were named after the months of their arrival or purchase. The surname 'van die Kaap' implied that a slave was born at the Cape.

Treatment differed widely, but it was only in the 1820s that effective control was obtained over physical punishment. The first execution of a European, accused of beating a slave to death on a farm near Stellenbosch, occurred in November 1822. Arson, poisoning, breaking tools and even embarking on a work slowdown were the most common 'tools' of resistance by slaves. Many sought freedom by running away. Yet many also identified with their owners

Only a few acquired a little money or livestock from earnings permitted by their owners, most lacked the resources with which they might have bought their freedom. By the time of their emancipation on 1 December 1834, they numbered about 35 000 which was almost equal to the free population, though higher figures have been stated.

The slaves impacted on the cultural and religious life at the Cape. Their languages are echoed in many of the Afrikaans words, phrases and songs, their Muslim customs – where they were Muslims - upheld in the communities which developed. The earliest Afrikaans texts were written by Cape Muslims in Arabic script.

In 1808, oceanic slave trading was abolished and increasingly slaves were drawn from those born in the Cape.

The emancipated slaves received neither land nor capital. Many moved to towns, villages and mission stations, but many remained on the farms as permanent or seasonal workers.

GLOSSARY OF AFRIKAANS WORDS

Algemene handelaar	general dealer
Ambulans	ambulance
Rivier	river
Bobbejaan	baboon
Boer	farmer
Boom	tree
Braai	barbeque, grill
Bundu	desert, wilderness
Burgher	citizen, inhabitant
Bushalte	busstop
Dames	ladies
Dankie	thank you
Diensstasie	service station
Dorp	village
Drostdy	magistrate's court
Einde – Dankie	end – thank you
Fynbos	'Fine bush'
Gat	hole
Gebruik Laer Rat	use lower gear
Geen Deurgang	no thoroughfare
Geen Deurpad	no through-road
Geen Ingang	no entry
Geen Staanplek	no stopping
Geen Toegang	no entry
Geen Uitgang	no exit
Geen Vure	no fires
Gesluit	closed
Gevaar	Danger
Groot	large, bit
Hek	gate
Here	gentlemen
Hoek	corner
Hou Links	keep left
Hou Regs	keep right
Ingang	entrance
Kafee	café
Kelders	cellars
Kerk	church
Kinders	children
Kerk	church
Khoikhoi	brave men
Klein	small
Kloof	ravine
Kraal	corral
Landdrost	magistrate
-laan	lane
Links	left
Lughawe	airport
Nagmaal	holy communion
Ompad	detour
Oord	resort
Oom	uncle
Oord	resort
-pad	road
Padstal	farm stall
Pasop	look out
-pas	pass
Poort	passage, way through

Plaas	farm
Robot voor	traffic light ahead
Ry stadig	drive slowly
Ry versigtig/Veilig	drive carefully
Slaggatte	potholes
Sondae gesluit	closed on Sundays
Stad	city
Stadig	slowly
Straat	street
Teekamer	rea room
Teerpad eindig	tarred road ends
Toegang verbode	no entry
Trek	to journey, travel
Uitgang	exit
Uitkyk	view, look-out
Ure	hours
Veld	field, grazing land
Vlei	inland lake
Vulstasie	petrol station
Wag	wait
-weg	road
Winkel	shop
Wynkelder	wine cellar

BUSINESS INDEX

Albertinia Tourism Bureau
P.O.Box 12
Albertinia 6695
+(0)28 735 1000

albinfo@telkomsa.net

Alcare Aloe Factory
P.O.Box 278
Albertinia 6695
+(0)28 735 1454

alcare@mweb.co.za

Amalienstein & Zoar
Aunt Carolina's
Amalienstein
P.O.Box 36
Ladismith 6655
+(0)28 561 1000

Aventura Holiday Resort
+(0)44 535 9912
plettres@aventura.co.za

Barrydale Wine Cellars
P.O.Box 59
Barrydale 6750
+(0)28 572 1012

sales@barrydalewines.co.za

Beaumont Wines
P.O.Box 3
Compagnes Drift
Botriver 7185
+(0)28 284 9733

beauwine@netactive.co.za

Birkenhead Brewery
Stanford
+(0)28 341 0183
info@birkenhead.co.za

Bloukrans Bungy Jump
+(0)42 281 1458
extremes@iafrica.com

Boesmanskloof Hiking Trail
see Genadendal Hiking Trail

Boland Hiking Trails
+(0)21 889 1560

Boplaas
P.O.Box 156
Calitzdorp 6660
+(0)44 2133 326

www.boplaas.co.za

Bouchard Finlayson
Hemel-en-Aarde Valley
Hermanus
+(0)28 312 3515

info@bouchardfinlaysonco.za

Bungy-Jumping
Gourits River and Bloukrans
info@faceadrenalin.com

Caledon Tourism Bureau
cnr Mill/Plein Street
+(0)28 572 1572

Calitzdorp Co-Op
P.O.Box 193
Calitzdorp 6660
+(0)44 213 3328

Calitzdorp Spa
P.O.Box 12
George 6530
+(0)44 213 3371

info@calitzdorpspa.co.za

Calitzdorp Tourism Info	+(0)44 213 3312 kannaland@telkomsa.net
Cape Agulhas Lighthouse	+(0)28 435 6078
Cango Caves	+(0)44 272 7410 reservations@cangocaves.co.za
Cango Ostrich Farm	+(0)44 272 4623 cango.ostrich@pixie.co.za
Cango Crocodile Farm P.O.Box 559 Oudtshoorn 6621	+(0)44 272 5593 cango@kingsley.co.za
Choo-Tjoe Train	+(0)44 801 8288
C.P.Nel Museum Oudtshoorn P.O.Box 453 Oudtshoorn 6620	+(0)44 272 7306 cpnmuseum@pixie.co.za
De Mond Nature Reserve Private Bag X16 Bredasdorp 7280	+(0)28 424 2170 dehoopinfo@sdm.dorea.co.za
Dias Museum Mossel Bay Private Bag X1 Mossel Bay 6500	+(0)44 691 1067 diasmuseum@mweb.co.za
De Rust Tourism 29 Schoeman Street De Rust	+(0)44 241 2109 derusttoer@xsinet.co.za
Die Krans P.O.Box 28 Calitzdorp 6660	+(0) 213 3314 diekrans@mweb.co.za
Die Poort P.O.Box 99 Herbertsdale 6505	+(0)28 7352 406
Dolphin Trail	+(0)42 281 1607 ext.219 dolphintrail@parks-sa.co.za
Elgin Valley Tourism Bureau	+(0)21 859 9030
Elim Tourism Bureau	+(0)28 482 1806
Erica Vineyards Remhoogte Stanford	+(0)28 341 0676 ericawine@telkomsa.net
Gamkaskloof/The Hell	see Swartberg Nature Reserve
Gamkaberg Nature Reserve	+(0)44 213 3367/ 44 874 2184 gamkanr@mweb.co.za
Gansbaai Tourism Bureau Main Street	gansbaaiinfo@telkomsa.net

P.O.Box 399 Gansbaai 7220   +(0)28 384 1439
Genadendal Hiking Trail   +(0)28 425 5020
dehoopinfo@sdm.dorea.co.za

George Tourism Bureau   +(0)44 874 4027
124 George Street
George 6529   info@georgetourism.co.za

George Museum   +(0)44 873 5343
Courtenay Street

George Crocodile Park   +(0)44 873 4302
York Street
George 6530

Goukamma Nature Reserve   +(0)44383 0042
goukamma@mweb.co.za

Grabouw Information Bureau   +(0)21 859 1398

Great Brak River Information   +(0)44 620 3338
gbrtourism@intekom.co.za

Greyton Tourism Bureau   +(0)28 254 9414
29 Main Road
Greyton 7233   greytoninfo@mweb.co.za

Groenefontein Nature Reserve   +(0)44 874 2184
george@cnc.org.za

Groenvlei Bush Camp/   +(0)44 383 0042
Goukamma Nature Reserve   goukamma@mweb.co.za

Grundheim   +(0)44 272 6927
P.O.Box 400
Oudtshoorn 6620   grundheim@abbsamail.co.za

Harkerville Trail
c/o Forestry Knysna   +(0)44 382 5466

Hartenbos Museum   +(0)44 695 2183
Majuba Avenue
Hartenbos 6520   hartenbos@atkv.org.za

Heidelberg Info Centre   +(0)28 722 2700
3 Eksteen St.
Heidelberg 6665   heidelinfo@telkomsa.net

Hermanus Tourism Bureau   +(0)28 312 2629
Old Station Building
cnr Mitchell/Lord Roberts Streets
P.O.Box 117 Hermanus 7200   infoburo@hermanus.co.za

Herrie Train Tours   +(0)44 272 2377

Highgate Ostrich Farm   +(0)44 272 7115
P.O.Box 94
Oudtshoorn 6620

Houhoek Inn
P.O.Box 95
Grabouw 7160
+(0)28 284 9646
houwhoek@iafrica.com

John Benn/Featherbed
P.O.Box 753
Knysna 6570
+(0)44 382 1693
bookings@featherbed.co.za

Kleinmond Tourist Bureau
Main Rd, Kleinmond
P.O.Box 81 Kleinmond 7195
+(0)28 271 4742
info@hangklip-kleinmondtoruism.co.za

Knysna Cycle Works
+(0)44 382 5153

Knysna Elephant Park
P.O.Box 1204
Knysna 6570
+(0)44 532 7732
kep@pixie.co.za

Knysna Museum
Queen Street
Knysna
+(0)44 382 5066

Knysna Historical Society
+(0)44 303 6320

Knysna Oyster Company
Thesen Island
+(0)44 382 6941
www.oysters.co.za

Knysna Tourism
Main Road
Knysna
+(0)44 382 5510
knysna.tourism@pixie.co.za

Knysna Reservations
+(0)44 382 6960
+(0)44 383 21609 fax

Kogelberg Nature Reserve
kogelbrg@mweb.co.za
+(0)28 271 5138
+(0)21 483 2949

Ladismith Wine Cellar
P.O.Box 56
Ladismith 6885
+(0)28 551 1042
lkws@telkomsa.net

Ladismith/
Kannaland Municipality
+(0)28 551 1023

Highgate Ostrich Farm
P.O.Box 94
Oudtshoorn 6620
+(0)44 272 7115/6
hosf@mweb.co.za

Lightleys Holiday Houseboats
+(0)44 386 0007
www.houseboats.co.za

Napier Museum
Napier Tourism
+(0)28 423 3894
+(0)28 423 3325

Marloth Nature Reserve
to top
P.O.Box 28
Swellendam 6740
+(0)28 425 5020
marlothnr@telkomsa.net

Monkeyland
P.O.Box 1190
Plettenberg Bay 6600
+(0)44 534 8906
monkeys@global.co.za

Mossel Bay Tourism Bureau   +(0)44 691 2202
P.O.Box 1556
Mossel Bay 6500   mbtb@mweb.co.za
Napier Tourist Bureau   +(0)28 423 3325
Sarel Cilliers St   www.capeoverberg.co.za

Nature's Valley Rest Camp   +(0)44 531 6700

Newton Johnson Wines   +(0)28 312 3862
Hemel-en-Aarde Village
Hermanus   capebay@netactive.co.za

Nelson Mandela Bay Tourism   +(0)41 585 8884
Port Elizabeth
Donkin Reserve
P.O.Box 357
Port Elizabeth 6000   info@nmbt.co.za

Old Harbour Museum, Hermanus   +(0)28 312 1475

Oudsthoorn Ostrich Show Farm   +(0)44 279 1861
P.O.Box 125
Oudtshoorn 6620   oosf@freemail.absa.co.za

Oudtshoorn Ostrich Show Farm   +(0)44 272 2522
P.O.Box 125
Oudtshoorn 6620   oosf@freemail.absa.co.za

Outeniqua Nature Reserve   +(0)44 870 8323 ?????
Private Bag X6517
George 6530

Outeniqua Power Van   +0()44 801 8239
   opv@mweb.co.za

Outenique Railway Museum   +(0)44 801 8224
Mission Street
George 6529

Overberg Conference Centre   +(0)21 859 5514
12 Hofmeyr Street
Caledon 7230   ppecbiti@iafrica.com

Palmiet Hydro-Electric
Pumped Storage Scheme&Visitor
Centre   +(0)21 859 2690

Paul Cluver Wines   +(0)28 844 0605
N2 Kromco turnoff,Elgin   info@cluver.co.za

Port Elizabeth Tourism   see Nelson Mandela Bay Tourism

Prince Albert Tourism   +(0)23 541 1366
P.O.Box 109
Prince Albert 6930   princealberttourism@intekom.co.za

Rein's Nature Reserve   +(0)28 745 3322
Gouritzmond   info@reinsouthafrica.com

Riversdale Tourism Bureau   +(0)28 713 2418
P.O.Box 29
Riversdale 6670   www.riversdaler.co.za

Riviersonderend Tourism   +(0)28 261 1511

Robberg Nature Reserve Private Bag X1003	+(0)44 533 2125
Plettenberg Bay 6600	robkeur@mweb.co.za
Safari Ostrich Farm P.O.Box 300	+(0)44 272 5896
Oudtshoorn 6620	safariostrich@mweb.co.za
Salmonsdam Nature Reserve	+(0)28 425 5020 dehoopinfo@sdem.dorea.co.za cncwbay@mweb.co.za
SANParks P.O.Box 787 Pretoria 0001	+(0)12 428 9111 +(0)42281 1629 reservations@sanparks.org www.sanparks.org
Sedgefield Coastal Reservations P.O.Box 882 Sedgefield 6573	+(0)44 343 2658 www.sedgefieldonsea.co.za
Shipwreck Museum Bredasdorp	+(0)28 424 1240
South African National Parks P.O.Box 314 Knysna 6570	+(0)44 382 2095
Stanford Tourism Bureau P.O.Box 84 Stanford 7210	stanfordinfo@overberg.co.za +(0)28 341 03340
Steenbras Dam Permits	+(0)21 859 2507
Stilbaai Tourism Bureau P.O.Box 245 Stilbaai 6674	+(0)28 754 2602 infosb@telkoms.net
St. Francis Tourism	+(0)42 294 0076 info@stfrancistourism.co.za
Storms River Mouth Rest Camp P.O. Stormsriver 6308	+(0)42 281 1607
Swellendam Hiking Trail	see Marloth Nature Reserve
Swellendam Tourism P.O.Box 369 Swellendam 6740	+(0)28 514 2770 infoswd@sdmdorea.co.za
Suurbraak Municipality P.O.Box 74 Suurbraak	+(0)28 522 1627
Suurbraak Information Office	+(0)28 522 1806
Swartberg Nature Reserve	+(0)44 279 1739 sberg.cnc.karoo@pixie.co.za
Transnet Heritage Preservation	+(0)44 801 8288

P.O.Box 150
George
2 Mission Street

Tsitsikamma Canopy Tours   +(0)42 281 1836
info@treetoptour.com

Villiersdorp Tourism   +(0)28 840 0169
P.O.Box 23
Villiersdorp 6848
Vindigo Wine & Décor   +(0)28 423 3069
108 Sarel Cilliers St
Napier   vindigo@isat.co.za

Walker Bay Nature Reserve   +(0)28 314 0062
Private Bag X13
Hermanus 7200

Waenhuiskrans Nature Reserve   +(0)28 424 2170
P.O.Box 277
Bredasdorp 7280   deMond@isat.co.za

Warmwaterberg   +(0)28572 1609
info@warmwaterbergspa.co.za

Whale Trail   +(0)28 425 5020
dehoopinfo@sdm.dorea.co.za

WhaleHaven Wines   +(0)28 316 1633
Hemel-en-Aarde Valley
Hermanus   whwines@hermanus.co.za

Wine Village   +(0)28 316 3988
Hemel-en-Aarde Village
Hermanus   wine@hermanus.co.za

Wilderness National Park   +(0)44 877 1197
www.george.co.za/parks

Wilgewandel Camelrides   +(0)44 272 0878

BIBLIOGRAPHY

Touring in South Africa, by Maxwell Leigh, Struik Publishers(pty)Ltd 1995
On Foot in the Garden Route, by Judith Hopley
The Great South African Outdoors, Readers Digest Association of SA, 1992
Garden Route Walks, by Colin Paterson-Jones, Struik Publishers (Pty)Ltd 1992
Place Names in the Cape, by Ed Coombe & Peter Slingsby, Baardskeerder 2000
Discovering Southern Africa, T.V. Bulpin, 1992
*Regional Indigenous Forest Management Plan,*Graham Durrheim, Dpt of Water Affairs and Forestry,
Knysna
A Short Historical Sketch of the Caledon Baths
Caledon Historical Walks
Breede River Revelations, by Chris Mellish, Mallard Publishers, 1996
Exploring the Southern Cape, by Neels de Ronde,Human&Rousseau, 1995
Coastal Holiday, a guide to SA seaside resorts, by Jose Burman, Human & Rousseau
The Historical Monuments of South Africa, by J.J. Oberholster, Rembrandt van Rijn Foundation for
Culture,1972
South Africa, a modern history, by T.R.Davenpot, Macmillan South Africa, 1985
Overberg, by Anna Rothmann-John Warner, Haum Publishers, Cape Town
SA Wildflower Guide Outeniqua, Tsitsikamma &Eastern Little Karoo, 1982
Roberts' Birds of Southern Africa, published by the Trustees of the John Voelcker Bird Book Fund, 1985
Whale Watching in South Africa, by Peter B.Best,Mammal Reserch Institute Pretoria University
Timber and Tides, by Winifred Tapson, Juta & Co.Ltd Cape Town, 1961
A History of St. George's Church, Anglican Church Records, Knysna
Guide Book to the Holy Trinity Church, Belvidere
Wandering through historical Knysna, by Margaret Parkes and Vicky Williams
C.P.Nel Museum Guide, Oudtshoorn

Explore Cape Nature Reserves, 2nd ed. by Cape Nature Conservation
*Various Field Guides, Information booklets on Nature Reserves and Hiking Maps,by Cape Nature
Conservation*
Museum Guide Books on Swellendam Drostdy, Mayville, Mossel Bay, Hartenbos
Information Guides on the Knysna Lagoon, published by SA National Parks
Birds of Southern Africa, by Kenneth Newman, Southern Book Publsihers, 1991
The Otter Trail Hiking Map
Walking and Information guide to the Robberg, Cape Nature Conservation
The Ostrich, by Anita Holtzhausen, Marlene Kotze, C.P. Nel Museum Oudtshoorn
*An Illustrated Dictionary of SA History,*Ibis Books and Editorial Services,1994
The Letters of Lady Ann Barnard, publ. by Balkema, Cape Town 1973
The Story of Millwood Gold, by Millwood Gold Society Knysna
Oyster Farming in Knysna – information leaflet, D.J.Krebser, 1988
A Walking tour of Port Elizabeth
Palmiet,forerunner in environmental engineering, Eskom
Cango Caves & the Little Karoo, published by Art Publishers
Elephants of Southern Africa, by Anthony Hall-Martin, published by Struik Timmins 1990
Garden Route Guide, Publ. by Jacana, 3rd. edition, Houghton 2003
Outeniqua, Tsitsikamma and Little Karro Flower Guide, publ. by Botanical Society of South Africa

ALPHABETICAL INDEX

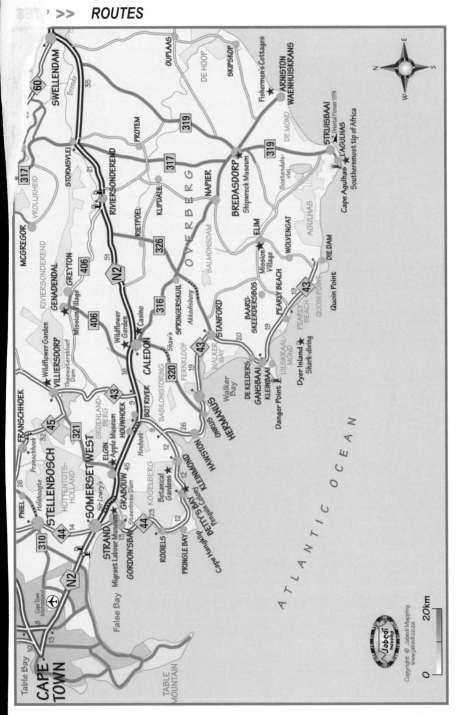

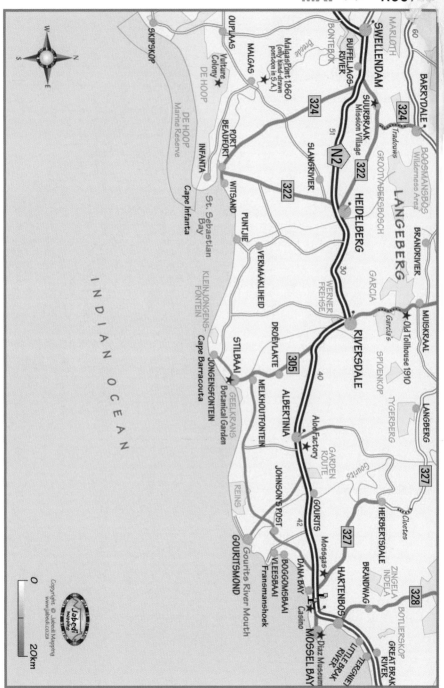

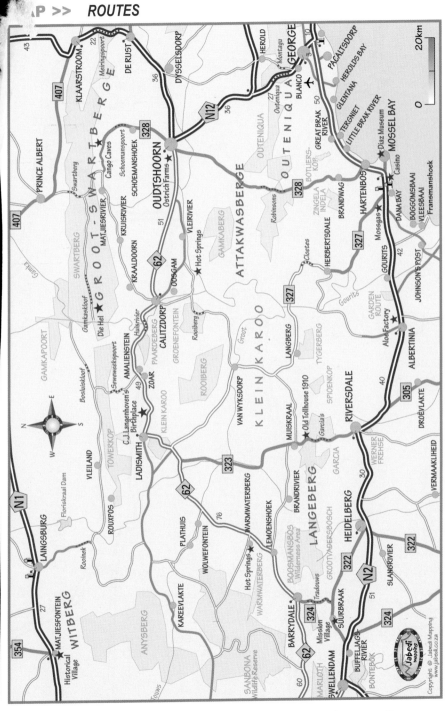

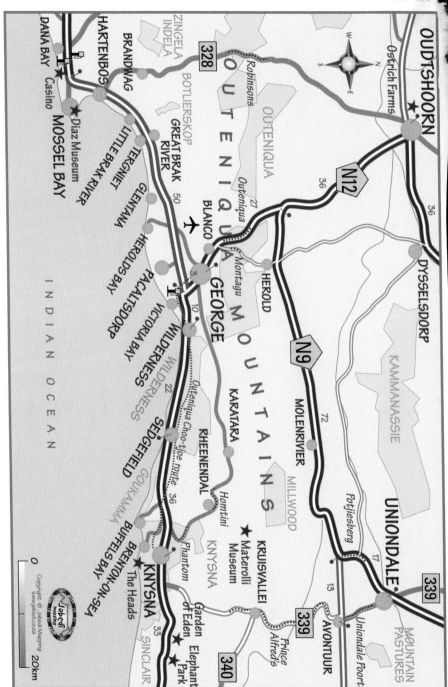

254 ᘓᘓᘓ

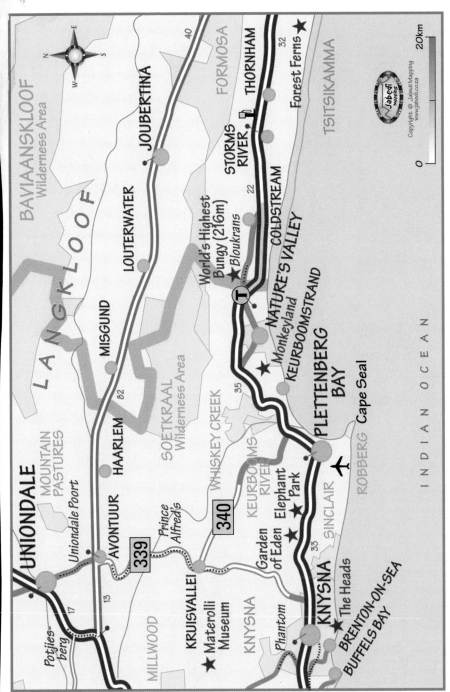

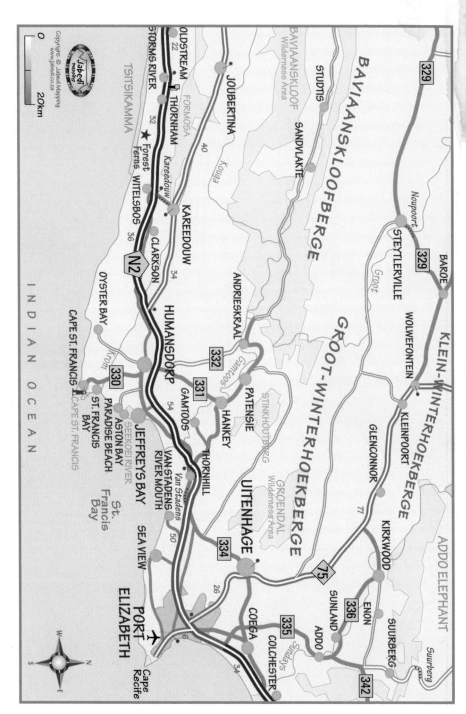